A COMMON CASE OF BEATLEMANIA

A Common Case of Beatlemania

A Memoir

Ursula Fuery Costa

© 2023 by Ursula Fuery Costa

All rights reserved. This book or any portion thereof may not be reproduced or used in any manner whatsoever without the express written permission of the publisher except for the use of brief quotations in a book review.

ISBN: 9798372484832

I would like to dedicate this book to my husband, Ronald Costa. He spent hours on end listening to me reminiscing about all the adventures that my girlfriends and I had chasing after The Beatles. In fact, he was the one that suggested that I should write a book. I could never have done it without his never-ending love, support, and encouragement.

CONTENTS

Chapter 1: In The Beginning 1
Chapter 2: The Beatles Revealed 7
Chapter 3: A Plan To Benefit Both Dad And Me 13
Chapter 4: Teenagers In Love 17
Chapter 5: Singing On The Bus 21
Chapter 6: Modernizing The Fuery Household 25
Chapter 7: Thank Your Lucky Stars 29
Chapter 8: Saturday Job 35
Chapter 9: Please Please Me Album 39
Chapter 10: The Elusive Magazine 43
Chapter 11: Best Present Ever 55
Chapter 12: My First Beatles Concert 59
Chapter 13: Beatlemania Is Now A Word 69
Chapter 14: Classified Information 77
Chapter 15: Our Very Special Magical Mystery Tour 85
Chapter 16: A Glance At Paul And George, ... 89
   And A Fun Day Off From School
Chapter 17: Two Christmas Presents From The Beatles 97
Chapter 18: The Fan Club Get Together 103
Chapter 19: Letters Galore 113

Chapter 20: Four Christmas Shows 121
Chapter 21: Sweets For The Beatles.. 127
Chapter 22: They're Off To France 133
Chapter 23: The Beatles In America 137
Chapter 24: London Airport 143
Chapter 25: A Tiny Fib 151
Chapter 26: Filming A Hard Day's Night 157
Chapter 27: Around The Beatles 161
Chapter 28: Ringo Admitted To Hospital 171
Chapter 29: Keeping Busy.. 175
Chapter 30: The Premiere Of A Hard Day's Night 177
Chapter 31: An Unforgettable Moment With Ringo 183
Chapter 32: Two Fancy Automobiles.. 187
Chapter 33: A Most Unreasonable Boss... 191
Chapter 34: The Arrival Of The Swedish Pen Pals 195
Chapter 35: Liverpool, Here We Come 203
Chapter 36: Wonderful And Heart- Wrenching 215
Chapter 37: Our Manchester Adventure..225
Chapter 38: Little Matchbox Cars 233
Chapter 39: Leaving My Beloved England....................................235
Chapter 40: Settling In, And Meeting Another Pen Pal 245
Chapter 41: Unhappy School Days 253
Chapter 42: Running Away From Home.......................................259
Chapter 43: Shea Stadium 1965..265
Chapter 44: Shea Stadium 1966..271
Chapter 45: Keeping Up With The Beatles...................................277
Chapter 46: Sad Times, And Good News 283
Acknowledgment: 291

CHAPTER 1
IN THE BEGINNING

I was blessed to be born in the great city of London, and to have loving parents who gave me the freedom to live my early teen years in the sixties, in the excitement that became a worldwide musical and cultural sensation -The Beatles. It was an experience that any girl would feel privileged to cherish in her heart forever.

I vividly remember the very first time that I heard The Beatles. My girlfriend Eileen and I had just jumped off the bus and were dawdling along after our busy day at school. We were both feeling very pleased with ourselves for having once again successfully managed to dodge the bus conductor and paying our bus-fare. Throwing my *thruppenny bit into the air and catching it with one hand, I shouted, "Hooray, we've done it again!"

We continued our snail's pace walk and chatted about the upcoming school dance. Suddenly, Eileen began to search through her blazer pockets. As soon as she found her money, she turned to me and said, "I don't know about you, but I'm feeling a little bit *peckish. Some licorice allsorts should do the job and keep me going until supper time." Always ready for something sweet, Eileen's suggestion sounded wonderful, and without hesitation, I replied, "Mmm, I do believe I'm in the mood for some pineapple chunks; they're my favorite, and they last forever."

With a knowing nod, Eileen replied, "There's nothing better than getting your money's worth." Without warning, Eileen took off running, and yelled, "Come on then, I'll race you there." We darted in and out, doing our best not to collide with the other pedestrians, and didn't stop until we had reached the sweet shop on Matthias Road. Opening the heavy glass door, I turned to Eileen and said, "I can't think of a better way to spend my bus fare."

Shaking her head in agreement, she replied, "It's like getting a present from The London Transport." Making a funny face, I answered, "After all the bleedin'* business we've given them, it's the least they can do." Laughing hysterically, we stepped into the tiny sweet shop, and inhaled deeply. The aromas coming from the toffee, the handmade chocolates, and the hundreds of other delicious treats made us dizzy with delight.

Minutes later, we were back on the street, holding our tiny white bags, each filled with *thruppence worth of our chosen sweets. We had at least another two hours before dinner time, so we were in no hurry. We continued our slow-paced walk, stopping every once in a while to gaze into the shop windows. And that's when it happened: We began to hear a faint, rhythmic throbbing in the distance. As we walked a little further, we could also hear the mysterious sound of a harmonica. This fascinating music seemed to be coming from a block of flats that were just up the road. As we got closer, we could hear voices singing in perfect harmony, and that's when we realized that this beautiful music was coming from somebody's radio. The radio was sitting on a tiny round table on a ground floor balcony, and the considerate owner had turned the volume all the way up.

Now, within a few feet from the radio, we stood motionless, as the beautiful music filled the air around us. And as we let the beat, the melody, and the voices carry us away, we began to tap our feet, and bob up and down. When the song ended, I twirled around to face Eileen, and cried, "That has to be the new song that everyone at school has been going on about." With a great big smile, she replied, "Yeah, that's it alright, my cousin bought the record the other day, and she hasn't stopped playing it.

Her Mum's complaining that she's driving the whole family bonkers!" Mimicking her Aunt, with hands on hips and chest out, Eileen spoke in her best cockney accent, "In our 'ouse, 'Love Me Do' can be heard morning, noon and bleedin' night! All I want is a bit of peace and quiet, is that too much to ask for?" Watching Eileen's brilliant performance, I was doubled up with laughter, and barely able to control myself, and Eileen was laughing even louder. Once she regained her composure, Eileen fired question after question at me, "So what do you think? Isn't it a great record? Don't you just love it? Isn't it the best song you've ever heard? Do you think you'll be buying it?"

Raising my hand to stop her incessant babbling, I yelled, "Cor blimey, * I feel like I'm being interrogated by a Scotland Yard detective. And to answer your questions, yes, I absolutely love it, and yes, I'll definitely be buying it. It's so different from the normal stuff that's on the radio. I wish today was Friday, between my pocket money, and my *saving stamps, I'd have enough money to buy it at this very moment." Eileen joked, "In the meantime, if you want to hear it again, you can always pop 'round to my cousin's, she's bound to be playing it."

Now that I'd finally heard the song that everyone at school had been raving about, I completely understood what all the fuss was about. 'Love Me Do' was released on October 5th, 1962 and before long, all the popular radio stations were playing this fabulous new song.

The following evening my girlfriends and I were sitting in Christina's living room, drinking cups of tea, and chatting about nothing in particular. Suddenly, 'Love Me Do' came on the radio, and we immediately stopped talking. Betty rushed over to the radio and turned the volume all the way up.

Sitting on her long couch, the five of us listened intently and began to sway from side to side. When 'Love Me Do' came to an end, Rita carefully placed her cup and saucer on the coffee table, and sounding like a musical expert turned to us and said, "Yes, it's definitely the harmonica that makes this song so unique." We all nodded in agreement, and the radio D.J. informed us that this new song had been recorded by an unknown group from Liverpool who went by the name: 'The Beatles.'

When we heard the funny name we all burst out laughing. Pouring boiling water into her mother's fancy rose covered teapot, Christina said, "I like the name, and because it's so silly, we're bound to remember it!" Laughing out loud, Valerie added, "I wonder why they didn't call themselves "The Spiders" or "The Ants", or why not "The Worms"? They're all catchy, and rather itchy names too."

Not long after 'Love Me Do' was released, articles about The Beatles began to appear in some of the London newspapers. We learned that this new group played in and around Liverpool, and that they were the house band at a club called "The Cavern". At this club, The Beatles had a huge, devoted following that showed up for every single show. After reading one article, I rushed to tell my girlfriends, "You're not gonna believe this; The Beatles perform at The Cavern, during lunchtime." Laughing hysterically, Christina said, "Well that's a new one, I've never heard of a night club that's opened for lunch." Frances reminded us, "Ah, but don't forget, it's in Liverpool, not London." Looking more than a little bit confused, Valerie asked, "But who's in the mood for a quick dance at lunchtime?"

Searching for the article, Rita said, "You must have read it wrong. I don't think I'd be in any condition to go back to work after eating my sandwich, having a dance, and watching The Beatles perform." In another newspaper article, we read that The Beatles had spent months playing in various nightclubs in Hamburg, Germany. After reading that, Valerie sighed, "Cor blimey, they've really been around, let's hope they're not a bunch of old geezers!" Hearing Valerie's comment, Rita cried, "Don't say that, now you've got me worried." With praying hands and looking up to heaven, Rita pleaded, "Oh dear God, let them be young, and let them be gorgeous."

The main people mentioned in this book. Left to right; Ursula, Christina, Eileen, Maroula, and Rita.

*<u>Thruppenny bit</u>…A coin worth three pennies, formerly used in Great Britain.
*<u>Peckish</u>…slightly hungry
*<u>Bleedin'</u>…mild swearing used for emphasis.
*<u>Cor blimey</u>…A way of expressing surprise, excitement, or alarm.
*<u>Saving stamps</u>…National saving stamps were a popular saving scheme aimed at children in the 1950s and 1960s.
*<u>Thrupence</u>… Three pennies.

CHAPTER 2
THE BEATLES REVEALED

My girlfriends and I absolutely loved listening to 'Love Me Do' and we read every single article that was published on The Beatles, but until we'd seen an actual picture of them, we couldn't be one hundred percent sure that they were the group for us. With a worried frown, Christina said, "I don't want to get my hopes up, I really need to know what they look like." Laughing hysterically, Valerie teased, "What if they're a bunch of ugly looking *teddy boys with *winkle pickers, long Edwardian jackets, and greasy quaff haircuts.

Giving Valerie a dirty look, Frances cried, "Now you've turned me right off." Brimming with confidence, I sighed, "With voices like that, they have to be dreamy." Crossing her fingers, Christina chirped, "Well let's hope that Valerie's wrong, and Ursula's right." On a lazy Saturday morning, while lounging in my bed, sipping a cup of tea, and thumbing through my latest copy of *Boyfriend' magazine, I heard a loud knock on the front door. My mother scurried down the hall to answer it. I heard a chirpy voice, "Hello Mrs. Fuery, is Ursula home?" In a cheery tone, my mother replied, "Of course she is, you know where to find her." Annoyed by the interruption, I rested my cup on the night table, and quickly pulled the *eiderdown up to my chin. I couldn't imagine who could possibly be visiting me at such an ungodly hour. All my girlfriends knew that on Saturdays I never got out of bed until well after eleven o'clock.

My mother yelled, "Ursula, Rita's here" and a second later, Rita came rushing into my bedroom. I said a quick, "*Allo" and continued flipping through my magazine. Without looking up, I asked, "What are you doing here so early? I know we've made plans to go down the High Street, but the plan was to meet at two o' clock, not *flipping ten o' clock!"

There was complete silence, so I looked up to see why Rita hadn't bothered to answer.

Normally, Rita was quite pale, but today her face was flaming red, and she was frantically waving a newspaper. Reaching for my cup of tea, I asked, "And what do you have there? Sales information for our shopping expedition?" Jumping onto the side of my bed, and almost spilling my tea, Rita shrieked, "I'm so excited. I've come all the way from *The Angel to show you something." She looked a little upset, and with a deep sigh continued speaking, "Please, don't tell me you've already seen the picture?"

Once again, I placed my cup of tea back on the night table, and giving her a puzzled look, I said, "Rita, what on earth are you going on about, what picture?" Rita croaked, "The picture of them!" Giving her a funny look, I snapped, "For God's sake, who's them?" Flushed with excitement, Rita shouted, "Why the Beatles, of course!"

As soon as she said, 'The Beatles,' I grabbed the newspaper right out of her hand. I was shaking with excitement, and even though I couldn't wait to see what they looked like, I was also more than a little bit scared. Before daring to look at the picture, I prayed out loud, "Dear Lord please let them be gorgeous!" Inhaling deeply, I ever so slowly unfolded the paper, and took a peek at the wrinkled page. My eyes shot open, and still holding the newspaper, I fell back onto my pillow, and looking up to heaven, I squealed, "Thank you dear Lord, not only have you answered my prayer, but this is way beyond my wildest expectations."

Still gawking at the picture, I glanced over at Rita, and cried, "To find four absolutely gorgeous, breathtaking boys all in the same musical group is nothing short of a miracle. Every other group has at least one member that's a little bit on the plain side!" Rita and I took another look at the picture, and together we began to scream with excitement. Hearing the commotion, my mother yelled from the hallway, "Ursula, what's going on in there?" Giggling, I yelled back, "Nothing to worry about Mum, it's just that Rita, and I are madly in love." Holding her sides and laughing hysterically, Rita opened the bedroom door, and quickly added, "But don't worry, not with each other Mrs. Fuery!" In a sarcastic tone, my mother replied, "I'm glad that's all it is. For a moment, I thought something dreadful had happened."

In this first picture The Beatles were posing, smiling, and looking absolutely gorgeous. They were dressed in identical grey suits that were very smart looking but had one very unusual feature: these suits were missing: A collar. Something we had never seen before. Underneath the collar-less suits John, Paul, George and Ringo wore snowy white shirts, dark ties, and their shoes were shiny black Chelsea boots (soon to be renamed Beatle boots!)

Admiring the picture, Rita said, "Not only do they sound different, but they look different too." Nodding in agreement, I replied, "You're right, they do look different. I've never seen anything like these suits before. I bet that's what all the boys in Germany are wearing." Smiling broadly, Rita sighed, "They look absolutely *smashing that's all I know!" Without taking my eyes off of the picture, I huffed loudly, "Why can't the scruffy boys that we know dress like this?" Laughing hysterically, Rita cried, "That untidy bunch, none of 'em even own a suit, let alone a nice pair of squeaky-clean shoes, and the only ties that they wear are their grubby school ties".

Feeling sorry for the harsh words we had just used to describe our male classmates, I reminded Rita, "We shouldn't be annoyed with them, after all the boys that we know are only fourteen, so there's hope for them yet." Giggling, Rita replied, "It certainly would make my school day a lot more pleasant if just one of the boys in our class resembled a Beatle."

We continued to discuss and admire the glorious picture of The Beatles for another ten minutes, and suddenly it dawned on us that it wasn't right to keep this wonderful discovery all to ourselves, and that sooner or later we'd have to share it with our best friends. Climbing out of my bed, I put on my

*dressing gown, grabbed a pile of clothes, and on my way to the bathroom, I yelled to Rita, "Stop staring at that bleedin' picture, and make my bed!" Rita was lost in her own private dream world and hadn't heard a single word that I'd said. Five minutes later, we were ready to go.

My mother was standing on the landing talking to our next-door neighbor, and as we headed towards the stairs, she asked, "Where are you girls off to, so early on a Saturday morning? Did you have your *Weetabix? Did you offer some to Rita?" Giving her a weary look, I sighed, "No Mum, we don't have time for Weetabix right now, we'll eat later."

Taking two steps at a time, we bounded down the stairs, and my mother shouted after me, "Young lady, don't forget you have to go to the launderette later. If you want your pocket money, you'll have to earn it." Without stopping, I yelled back, "I'll be back in a couple of hours, then I'll be your slave for the rest of the day."

Rita and I were on our way to Teresa's house, and lucky for us she lived less than a quarter of a mile away. On the way, we ran past Michael, who was a classmate of ours. He was leaning up against a wall and puffing away on a cigarette. When he spotted us, he yelled out, "Allo girls, what's your big rush then? Come and have a chit chat and share a *fag with me. I haven't seen the pair of you in ages." Without slowing down, I replied, "Sorry mate, we can't talk now, we're on a very important mission." Rita added, "Besides, we just saw you in school yesterday." The two of us kept running, and Michael shouted after us, "Cheeky!"

Turning onto Princess May Road, we spotted Teresa. She was on her way home from the Laundromat and lugging a big bag of laundry. We caught up with her, and without saying a word, we handed her the newspaper. With a puzzled look, she asked, "What's this?" Rita cried, "Take a *gander at page four, and you'll see!" Teresa dropped the bag of laundry onto the ground and opened the paper.

When she saw the picture, her expression went from puzzled to ecstatic. Rita and I stood quietly while our girlfriend stared dreamily at the picture. Finally, Teresa looked up and waving the newspaper, she turned to us and squealed, "We've got to show this to Christina. She's gonna die when she sees how beautiful they are! Ever since the first time Christina heard 'Love Me Do' she's been raving about The Beatles." Looking puzzled, I snapped, "She's not the only one!"

We hurried to Teresa's house, threw the bag of laundry into her hallway, and Teresa yelled to her mother, "I'll be right back Mum." Minutes later, the three of us were running down Wordsworth Road, on our way to Christina's house. Christina lived on Beatty Road which was only six streets away from Teresa's house. Turning the corner and running at top speed, I yelled, "Let's hope we don't bump into any more boys who want to slow us down."

In what seemed like a flash, we were standing outside Christina's house. We rang the doorbell, stood back, and waited anxiously for someone to answer it. Gasping for breath, I turned to my girlfriends and cried, "I think we've had more than enough exercise for one day!" Holding their sides and panting, Rita and Teresa nodded in agreement.

Finally, Christina's mother opened the door, and when she saw us standing there, she chirped, "Well hello girls, what a pleasant surprise. I've just put the kettle on, so you're just in time for a lovely cup of tea." Walking passed Mrs. Maher, Rita purred, "Thank you Mrs. Maher, that sounds wonderful."

Bolting down the hall, the three of us ran straight into the kitchen. Christina was slicing a loaf of bread, and when she saw us, she quickly put the knife down. With a worried look, she asked, "What are you lot doing here? Is something wrong? Please tell me everything's alright!" Bursting with excitement, Teresa answered, "Everything is fine, in fact today's the day that you've been waiting for, and we've brought you the most wonderful surprise." Looking totally confused, Christina answered, "Oh yeah, and what might that be?" Without hesitation, Teresa handed the newspaper over to

Christina, and the three of us stood back, and waited to see her reaction.

Examining the now very wrinkled picture, Christina's face lit up, and squealing with delight, she cried, "Ah, finally I get to see The Beatles. And I must say, they're the dreamiest group I have ever seen." Jumping up and down, I cried, "Isn't it amazing? None of us expected them to be this gorgeous." Grabbing the newspaper, Rita added, "There's only two words to describe The Beatles, they are without a doubt, 'Absolutely Smashing!'"

While we sipped our tea and nibbled on chocolate digestive *biscuits, I said to my girlfriends, "Maybe this is what they mean when they say: love at first sight!" Giggling, Rita cried, "It definitely is for me." Teresa added, "I couldn't agree more!" Not to be left out, Christina chimed, "I've never been in love, and I must say, I'm liking it!" And all I could say was: "Yep, me too!"

*<u>Teddy Boys</u>...*Young men characterized by a style of dress based on Edwardian fashion.*
*<u>Winkle Pickers</u>...*Shoes that feature a very sharp and long pointed toe, reminiscent of medieval footwear.*
*<u>Eiderdown</u>...*A quilt filled with down or some other soft material.*
*<u>Allo</u>...*Cockney word for hello.*
*<u>Boyfriend magazine</u>...*was launched in 1959 and was the first girls' magazine to put music first.*
*<u>Flipping</u>...*used for emphasis or to express mild annoyance.*
*<u>The Angel</u>...*An area in Islington.*
*<u>Smashing</u>...*another word for attractive.*
*<u>Dressing gown</u>...*Bathrobe.*
*<u>Weetabix</u>...*A whole grain wheat breakfast cereal.*
*<u>Fag</u>...*another word for a cigarette.*
*<u>Gander</u>...*another word for have a look.*
*<u>Biscuits</u>...*Cookies.*

CHAPTER 3
A PLAN TO BENEFIT BOTH DAD AND ME

Not long after that first picture was published, all the London newspapers and teen magazines began to carry pictures of The Beatles. Being a poor schoolgirl, I knew that I'd have to come up with a really good scheme in order to obtain some of these fabulous, never before seen pictures. The Daily Mail always seemed to have wonderful new pictures of The Beatles. So, after much thought, I came up with an ingenious plan! My plan was to persuade my father into buying the newspaper on a daily basis.

I patiently waited for the perfect opportunity and when the right time came, I took my father to one side, and with a concerned face said, "Dad, I'm a little bit worried about you. There's a lot going on in the world, and I really don't think the evening news on the telly is adequate. If you really want to keep up with everything, and be well informed, I think you're going to have to buy a daily newspaper. So here's what I'm suggesting. On your way out to work leave the money on the kitchen table, and on my way to school I'll stop by the *newsagents and pick up The Daily Mail. This way, after your long, hard day, your newspaper will be waiting for you when you get home."

Scratching his head and with a pensive look, my father sighed, "Yes, you're probably right, I should try to keep abreast of what's going on in the

13

world, and as long as you're willing to pick it up for me, I've nothing to worry about." As he sat in his cozy armchair, I stood behind it, and with a gleam in my eye I began to rub his shoulders, and purred, "That's right Daddy, just leave everything to me."

From that day on, my early morning routine changed. On my way to the bus stop, I'd *pop into the newsagents on Matthias Road, and pick up the morning edition of The Daily Mail. On that first day while sitting on the bus I thumbed through the newspaper, and found two fabulous, never before seen pictures of The Beatles. As soon as I got to school, I rushed into the sewing room, found a pair of scissors and cut out the pictures. Then, I carefully placed them in between the pages of my thick poetry book.

Later that evening, my father sat down in his overstuffed armchair, opened his newspaper and with a contented sigh, began to read. But as soon as he discovered the two gaping holes on page seven, the smile left his face, and he went completely bonkers. Waving the damaged newspaper and in a rather loud voice, he threatened to never buy another newspaper for as long as I lived in his house. I'd never seen my father this angry, and I couldn't understand why he was making such a huge fuss over such a tiny thing. After all, everyone knew that all the important stuff was right there on the front page!

His ranting and raving continued, and I was getting quite a headache, so I had no choice but to resort to crying. Crying usually did the trick, but to my surprise, this time it wasn't working. He was furious, and instead of handing me a hankie and consoling me, he stormed out of the living room, and shouted to my mother, "Nora, put the kettle on, I need another cup of tea."

Ten minutes later, while sipping his steaming hot tea, he finally managed to calm down. I waited for several hours before I plucked up the courage to approach him, and after much negotiations my father and I came to an understanding. I agreed to let him read his newspaper intact, and he agreed that after he was finished reading it, he'd hand it over to me, and I could do whatever I wanted with it.

One morning, Mr. Monroe the newsagent, was in a rather jovial mood, and as I picked up my newspaper from the stack, he joked, "Cor blimey, look at you, reading the newspaper on a daily basis. What's next *clever dick, Oxford?" Trying not to laugh, I handed him the money, and in my poshest voice, replied, "I can't help it if I'm brilliant, and thank you very much but I do believe I'd prefer Cambridge." Walking out the door, I looked back at Mr. Monroe, and began to giggle. And all he could say was, "Cheeky!"

By now, several of the girls in my class were also buying newspapers, and we spent more time drooling over the pictures of The Beatles, than we had ever spent on our schoolwork. Staring dreamily at the latest picture, Valerie sighed, "They always look so happy, they seem more like brothers than a singing group." Carefully folding her newspaper, Frances added, "I can't think of a better way to start the day than to see a brand-new picture of these four gorgeous faces." We realized that even though The Beatles were a close-knit musical group, they were also separate individuals. And just from looking at the pictures, their own distinct personalities came through, and it didn't take us long to figure out who was who:

Paul was definitely the charmer of the group. George came across as the strong, silent type. John gave the impression of being the leader. And Ringo seemed more reserved than the others. After several lengthy discussions, (usually during our history class) Betty sighed, "It's obvious that there's at least one Beatle that fits every girls' notion of 'The Perfect Man.'"

We all knew that The Beatles had amazing talent, wore fabulous clothes, and were the four best looking boys in all of Great Britain. But there was one other feature that was uniquely theirs and that was: their gorgeous hair. Before The Beatles, none of us had ever seen such a fabulous hairstyle, and we absolutely loved it. Up until now, all of the popular male singers in England wore their hair very similar to Elvis Presley's hairstyle. Remembering the television commercial, Rita joked, "With The Beatles' hair, not even a little dab of *Brylcreem is necessary!" Girls all over the country loved The

Beatles' hair, and we were certain that before long every boy in England would be copying this fabulous new hairstyle.

Another thing that we loved about The Beatles was the fact that they were older men. They had been out of school for quite a few years, they had travelled, they had worked in Europe, and they were living on their own.

Betty chirped, "George is the baby of the group, and he's five years older than us." Flipping through the latest edition of 'Boyfriend' magazine and drooling over yet another never before seen picture of The Beatles, Valerie sighed, "Yes, without a doubt they're sophisticated men of the world." Eileen purred, "They're absolutely perfect, not too young, but certainly not ancient." Valerie reminded us, "And don't forget, I've always preferred older men." With all of these amazing qualities: The talent, the good looks, the gorgeous hair, the ideal age, and the fabulous clothes, my girlfriends and I all agreed that The Beatles were indeed: 'The ultimate package.'

*_Newsagents_…is a business that sells newspapers, magazines, cigarettes, snacks etc.
*_Pop_…Go inside a building or room.
*_Clever dick_…A person who tries too hard to impress with their cleverness.
*_Brylcreem_… a brand of hair styling products for men.

CHAPTER 4
TEENAGERS IN LOVE

In 1962, when The Beatles first came onto the English music scene, I was a fourteen-year-old schoolgirl at Cardinal Pole R. C. Secondary School in Hackney, London. My girlfriends and I had finally reached the fourth year and knowing that at the end of the school year we'd all be fifteen, and legally old enough to leave school and get full time jobs, which made us feel quite grown up.

Fourteen was also the perfect age for your first crush. (Even though I have to admit my very first crush was Cliff Richard, so I must have been more mature than most fourteen-year-old girls.) So, to have your first crush on a member of a musical group rather than someone you actually knew, made life a lot easier.

Valerie groaned, "When you *fancy a boy in your class, you're just waiting for everyone to take the *Mickey, and who needs that all day long?"

Every girl in my fourth-year class had fallen madly in love with at least one member of The Beatles, and some were having trouble making up their minds which one they actually preferred.

Betty was in a real quandary, "Do I fancy George, or is Paul the one for me? They're both so dreamy, so this could take me months to decide." Laughing out loud, Eileen turned to Betty, and asked, "You like more than one kind of cake, don't you? Betty shook her head yes, and Eileen continued, "So then you're allowed to like more than one Beatle, it's the exact same thing!"

After hearing Eileen's perfectly logical reasoning, it was plain to see that Betty completely understood, and looking relieved, she said, "You're absolutely right, there's nothing wrong with fancying two gorgeous *blokes at the same time!"

Because of our never-ending chatter about The Beatles, there were times when we'd completely forget that we were in school. It was almost impossible to stay focused, and our studies definitely suffered. The boys in our class constantly complained to the teachers about our nonstop yapping, but it didn't change anything. After much thought, and many discussions, my girlfriends and I each picked our favorite Beatle.

With a surprised look, Rita said, "I thought we'd all pick the same one, but it's nice to know we've all got completely different taste when it comes to men!" Eileen laughed, "It's a good job too, at least we won't all be fighting over the same Beatle." Valerie and I both chose Ringo, and during our *domestic science class we always made sure that we sat next to each other so that we could talk about him all through the lesson. In between the baking, the cleaning, and copying down dozens of recipes, we chatted nonstop about Ringo.

Before The Beatles came along, we had both adored Cliff Richard. One day, while we were busy making *fairy cakes, Valerie whispered, "Remember when we went 'round to Cliff's house in Winchmore Hill. He wasn't home, but we had a lovely chit chat at his front door with his little sister. By the way, how did we find out where Cliff lived?" Adding a quarter of a cup of sugar to the batter, I answered, "Don't you remember? We went up the West End to see him and The Shadows going into the theatre for the premiere of *The Young Ones, and while we were standing in the crowd, we started talking to a girl, and she gave us his address. So, the very next day right after school we took the bus to Winchmore Hill and popped 'round to see him! But he wasn't home, and we were both heartbroken."

With an admiring glance, Valerie squealed, "Ursula, what an amazing memory you have." Giving her a puzzled look, I hissed, "Valerie, it wasn't that long ago." "Isn't it funny how we've always fancied the same blokes?" She added. Giggling, I answered, "What can I say? We've got great taste in men!" Valerie replied, "Now that we've gone off Cliff, isn't it nice that we have Ringo to dream about?"

Sighing deeply, I answered, "We'll always love Cliff, it's just that these days, we're a lot more sophisticated."

And grabbing a handful of flour out of the canister, I threw it all over Valerie. Laughing hysterically, she picked up an egg, and aiming it straight at me, yelled, "What can I say? You can't get more sophisticated than the two of us!"

*<u>Fancy</u>…Another word for like.
*<u>Take the Mickey</u>…To tease, mock, or ridicule someone.
*<u>Blokes</u>…Another word for man.
*<u>Domestic science class</u>…Cookery class
*<u>Fairy cakes</u>…Similar to a cupcake.
*<u>The Young Ones</u>…A movie starring Cliff Richard and The Shadows.

CHAPTER 5
SINGING ON THE BUS

Cardinal Pole Secondary School was on Wenlock Road, right across the street from Wenlock Brewery. The school building was ancient, and the playground was a tiny, asphalt covered space which was divided into two sections: one for the boys, and the other for the girls. A fifteen-foot fence kept the boys and girls well separated. Because of the pungent odors coming from the nearby brewery, standing in the playground was sheer agony. Most days it smelled like burnt porridge mixed with rotting fish, and buckets of yeast. And just when you were getting used to that horrible smell, a new one wafted over! I just couldn't bear the smell, so I did whatever was necessary to avoid standing outside in the stinky playground.

During our twenty-minute morning and afternoon breaks, my girlfriends and I volunteered to work in the *tuck shop. The tuck shop was nothing more than a large cupboard, with a wooden counter that had hinges, and when not in use was tied to the wall. A couple of the boys had made it in their carpentry class. In the tuck shop we sold chocolate bars, *crisps, polo mints, and all sorts of other delicious snacks. It was very popular with the students, and it made quite a nice profit for the school.

While serving the customers, my girlfriends and I chatted constantly about John, Paul, George and Ringo, and while the boys looked annoyed, most of the girls couldn't help but join in the conversation. During the lunch hour, I volunteered to teach Irish dancing to the younger girls, and while they practiced their steps, I happily sat in the corner reading the latest teen magazines.

By now, all of the magazines carried fabulous pictures of The Beatles, and the most interesting articles. I learned so many fascinating facts about John, Paul, George, and Ringo, while on the other side of the room the girls kept tapping away.

When I wasn't teaching Irish dancing, you could find me in lunchroom. The lunchroom was always lovely and warm and being as the boys and girls never had lunch together, by serving the boys their lunch it was the perfect way to stay inside for the entire lunch hour. After the main course was over, the lunch ladies cleaned up, and brought out the dessert and all of the equipment that went along with it.

This procedure took a good ten minutes, so once again I had some time to put my feet up and read the latest news on The Beatles.

Between all my volunteering I hardly ever went outside, which was exactly why I volunteered to do so much.

Because of the wafting stench coming from Wenlock Brewery, plus the lack of space in the playground, our physical training class became a weekly outing. Every Wednesday morning, the fourth-year girls got on a bus, and travelled to the wide-open fields of Victoria Park.

At the park, we were forced to participate in several unpleasant physical activities, which we had no choice, but to endure. Playing a game of *rounders or running around a large open field over and over again, felt more like a punishment than a fun day out. But there was one part of the P.T. morning that made up for all of the discomfort we suffered at the park, and that was the bus ride.

Every week, quite a few of the girls would buy the 'Record song book.' This magazine cost nine pence, but it had all of the lyrics to all the songs that were on the current hit parade, and it was worth every penny. The girls who had the magazine, shared with the others, and as we drove through the streets of London, the entire busload of girls joined in singing all of the latest popular songs. It was plain to see that the bus driver loved our singing, and he and occasionally even the teachers joined in.

Once 'Love Me Do,' was released, it soon become our favorite sing along song, and we'd sing it countless times until we arrived at the park. On the journey back, we were all in a much better mood, and once again, we'd sing 'Love Me Do' at the top of our lungs all the way back to school. Even though the bus driver didn't have a copy of the 'Record song book,' it didn't take him too long to memorize all of the words to 'Love Me Do', and at times he would be singing louder than any of us girls.

*<u>Tuck shop</u>…*A small shop selling food.*
*<u>Crisps</u>…*Potato chips*
*<u>Rounders</u>…*A ball game similar to baseball, played chiefly in British schools.*

CHAPTER 6
MODERNIZING THE FUERY HOUSEHOLD

In 1962, my record player was an old-fashioned wind-up gramophone player which my father had bought long before any of us kids were born. Whenever my girlfriends came for a visit, they'd beg me to put on a record. Just to wind the crank on that old machine took all of my strength, and by the time the music began, I was exhausted. I'd plop down on the couch, and my girlfriends would be laughing their heads off! After each song I'd have to wind the crank all over again. The other bad thing about that old machine was that the thick, old-fashioned needles would ruin all of my brand-new records.

So, you can imagine my delight when on Christmas day my parents surprised us with a brand-new Dancette electric record player. Noticing my excitement my mother reminded me, "Now don't forget this is a family present, it's for your brother and sisters too."

This record player was so sleek and modern, and it was definitely the most up to date piece of furniture in our entire flat. Overcome with sheer happiness, I cried, "I've never in my life seen anything so beautiful, and I'm happy to say my cranking days are finally over for good!" Together, my father and I read the brochure and soon discovered a feature that neither one of us had ever seen before. This amazing new record player had an arm that allowed you to stack five single records at a time. When the record was over, the next one dropped down onto the turntable, and automatically started to play.

My dad and I watched in awe, as each record dropped into place. As I hit the reject switch, I shrieked, "I've never seen such a magical thing, this is unbelievable." Scratching his head in disbelieve, my father said, "With that old phonograph, we were living in the dark ages!" I nodded over and over in complete agreement.

Knowing that The Beatles' second single would be coming out on January 11th, 1963, I'd saved the pound note that my Godmother had sent me for Christmas, and on the day of its release, I was at the record shop an hour before opening time. About fifty people were lined up outside the shop, and it suddenly dawned on me that everyone in the *queue was there to buy exactly what I wanted: The Beatles' new single. An hour later, I was skipping along on the streets of London, carrying my new prized possession!

When I arrived at *Emerson House, one of my neighbors was just about to go into his flat, and noticing my huge grin, he said, "What's that you've got there Ursula? You look *as pleased as punch." Gushing, I answered, "Ah, it's the new Beatles' record. I've been waiting such a long time for it to come out, and now that I have a new record player, it's gonna sound even better." Opening the door to his flat, he said, "Ah, that's the record my daughter's been going on about. Let me know how it is?" Ready to leap up the stairs, I replied, "I already know, it's gonna be great."

Taking two steps at a time, I galloped upstairs and hurried into my house. I immediately went into the living room, unplugged the record player, and carefully carried it into my bedroom. I placed the shiny new disc on the spindle, pushed the eject button, and the magical machine gently dropped the record onto the spinning platter. As the tone arm gracefully descended, I closed my eyes and was instantly transported. The first few notes of 'Please Please Me' gave me the shivers. It began with the haunting harmonica sound that I'd heard in 'Love Me Do' but the beat was much faster, and more forceful.

I instantly knew that this would be a great song to dance to, and the melody was really easy to sing. The words were catchy and very easy to understand. Now, all I had to do was write down the words, and in no time at all I'd know the song off by heart!

On our next trip to Victoria Park, every girl on the bus knew all of the lyrics to 'Please, Please, Me' and it became our new favorite song to sing, and of course, the bus driver loved it too.

By the beginning of 1963, my Beatle obsession was getting serious. I read every single article that I could possibly lay my hands on, and I spent hours carefully cutting out each and every Beatle picture, whether big or small. My bedroom's pink and blue flowery wallpaper was quickly disappearing under the images of John, Paul, George and Ringo, and the bigger the picture, the happier I was. There was only one word to describe my latest bedroom decor, and that word was: 'Fab' (the new word from Liverpool, that everyone was saying!)

*Queue…A line of people.
*Emerson House…The name of my apartment building.
*As pleased as punch…A saying in England that means: Very pleased, delighted.

CHAPTER 7
THANK YOUR LUCKY STARS

Saturday, January 19th, 1963, was the big day that my girlfriends and I had been anxiously waiting for. The Beatles were scheduled to make their first televised, national appearance on the popular show: 'Thanks your Lucky Stars'. After hearing the wonderful news, Rita could barely contain her excitement, and jumping up and down, she squealed, "Finally we're going to see The Beatles perform. I just can't wait!"

The week of the show, we were counting the days until the weekend, and the closer it got to Saturday the more difficult it became to concentrate on our schoolwork. As she tore up her third attempt at writing an essay, Francis cried, "How am I supposed to write a composition, when all I can think about is seeing The Beatles?" Valerie snapped, "Oh stop grumbling, we're all in the same boat."

By Thursday, all of our teachers had noticed our mounting excitement, and I'm sure that they realized that until the weekend was over, it was highly unlikely that anything would be learned. Miss Goddard warned us, "I don't mind you talking about The Beatles, but girls, please keep the volume down. "With a flushed face, Mary cried, "Thank you Miss, we don't mean to be like this, it's just that we're so excited. "With a faraway look, Miss Goddard replied, "Believe it or not I completely understand, it wasn't that long ago that I was young myself! " Hearing Miss Goddard's unexpected response Valerie and I had a sneaky giggle.

During our French class, while Miss LaVerne wrote foreign words on the blackboard, we made plans to turn The Beatles' first television appearance into a celebration. In a hushed voice, I whispered to my girlfriends, "My Mum and Dad said that everyone's invited over to our house to watch them." Valerie squealed, "Being all together for the big occasion will make it super special." I quickly added, "Just remember no latecomers will be allowed in. Once the show starts, we're not budging. After waiting all this time to see them, we're not gonna miss a single minute."

Realizing that we were still in The French class, Valerie whispered, "And I think it would be very nice if everyone brought something to nosh on." In her usual shy manner, Cecilia asked, "What kind of things shall we bring?" Giggling, Rita answered, "Whatever you *fancy, cakes, biscuits, pies, anything that's been made with lots of sugar." Shaking my finger, I added, "That's right, no fruits or vegetables allowed. If it's good for you, we don't want it."

Finally, the long-awaited day had arrived. I was up bright and early and because I wanted everything to be gleaming, I spent hours dusting, hoovering, and scrubbing the floors. Sitting with her feet up and enjoying her third cup of tea, my mother joked, "I never thought I'd see the day when you'd be spring cleaning in January. "From behind his newspaper, my father commented, "It's lovely to see your poor mother having a break on a Saturday morning. "My mother quickly chimed in, "I think if The Beatles were on the *telly more often, I'd have a lot less housework to do!"

Before everyone arrived, I covered the dining table with our best tablecloth. My mother watched as I carefully arranged the shining plates, the gleaming glasses and the polished cutlery on top of her fine, embroidered tablecloth. I stood back to admire the table and nodded my approval. Finally, my mother spoke, "You know it's not Christmas. We've got lots of other tablecloths that are perfectly suitable. You don't have to be showing off to your friends," I promised my mother that the minute the party was over I'd wash the tablecloth by hand.

After a long pause, she finally said, "Oh alright, you can use it."

An hour before show time my girlfriends began to arrive. Placing a giant platter of chocolate goodies on the table, Betty squealed, "This is gonna be so much fun. To watch The Beatles on the telly with your best friends is something we'll remember forever." As they entered the house, each of my girlfriends handed me assorted containers filled with delicious treats. I immediately handed them to Rita, who carefully placed each item on the celebratory table.

As soon as everyone had arrived, we stood back and admired the table full of colorful, sugary desserts. We had all agreed that we wouldn't eat anything until after The Beatles' performance was over. Licking her lips, Valerie sighed, "I don't know what I'm more excited about, seeing The Beatles or tucking into these yummy sweets." Noticing our disapproving looks, she quickly added, "I'm only joking. Of course, it's The Beatles!"

By the time 'Thank Your Lucky Stars' came on, there was quite a crowd in our living room. My parents and sisters wanted to see The Beatles too, so they sat squashed together on the small couch, while my girlfriends and I sat on the floor. Shouting at the television set, Eileen yelled, "Hurry up Beatles" Valerie added, "Come on, get on with it, start the flipping show already."

After what seemed like an eternity it was finally time, and when John, Paul, George and Ringo appeared on the screen, my girlfriends and I gave a collective gasp, and crawled up even closer to the television set!

Wearing identical V necked suits, white shirts and dark ties, the four of them looked absolutely *smashing. I couldn't believe my eyes, seeing them on the telly it was plain to see that The Beatles were even more gorgeous than any of us had ever imagined! The Beatles began by singing their new hit, 'Please Please Me' and after the first few beats, my girlfriends and I began to sway to the music, and to sing along with them.

In what seemed like a flash the three-minute song had come to an end, and without taking our eyes off of The Beatles, we tried to guess which song they'd be performing next. Mary thought it would be 'Love Me Do,' while Christina was positive it would be a new song that none of us had ever heard. Soon everyone was shouting out their predictions, and Valerie yelled, "If you'd all stop shouting maybe we'll be able to hear the song."

None of us had taken our eyes off of the television screen, and when The Beatles began to bow and wave, we gasped in disbelief! Christina cried out, "It can't be over!" Valerie screamed, "One bleedin' song, that's it? We've been waiting for such a long time to see them, and now after singing just one song, it's all over! "Rolling on the floor, Francis moaned, "This is too hard to believe, I'm heartbroken!" And Rita added, "I was just getting comfortable. I thought I'd be admiring George for at least two more songs." In unison, everyone shouted, "Yeah, so did we!"

My father tried to lighten the mood, "Now girls, you know what they say, time flies when you're having fun!" Giving him a sideways glance, I snapped, "Please Dad, this is not the time for jokes." Getting up from the floor, Mary chirped, "We've finally seen The Beatles perform, so let's be happy, and have a party."

Running to the table, Valerie grabbed a chocolate eclair, and announced, "It's time to eat these delicious goodies, this should make us all feel a little bit better." Smiling broadly, Christina whispered, "And we all know how much Valerie loves her chocolate eclairs."

The remainder of the evening was spent eating all of the yummy treats, drinking glasses of *Tizer, and cup after cup of streaming hot tea, and of course, reliving The Beatles' all too brief television debut. Devouring her third eclair, Valerie sighed, "There's nothing like a piece of cake to help you get over a huge disappointment"

Munching on half a jam donut, I couldn't answer so I just shook my head in agreement.

At the end of the night Francis said, "We'll definitely have to this again, I've had a wonderful time, and I absolutely loved all the goodies" Gobbling up the last of the chocolate digestive biscuits I joked, "It's alright for you lot, you get to go home, and now I have to wash the bleedin' tablecloth." Speaking in a very *posh voice, Valerie added, "Everyone knows that being the perfect hostess is a lot of hard work, and you my dear, have done a marvelous job." Handing her back her empty container, I replied, "Why thank you darling, and next time you can play hostess, and I'll be sure to give you loads of compliments."

The following day, people everywhere were talking about The Beatles' television performance. It seemed as if the whole of London had tuned in to watch them on 'Thank Your Lucky Stars.' Now, everyone knew what my girlfriends and I had known for ages: 'The Beatles were indeed absolutely FAB!

*<u>Smashing</u>…Another word for gorgeous
*<u>Fancy</u>…Whatever you like.
*<u>Hoovering</u>…vacuuming
*<u>Telly</u>…English word for television.
*<u>Tizer</u>…Is a red-colored, citrus-flavored soft drink sold in the U.K.
*<u>Posh voice</u>…Upper class voice.

CHAPTER 8
SATURDAY JOB

On March 18th, 1963, I turned fifteen. I was now legally old enough to seek full or part time employment. As I was leaving to go to school my mother wished me a happy birthday for the tenth time, and said that she'd meet me at 4:30. Looking puzzled, I asked, "Whatever for?" "So that we can get you a Saturday job," she replied. Giving her a sideways glance, I answered, "Okay Mum, we'll find me a job, but surely not today! Not on my birthday! Once I get to school, I'll probably be getting the *bumps, and as you know my friends can be quite rough, so I'll be in no condition to walk! And besides, nobody goes looking for a job on their actual birthday." I left to go to school, thinking that was the end of that!

My girlfriends and I had decided that straight after school we'd go to the Wimpy Bar to celebrate my very special birthday. At 4:30 sharp we met up in the playground, and as we walked out of the school gate, I immediately spotted my mother standing across the street. Looking confused, Rita turned to me and asked, "What's your Mum doing over there?" I was so annoyed all I could do was huff, "She's determined to get me a job. She's not gonna be happy until she has me slogging away every single Saturday. So there go all the plans for my little birthday bash." Trying to cheer me up, Eileen sighed, "Don't worry, we'll celebrate on another day."

I somehow managed to control my temper, and mumbled through gritted teeth, "What a pain in the *arse, I was really looking forward to a delicious Wimpy cheeseburger." Valerie moaned, "Yeah, I was fancying one too." Seeing how irritated I was, my girlfriends scurried off in the opposite direction. I stomped across the street and when I reached my mother, I put my hands on my hips, and yelled, "Alright, let's get this over with!" Looking surprised, my mother huffed, "Well, I must say you're in a lovely mood, and on your birthday too." I snapped, "And what did you expect?"

In silence, we walked down Murray Grove and onto New North Road. Ten minutes later we were on a bus and on our way to Dalston Junction. I stared out of the window and refused to talk. Finally, my mother broke the silence, "There's bound to be some kind of suitable position for you on Kingsland High Street". Still staring out the window, I answered, "Maybe I can get a job cleaning the public lavatories near Ridley Road. Would that be suitable enough for you, Mother?"

My silly comment made both of us laugh, and I turned to my mother and cried, "You could have waited until tomorrow, you knew that my girlfriend and I had plans. "Looking quite guilty, she replied, "Well it's too late now, so we might as well make the most of it."

Ten minutes later we were off the bus and walking down the High Street. As we were walking by 'Boots the Chemist', my mother noticed a 'help wanted' sign in the window. The sign stated that they were looking for a part time sales assistant. My mother cried, "That's absolutely perfect," and before I had a chance to think about it, she dragged me into the shop.

Looking at the shelves filled with bottles of medicines, and all sorts of tablets, I whispered to my mother, "I don't know about this! It's a chemist shop, and you know how I feel about being anywhere near sick people with germs." My mother didn't answer and before I had the chance to run out of the shop, the manager came waltzing over to us. In a very cheery voice he said, "Good afternoon ladies, how may I help you?"

While my mother did all the talking, I walked over to the cosmetic counter, and stared at the beautiful powder compacts that were in a glass display case. Giving me a knowing smile, the manager handed me a clipboard that had an application and a pen attached to it. "Fill this out for me love" he said. I found a seat in the corner of the shop, and scribbled down all of my insignificant information.

After a hasty interview, where he asked me all of two questions, the manager blurted out, "I've got a good feeling about you young lady, so let's give it a try," Hardly able to believe what I was hearing, the manager hired me on the spot. He shook my hand, and told me that my pay would be one *pound for an eight hour day, and I'd work on Saturdays, and on the occasional school holiday.

The idea of getting one pound every single week was simply too hard to comprehend. As the manager kept talking about what my responsibilities would entail, my head was spinning, and all I could think of was: What will I do with all that money? And to my mother's delight, her eldest daughter was now part of the working force. So, as we walked home, we were both feeling rather happy.

The following Saturday I started my part time career at 'Boots The Chemist.' I didn't have a clue about makeup, and I was dying to get some professional advice from my coworkers on the cosmetic counter. But, to my dismay, Mr. Jones (the manager) decided to put me on the drug and preparation side of the shop.

With so many more experienced assistants already working behind the counter, Mr. Jones decided that my main task at 'Boots' would be to repack their bestselling cough drops. I was given a small space in the dark, musty smelling attic, and for this chore the only equipment necessary was a rickety chair for me to sit on, and an old-fashioned weighing scale. Every Saturday, gigantic boxes full of colored cough drops were waiting for me in the attic, and I'd spend the day weighing the drops, and repackaging them into small see through bags.

On my first day the manager told me, "Now Ursula, if you *fancy a couple of drops, please don't be shy, help yourself. As you can see, we have thousands of them." Delighted to hear this, I chirped, "Why thank you Mr. Jones, don't mind if I do."

While weighing the never-ending supply of tasty cough drops, I'd gaze out of the seventeenth century bow window, and when I'd see my school friends who were on their way to Ridley Road Market, I'd bang on the window, and wave to them. Packing and munching the cough drops was quite a pleasant task, and from my window, high above Kingsland High Street, my social life never skipped a beat. At the end of the workday, Mr. Jones would hand me a crisp one-pound note, and to me it was like getting a small fortune.

I now had enough money to buy every Beatle record that came out, and every magazine that had an article or new pictures of John, Paul, George and Ringo. I also had enough money to buy some new mod clothes, and to go to *The Tottenham Royal with my girlfriends on a Saturday night.

We were always hoping that one day The Beatles would perform there, but alas, they never did. However, to our delight The Dave Clark Five were the resident band, and we thoroughly enjoyed dancing to their amazing hits when they performed on stage.

---

*<u>The bumps</u>...Friends taking the birthday boy/girl by the arms and legs and bumping them up into the air, and down onto the floor for as many times as it is their age.
*<u>Arse</u>...British spelling of ass. (your bottom)
*<u>One pound</u>...Equal to approximately 3 dollars in 1963.
*<u>The Tottenham Royal</u>...a North London entertainment venue.

CHAPTER 9
PLEASE PLEASE ME ALBUM

The Beatles' first *LP titled: 'Please Please Me' was released on Friday, March 22nd 1963. Lucky for me, my first day at 'Boots' was the day after its release. The price for the LP was one pound, ten shillings and eleven pence. My parents had given me a pound for my birthday present, so between my birthday money, and my first hard earned pound, I'd have more than enough money to buy the LP.

I wanted to buy it during my lunch hour, so I had to borrow twelve shillings from my mother. As she handed me the money, she gave me one of her over exaggerated concerned looks, and before she had a chance to say anything, I laughed, "Don't worry Mum, I'm a working girl now! You'll get the full twelve *bob back as soon as I walk in the door tonight!" I put the money in my coat pocket along with my pound note, and I stuffed my bright yellow net bag into my other pocket, and off I went to work.

At lunch time, I ran all the way to the record shop. As I walked into the shop, the saleslady chirped, "Allo ducky, how can I help you?" Barely able to contain my excitement, I gasped, "I'd like to buy The Beatles' new LP." Her face lit up and she cried, "Oh *darlin' you're gonna love it. I've been playing it all morning, and everyone's been coming in to buy it. You're a very lucky girl, cos we've only got a couple of 'em left." I gave the saleslady my money and little did she know that this was a monumental day for me, for this was the very first long playing record I had ever bought. I carefully placed it into my net shopping bag, and as I walked out of the shop, the saleslady shouted after me, "*Enjoy it luv!" I turned to face her, and with a big smile, chirped, "Oh, I know I will!"

With my precious LP swinging in my bag, I skipped all the way back to 'Boots The Chemist.' I went into the staff room, hid the precious album in a safe place, gulped down a sausage roll and hurried back upstairs to the attic. Now that I had The Beatles' LP, I couldn't wait for the workday to end.

Later that night, my girlfriends came over, and for hours on end, we happily listened to the amazing new album. Reading the album cover, Rita burst out laughing, "You're not gonna believe this, one of the songs is titled 'Anna' and now my sister is gonna think that The Beatles have written a song especially for her.

Within days after buying it, I knew every song on the 'Please Please Me' album, and all I wanted to do was to lie on my bed, stare at my Beatle pictures, and listen to the album over and over again!

By the spring of 1963 all of the teen magazines were publishing full length articles, and fabulous pictures of The Beatles. Every weekend, I bought my three favorite magazines: 'Valentine' 'Fabulous' and 'Boyfriend' and now a new one was added to my list. This new magazine was called 'Mersey Beat' and instead of looking like the other magazines, this one looked more like a small newspaper. 'Mersey Beat' was published in Liverpool, and because it carried the latest, most up to date information on The Beatles, and all of the other new groups from Liverpool, it soon became the most sought-after magazine among teenagers. We enjoyed reading and learning all about The Liverpool music scene. And even though the distance from London to Liverpool was less than two hundred miles, to us Liverpool seemed like a different world, and a million miles away.

On April 12th, 1963, The Beatles third single 'From Me To You' was released. This single would soon be their first record to reach number one on the Hit Parade.

As soon as it came out, The Beatles' new song was being played continuously on every pop music radio station, and record shops had set up outdoor loud- speakers, to let the people know that they had The Beatles' latest record in stock, and lucky for us, 'From Me To You' was blasting at high volume up and down the High Street all day long. 'From Me To You' was a really happy, bouncy, upbeat kind of love song. It had a simple, honest message that said the lovely things that all of us girls wanted to hear.

The first time I heard 'From Me To You,' right away I noticed the familiar harmonica sound, and to this day when I hear: 'da-da-da-da-da-dum-dum-dum,' I still get dizzy with excitement.

*<u>LP</u>... Long playing album.
*<u>A bob</u>...A slang word for a shilling.
*<u>Allo</u>...Hello.
*<u>Darlin</u>...Darling.
*<u>Luv</u>...Love.

CHAPTER 10
THE ELUSIVE MAGAZINE

For months, everyone had been reading about a new monthly publication that would be coming out sometime in the summer. This new magazine titled: 'The Beatles' monthly Book' would be entirely about for The Beatles. The publishers assured the fans that this new magazine would have brand new articles, up to date interviews, and never before seen photos of The Fab Four each and every month all for the bargain price of one shilling and six pence.

My girlfriends and I were so excited, and we couldn't wait to get our hands on this fabulous new magazine. Before long, we learned that August 1st.1963 was the date that this new magazine would finally be on sale.

On the morning of August 1st. my alarm went off at 7a.m. I jumped out off bed, grabbed my dressing gown, and staggered into the kitchen. My father was sitting at the table, and with a puzzled look, asked, "What on earth are you doing up at this hour? Grabbing the box of Weetabix, I answered, "I'm about to pop round to the newsagents and pick up the new Beatles' magazine. I've been waiting for it to come out for what seems like forever, and finally, today's the lucky day. I'm so excited, I hardly slept a wink all night."

Reaching for the teapot my dad replied, "Well that's great, now how about a nice cup of tea to get you going?" "Yawning loudly, I answered, "Yes please." After gulping my tea, I ran into the bathroom and got dressed. Then I hurried back to the kitchen and finished my bowl of cereal. While tying up the laces on my *plimsolls, and said to my father, "Keep the kettle on. I should be back within ten minutes, and then I'll have another cup." Grinning, he gave me the thumbs up, and said, "Right you are."

Skipping down the four flights of stairs, I realized how lucky I was to live so close to the shops, and in less than five minutes I was standing at the newsagent's counter. Barely able to contain my excitement, I held out my money, and said to Mr. Monroe, "I'd like to buy the new Beatles' Monthly please." Leaning over the counter Mr. Monroe sighed deeply, "Sorry dear, I'm afraid you're out of luck, we've completely sold out. We only got a few copies, and they were gone like bleedin' hot cakes."

I couldn't believe what I was hearing, my lower lip started to quiver, and I blurted out, "But it's not even eight o'clock! "In a fatherly voice, Mr. Monroe replied, "Well don't worry darling, just go down the High Street you're bound to be able to find one down there." Mr. Monroe's unexpected reply had ruined all of my well thought out plans. Ten minutes from now, I was supposed to be back in bed, under my lovely warm eiderdown, sipping my second cup of tea, and enjoying my copy of the first edition of 'The Beatles' Monthly Book.'

I staggered out of the shop onto the street, leaned up against the newsagent's building, and tried to get over my huge disappointment. There were lots of newsagents along the High Street, and so if I really wanted to get this magazine, I'd better get a move on, and start walking to Dalston. It was still early in the morning, and I had no doubt that finding The Beatles' Book wasn't going to be a problem.

Suddenly, a voice bellowed from behind me, "Hello Ursula, you're out bright and early this morning, so where are you off to?" I turned around and there stood Mrs. White, our old and rather deaf neighbor. She was holding onto her rickety shopping cart and was about to go into the green grocers. Knowing how deaf she was, I screamed, Hello Mrs. White, I'm on my way to buy the new Beatles' magazine."

Mrs. White replied, "Well fancy that, I bet my granddaughter will be wanting to get one of those too, she's mad about those Beagle boys." After hearing Mrs. White's funny comment, I couldn't help but laugh, and now thanks to her I was in a much happier mood. Waving goodbye to her, I began my totally unexpected hike to Dalston.

Two hours later, I was still searching for the new Beatles' Monthly Book. Dragging myself from one shop to the next, I pounded along both sides of Kingsland High Street, and on the way, I managed to dodge hordes of fast-moving pedestrians. At every newsagents, I heard the same story: "Oh dear, I just sold the last one five minutes ago."

By the time I reached Dalston Junction, I'd been into every paper shop, sweet shop and stationary shop along the High Street, and I realized that if I wanted to get 'The Beatles' Book' I'd have to take a bus to a different part of London. Exhausted but still determined I jumped on a bus that was going to Stoke Newington. I didn't have the energy to climb up the stairs, so I plunked down on the first empty seat on the *bottom deck. Leaning my pounding head against the cold window, I rubbed my aching feet and quietly moaned to myself. Reeling out my ticket, the conductor chirped, "Don't look so glum, it can't be that bad."

I was in no mood for this man's jolly banter, and I snapped, "Oh yes, it is, in fact it's bleedin' worse!" Allowing me to wallow in my self-pity, the conductor handed me my ticket, and hastily scurried away. Ten minutes later, I was off the bus, and virtually running down Stoke Newington High Street. Along the way, I went into at least a dozen newsagents, and repeated the same question to each of the shopkeepers, "Do you have the new Beatles' Book?" And each shopkeeper gave me the exact same answer, "Sorry love, we've sold out."

By the time I'd reached the last newsagent, I was in tears. I had wasted an entire morning, and now I had to face the facts that I was not going to be able to get this fabulous new magazine that I'd spent so much time dreaming about! And when the lady behind the counter gave me the same old answer, "Sorry dear, they're all gone." I stomped out of the shop, and screamed, "Blooming hell, this is a bloody nightmare!"

After traipsing from one end of the High Street to the other for hours on end, I didn't know what to do. I knew that I could get on a bus to Wood Green, there were lots of paper shops there, but I also knew it would be too late, and I'd have to listen to the now all too familiar mantra: "Sorry love, we're all sold out!" And then, as if things weren't bad enough it began to rain. My body was aching, and I felt like a ninety-year-old granny. All I wanted was a nice cup of tea, and something super sugary to eat. So, I took the bus back to Kingsland High Street, and somehow managed to drag myself home.

My mother was waiting at the front door, and in an anxious tone, cried, "*Crikey, what on earth happened to you? Your father told me that you'd be back in a few minutes, and the kettle's been boiling away for hours." I didn't have the energy to answer, so I staggered into the living room, and threw myself onto the couch. Fluffy, my cat jumped up and snuggled his head into my neck. With a sympathetic look, my mother suggested, "Why don't you have a nice hot bath for yourself, it'll do you the world of good, and you'll be as a right as rain in no time. And while you're in there, I'll make you a nice cup of tea."

Massaging my throbbing head, I sighed, "Thank you Mummy, that sounds perfect." Poor Fluffy who had just made himself comfortable, looked more than a little upset when I tumbled off the couch. I dragged myself into the bathroom, turned on both taps, threw two packets of rose scented bath salts into the running water, and somehow managed to climb in. Five minutes later, I was soaking in a lovely warm bubble bath, sipping a mug of steaming hot tea, and trying ever so hard to forget about the harrowing experience I had just gone through.

Later that night some of my girlfriends came over, and between all of us, not one of us had been able to buy the new Beatles' Book. Slumped on the couch, Valerie grumbled, "We can't even share a copy." Turning to my girlfriends, I sighed, "It's just dawned on me, there's a lot more Beatle fans out there than any of us had realized." The four of them looked at me and nodded in complete agreement.

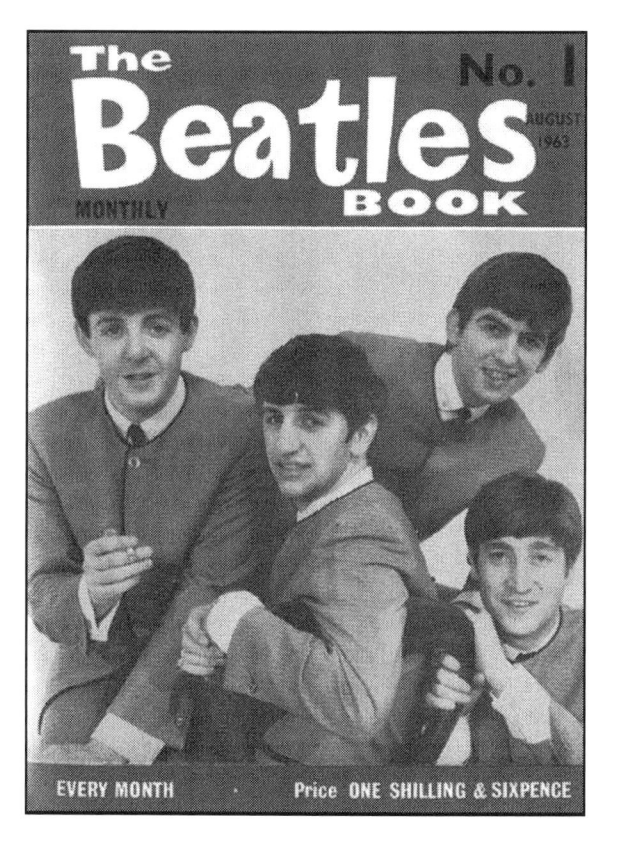

The new, impossible to find Beatles Monthly Book.

The following morning, I went to the newsagents to buy the Daily Mail, and as soon as I walked into the shop the awful memory of the previous day came rushing back. Mr. Monroe immediately noticed the disappointment on my face, and leaning over the counter, he said, "Oh Ursula you look so sad. Don't tell me you didn't get that new Beatles' Book." My lip started to quiver and shaking my head from side to side all I could mutter was, "Nope!" Mr Monroe's face looked as unhappy as I felt.

Scratching his head, it was obvious that he was deep in thought, and all of a sudden, he snapped his fingers and said, "Tell you what I'm gonna do, me darling. From now on, I'm gonna keep a copy of The Beatles' Book right here behind the cash register. It'll be for you and nobody else, but you have to promise me that I'll never see that sad little face again." Gulping back the tears, I managed to say, "Thank you, Mr. Monroe, I'm ever so grateful." And before my emotions got the better of me, I picked up the newspaper, dropped the money on the counter, and ran out of the shop.

A few days later, my girlfriends and I read in the newspaper that the Beatles' Monthly Book had been a huge success, and that every single issue had flown off the newsagents' shelves in record time. Thousands of girls all over England were unable to obtain the new magazine, and just like us they too had been so disappointed.

The following month, my copy of The Beatles' Book was waiting for me at the paper shop. As soon as I stepped into the shop, Mr. Monroe held up the magazine and waving it from side to side, cried, "'I've been waiting for you. 'Here it is me love, are ya happy now?"

This new magazine was much smaller than I had expected, but the picture of John, Paul, George and Ringo on the front cover more than made up for the size. I jumped up and grabbed the magazine right out of Mr. Monroe's hand, and as I gave him the one shilling and six pence, I chirped, "Thanks to you, I'm the happiest girl in the whole of England." Walking out the door I overheard him say to his assistant, "Teenagers, it doesn't take much to keep the little darlings happy."

The Beatles' Book was even better than any of us had imagined. Each and every month, the new magazine had the most up to date information on The Beatles, plus the most beautiful pictures that had been taken especially for The Beatles' monthly book. The highlight of the magazine was definitely the centerfold. Each month a glorious double page picture of one of The Fab Four was featured in the middle of the magazine.

Carefully removing the staples, I'd find the perfect spot to display the gorgeous new picture on my bedroom wall. The Beatles' Monthly kept all of us occupied for hours on end. My girlfriends and I devoured every single word that was written and afterwards we'd have lengthy discussions on each and every article. Almost every page had at least one picture, and we spent hours drooling over each and every one of them.

The Beatles' Book also had a special section devoted to fan mail. The fan club secretaries Anne Collingham and Bettina Rose received thousands of letters every month, and after sifting through the stacks of mail, they'd select a few to be published in the latest edition. I always enjoyed reading the fan's letters. It was the perfect way to find out what other Beatle fans all over the country were thinking.

In the summer of 1963, my girlfriends and I decided that it was time to join The Beatles' Fan Club. The cost was five shillings a year, and we all agreed that the price was a true bargain. I went to the post office, bought a five-shilling postal order, and mailed it along with my membership application to the fan club headquarters.

A week later I received my official fan club card, and proudly became Beatle person number 20,209.

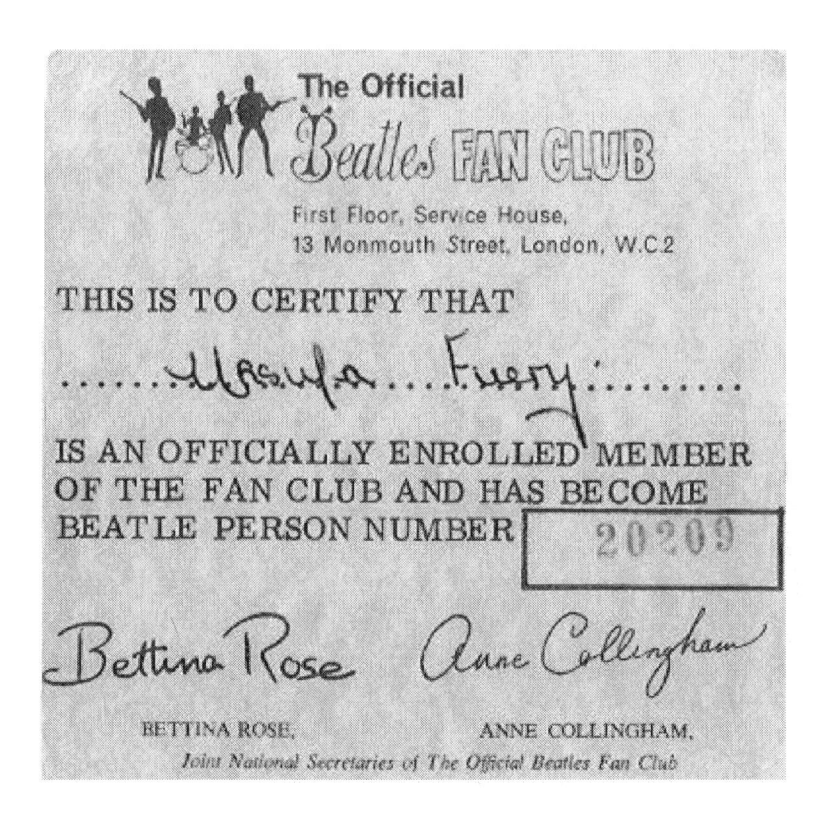

My Offical Beatles Fan Club Card- #20209

OFFICIAL BEATLES FAN CLUB

THE BEATLES .... topped their first popularity poll in November 1961 when readers of the magazine 'Mersey Beat' voted them the North West's favourite outfit... recorded their first Parlophone disc - "Love Me Do" - in September 1962 (released 5 October 1962) ... topped the nation's hit parade for the first time with their second disc – "Please Please Me" - in the third week of February 1963... won their first Silver Disc Award in March 1963... topped the nation's LP charts for the first time with their first LP album (named after that fabulous "Please Please Me" single) in May 1963... have held down the Number One spot in the Top Twenty for more weeks than any other artist or group this year.

● GEORGE HARRISON

GEORGE HARRISON was born in Liverpool on 25 February 1943. He is 5'11" tall and weighs 10 st. 2 lbs. His eyes are hazel and his hair is dark brown. He attended Liverpool Institute and left school to become an apprentice engineer. George SINGS and PLAYS LEAD GUITAR. He met John and Paul at school in 1954 and the trio stayed together in a variety of skiffle and Rhythm & Blues groups before the formation of THE BEATLES in December 1960. George likes smallish blondes, driving, sleeping, watching television, guitar recordings by Chet Atkins and Segovia, the singing of Eartha Kitt, wearing casual clothes, Brigitte Bardot, egg and chips, films produced by Alfred Hitchcock. George dislikes girls who do not dress flatteringly, having his hair cut, travelling long distances at night. Favourite colours:- blue and black.

● JOHN LENNON

JOHN LENNON was born in Liverpool on 9 October 1940. He is 5'11" tall and weighs 11 st. 5 lbs. His eyes and his hair are brown. He attended Quarry Bank High School and Liverpool College of Art. He bought his first electrified guitar with money earned when he was working on a Liverpool building site during his school holidays. John SINGS and PLAYS RHYTHM GUITAR and HARMONICA. Also provides most of those remarkable falsetto voice effects for the group's vocal arrangements. John likes steak, chips, jelly, curries, painting, listening to modern jazz, cats, suede and leather clothing, Juliette Greco, The Shirelles, blondes who are intelligent, reading books, writing off-beat poetry, composing songs in collaboration with Paul. John dislikes thick heads, traditional jazz and anyone who can't make reasonably interesting conversation with him. Favourite colour:- black.

● PAUL McCARTNEY

PAUL McCARTNEY was born in Liverpool on 18 June 1942. He is 5'11" tall and weighs 11 st. 4 lbs. His eyes are brown and his hair is very dark brown. Paul attended Liverpool Institute and collected five passes in his G.C.E. examinations. He went on to pass English Literature at Advanced Level, and he speaks German and Spanish. Paul SINGS and PLAYS BASS GUITAR. He likes Kraft Cheese Slices, steak, chips, all types of well-performed music, watching television, writing new songs with John, almost all girls but particularly those who have long hair and wear short tight skirts with high-heeled shoes, Little Richard, Dinah Washington, Natalie Wood, Sophia Loren, doodling about on Ringo's drum kit, reading adventure stories. Paul dislikes shaving and all types of dishonesty or falsehood. Favourite colour:- black.

● RINGO STARR

RINGO STARR was born in Liverpool on 7 July 1940. He is 5'8" tall and weighs 9 st. 4 lbs. His eyes are blue and his hair is brown. His real name is Richard Starkey - the nickname, Ringo, came about because he collects a fantastic number of rings to wear on his fingers. He attended Dingle Vale Secondary Modern School. Ringo PLAYS DRUMS and (occasionally) SINGS. He joined THE BEATLES in 1962. Has a streak of naturally grey hair. Was in the same class as Billy Fury for a spell at school. Likes light or dark-haired girls so long as they are neat in their appearance, steak and chips, fast cars, Ray Charles, "anyone who likes me", sleek suits, Dinah Washington, Brigitte Bardot, television Westerns. Dislikes onions, tomatoes, chinese food, motor bikes and Donald Duck. Favourite colour:- black.

- o - o - o - o - o - o - o - o - o - o - o - o -

THIS INFORMATION SHEET AND PRESENTATION PHOTOGRAPH IS ISSUED FREE OF CHARGE TO ALL MEMBERS OF THE OFFICIAL BEATLES FAN CLUB.

- o - o - o - o - o - o - o - o - o - o - o - o -

LATEST CLUB INFORMATION AND NEWS IS PRINTED ON THE SPECIAL FAN CLUB PAGE OF THE NEW 'BEATLES MONTHLY BOOK' OBTAINABLE FROM ALL NEWSAGENTS AND BOOKSTALLS.

- o - o - o - o - o - o - o - o - o - o - o - o -

THE OFFICIAL BEATLES FAN CLUB ISSUES FULLY ILLUSTRATED NEWSLETTERS TWICE A YEAR - IN APRIL AND DECEMBER - AND THE ANNUAL SUBSCRIPTION IS FIVE SHILLINGS (RENEWABLE EACH YEAR ON 1 MAY).

- o - o - o - o - o - o - o - o - o - o - o - o -

ALL APPLICATIONS FOR MEMBERSHIP SHOULD BE ADDRESSED TO THE CLUB'S NATIONAL SECRETARY:-

ANNE COLLINGHAM,
THE OFFICIAL BEATLES FAN CLUB,
First Floor, Service House,
13 MONMOUTH STREET,

The Beatles Fan Club Fyler that came with the Official Fan Club Card

Now that I was a member of the fan club, I received special newsletters that gave me even more information on The Beatles. The fan club also informed us about upcoming shows and appearances. Between the fan club newsletters and the Beatles' Book, my girlfriends and I were always right up to date on all of The Beatles' news.

I had managed to save over two pounds, so I decided to treat myself, and I bought the official Beatles' sweater. It was so fabulous I didn't want to take if off, and I wore everywhere I went. I could tell that everyone who saw my beautiful Beatle sweater loved it too!

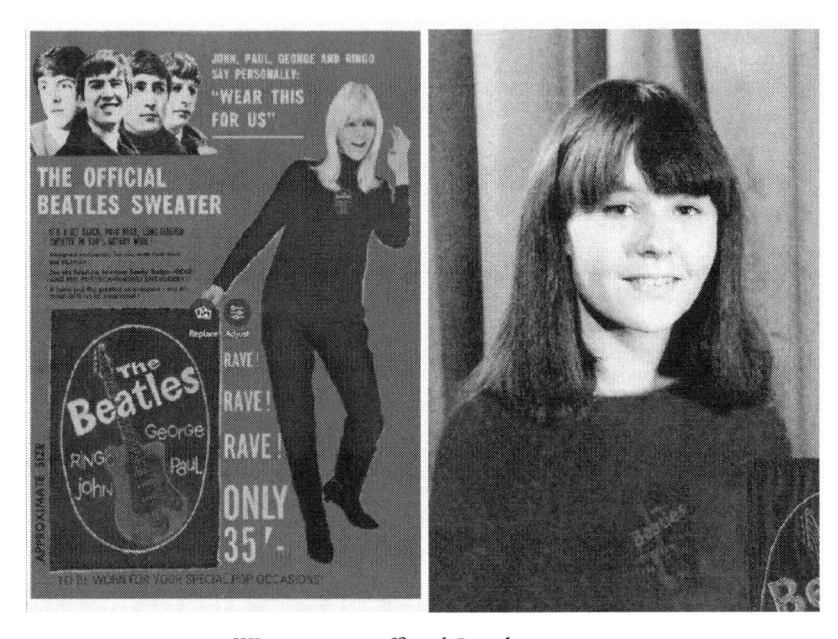

Wearing my official Beatles sweater.

On August 23rd. 1963, The Beatles' long awaited next single was finally released. Its title was: 'She Loves You'. I bought the record on the very day that it was released, and after playing it over and over, and writing down all of the words, It didn't take me too long to learn the entire song. All of the popular radio stations played 'She Loves You' continuously, and it was so much fun to sing along with the radio.

A week after its release, no matter where I'd go, I could hear people humming 'She Loves You' and by September 12th, the new song had skyrocketed to the number one position on the hit parade. Once again, the record shops blasted the new Beatle song from their outdoor speakers, and on hearing the song, my girlfriends and I would break into spontaneous dancing, and sing along. But instead of singing 'She Loves You', we changed the lyrics to: 'We Love You.'

We also began to answer every question by singing, "Yeah, Yeah, Yeah!" until one day, Valerie read that thousands of girls all over England were doing the exact same thing. Throwing the newspaper into the rubbish bin, Valerie cried, "These days, it's just impossible to be original!"

My father too, enjoyed 'She Loves You' and it soon became his favorite song to whistle. Listening to him, I'd tease, "Fancy you, whistling a Beatle song, I had no idea you had such great taste in music."

*Plimsolls…a light rubber-soled canvas shoe, worn mainly for sports. (Similar to sneakers.)
*Bottom deck…The downstairs of a double decker bus.
*Crikey…An expression of surprise:

CHAPTER 11
BEST PRESENT EVER.

One afternoon I arrived home from school, and my mother came rushing out of the kitchen holding up a big brown envelope. Handing it to me, she said, "The postman delivered this an hour ago, and it's addressed to you." I couldn't imagine what could possibly be inside this official looking envelope. I certainly wasn't in any kind of trouble, and other than talking a little too much in class I was the perfect student. Noticing the worried look on my face, my mother began to laugh, and teased, "Oh for God's sake, just open it!"

I ran into the kitchen and grabbed a knife, and in one swift motion ripped open the envelope. Two tickets came tumbling out of the envelope and fell to the floor. I quickly scooped them up and began to read what was written on one of them. I couldn't believe my eyes; these tickets were for 'The Great Pop Prom' and the headline act was none other than The Beatles. The show was going to take place at the world-famous Royal Albert Hall on Sunday, September 15th. 1963.

Suddenly it dawned on me: I was finally going to see The Beatles in person, and the very thought made me giddy with excitement! My legs began to shake, and I could barely breathe. I grabbed a chair and somehow managed to sit down. For the longest time I just sat there staring in disbelieve at the precious tickets. I couldn't imagine who'd sent them to me, and I was in a complete state of shock. When I finally looked up and saw my mother's beaming face, I instantly knew that she was the one who'd bought them.

I held up the tickets and cried, "Ah, the mystery is solved, you're the one who got them!" Smiling broadly, she replied, "Well your father and I know how much you love The Beatles. You're constantly talking about them, so it's plain to see that you're just dying to see them." I was still a bit shaky, but somehow managed to get up, and giving her a huge hug, I cried, "Thank you mummy, it's the best present I've ever received!"

After I'd finished hugging her, my mother straightened out her cardigan, and just by the look on her face I knew that she was about to tell me something unpleasant. Finally, she spoke, "As you can see there are two tickets, one is for you, and the other one is for Angela. "I knew it was too good to be true, and giving her a sideways glance, I pleaded, "Oh mum, do I have to go with her? Please, couldn't I take one of my girlfriends instead?"

My mother didn't answer, and that's when it dawned on me, that thanks to my parents I was going to see The Beatles. If I had to take my little sister with me, it wouldn't be so bad. I'd go with my Great Grandfather if that's what my they wanted. Turning to face her, I said, "You're absolutely right. Of course, Angela can come with me, and don't worry I'll make sure that she doesn't wander off and get lost up the *West End." My mother went back into the kitchen, and heading to the front door I yelled, "I'll be right back, I'm just going to show Teresa the tickets." My mother shouted after me, "Don't be giving Angela's ticket away now!"

Staring at the ticket Teresa sighed, "I wish my mum had got me a ticket. Imagine all the fun we'd have if we went to the show together." With a sympathetic sigh, I replied, "One day we'll see them together, just you wait and see."

After dinner, I steered my mother over to the couch, and placed a cushion under her feet. In a dramatic tone, I cried, "Please mum sit down, and relax and leave everything to me. After the wonderful present you've given us today, the least I can do is the *washing up." Practically purring, my mother sighed, "Don't be spoiling me now."

Looking over at Angela, who's head was buried in an Enid Blyton book, I shouted, "And I'm sure tomorrow night your other daughter will show her gratitude by doing the exact same thing." Angela didn't look up, but I knew that she'd heard every single word that I'd said.

*<u>West End</u>…London's busy entertainment area.
*<u>Washing up</u>…Cleaning the dishes, glasses etc.

CHAPTER 12
MY FIRST BEATLES CONCERT

The night before The Great Pop Prom, Angela and I spent hours rummaging through the bedroom *cupboard, our wardrobe, and the chest of drawers. We were searching for the perfect outfit for Angela to wear for tomorrow's big event. As she threw another pile of clothes onto her bed, I thoroughly examined each and every item. Angela began to yawn, and it was obvious that she'd had enough. Throwing another unsuitable top onto the reject pile, I snapped, "You don't seem to understand, tomorrow's a very important day, and we must look absolutely fabulous.

Everyone at the concert will be wearing gorgeous clothes, and *by hook or by crook, so will we."

Instead of helping me, Angela sighed deeply and said, "You can pick out my outfit, I've always trusted your great taste when it comes to fashion, so whatever you select will be fine with me." Giving her a sideways glance, I cried, "Oh no you don't, I know what you're up to. You just wanna watch the *telly and leave all the work to me." Handing her two dresses, I snapped, "Now go and try these on, and hurry up about it!" Stomping out of the bedroom, she cried "Golly, you can be so bossy. "I already knew what I'd be wearing. My fabulous new outfit was draped on a hanger, ready for me to slip on.

That afternoon, during my lunch hour at 'Boots The Chemist,' I ran to Ridley Road Market, and at one of the clothing stalls I'd bought a French sailor's *jumper. These jumpers were the height of fashion, and all over London both males and females were proudly wearing their blue and white striped tops. I'd been dying to own one of these fabulous jumpers, but the expensive price tag had kept me from splurging. Thanks to 'The Great Pop Prom' I now had the perfect excuse to be extravagant. Between my fabulous new top, my gorgeous navy-blue trousers, and my mod *hush puppies, I was confident that I was right up to date with the latest clothing style.

Now Angela was in need of my fashion expertise, and after three agonizing hours, the final selection was made. We both agreed that her red and white flowery blouse, and her new navy- blue pleated skirt was the perfect outfit for a modern, up to date girl.

Posing with my cat Fluffy, just before leaving for The Great Pop Prom. I thought I looked so stylish!

At long last, September 15th.1963 had finally arrived. The concert was an afternoon event. Knowing that we'd probably have to wait for a bus, endure a very long bus ride, and have to wait again on the queue once we had arrived at The Royal Albert Hall. So, with all the plans in my head, and not wanting to be late I decided that we'd better leave the house at least two hours before the start of the show.

As the clock struck twelve, Angela and I were at the front door ready to go. Buttoning up our jackets, we said goodbye to our mother, and in an excited, and rather loud voice, I yelled out to my father, "*Ta ta Dad, we're off to see The Beatles!"

Angela whispered to me, "I think you're shouting on purpose so that all of our neighbors will know where we're going." Giving her a little wink, I whispered back, "You know, you could be right." From the kitchen, my dad yelled back, "Hold on a minute girls, I've got something for you." Angela and I looked at each other and shrugged our shoulders. I could hear him rummaging through the cupboard, but I couldn't imagine what he was going to give us.

Finally, he came running out of the kitchen holding the biggest bag of sweets I had ever seen.

With a twinkle in his eye, he handed the enormous bag over to Angela, and joked, "Just in case you girls get a little bit *peckish, here's a treat for both of you." Angela gave him a huge hug, and cried, "Thanks Dad, you're the best." I immediately grabbed the bag out of Angela's hand, and in a rather bossy tone, snapped, "I'd better take them, you know how you are when it comes to sweets? They're for when we're watching the show, and if you're holding them, they'll be gone by the time we get off the bus."

Twenty minute later, Angela and I were boarding the number 73 bus. We bounded up the stairs, ran to the front of the bus, and plunked ourselves down on the front seat. Driving along, I gazed out of the large double windows, and it suddenly dawned on me where we were heading. We were on our way to the West End, we were on our way to 'The Great Pop Prom' and best of all, we were on our way to see John, Paul, George and Ringo. Just thinking about it made my stomach jump with excitement, and I whispered to Angela, "I can't believe we'll be seeing The Beatles this afternoon. I'm so excited, I feel quite nauseous."

With a concerned look, Angela replied, "I know what'll fix that. Have a few sweeties, and while you're at it I'll have some too." Giving her a dirty look, I shrieked, "Oh no you don't, I know what you're up to. You'll have 'em all gone before we get off this bleedin' bus!" All the other passengers on the upper deck had heard my loud response, and each and every one of them were laughing hysterically.

Blushing from embarrassment, Angela snapped, "Why do you have to be so bloody loud?" I was so excited about preparing myself to see The Beatles that I had completely forgotten that other people were even on the bus. I was embarrassed too, so I whispered in Angela's ear, "Sorry."

We stayed on the 73 bus until we reached Marble Arch, and then we had to take another bus which left us off right outside the Royal Albert Hall. The ornate, orange colored circular building was a spectacular sight to see. It was named after Queen Victoria's late husband, and I had read that it held at least 5,500 people. I was so excited; I couldn't wait to get inside.

The Royal Albert Hall.

Looking at my watch, I said to Angela, "It's getting late, we'd better get a move on, and find the end of the queue." The queue moved along quite nicely, and in what seemed like a flash, we were standing at the main entrance. A uniformed usher checked our tickets and directed us to the rear end of the main section. Ten minutes later, we were finally sitting in our reserved seats.

Standing up to look around, Angela whispered, "Well, we're definitely in the cheap seats." I replied, "As long as we can see the stage, I'm happy."

While sitting in the super comfortable seats, Angela and I stared in awe at the interior of this magnificent venue. Neither one of us had ever seen anything like this before: the lavish decor, the opulent gold leaf ornamentation, the private balconies with the perfectly hung drapes, and the soft, red velvet fabric which seemed to cover the entire place. Angela cooed, "I feel like I'm in Buckingham Palace". Nodding in agreement, I whispered, "I can't get over it, I've never seen anything so luxurious. Come to think of it, this whole afternoon is like one big dream."

The interior of The Royal Albert Hall.

Now all we have to do is keep our fingers crossed that nobody really tall sits in front of us, and ruins the view of the stage." Angela leaned over, and whispered, "Now that we're settled do you think we could eat some of the sweeties?" Moaning loudly I replied, "I think you care more about these bloody sweets than you do about seeing The Beatles." Angela cried, "Your language is appalling! It's a good job mum can't hear you."

I opened the enormous bag, handed it over to Angela, and sighed, "Well go on then, help yourself. Eating handfuls of tiny *dolly mixtures, we sat back, and watched as the crowds kept pouring into the concert hall. Finally, two petite girls sat down in front of us, and smiling broadly Angela and I gave each other the thumbs up, and I breathed a deep sigh of relief.

Thirty minutes later, the show began.

The moment the curtains went up, the audience cheered loudly, and the atmosphere was electrifying. The master of ceremonies was none other than the popular D.J. Alan Freeman. The first act that Alan introduced was a new group from London called "The Rolling Stones". This new group was becoming quite popular, and their first single titled: 'Come On' was slowly climbing up the hit parade. While The Rolling Stones performed, the audience became very loud, and some of the girls were actually screaming.

I had never been to a pop concert before, so this was a whole new experience for me, and while The Rolling Stones performed, I divided my time between watching them on stage, and staring at the screaming girls. After The Rolling Stones, The Viscounts, Kenny Lynch, Susan Maughan, Shane Fentone, The Vernon Girls, and several other performers entertained us.

All of these acts were very talented, but I couldn't wait for them to hurry up and get off the stage. In anticipation, I kept checking the program and I knew that it was only a matter of time before The Beatles would be coming out. It was plain to see that Angela too was thoroughly enjoying her first pop concert, and the gigantic bag of dolly mixtures only added to her enjoyment.

The Beatles were the last act to perform, and when John, Paul, George and Ringo finally came out onto the stage, the entire audience immediately leapt to their feet. Before The Beatles had played a single note, everyone was screaming loudly. Being in the middle of all this excitement was highly contagious, and Angela and I screamed along with the rest of the audience. The screaming was deafening, and it was nearly impossible to hear which songs The Beatles were singing. But I didn't mind one bit, just to be able to see them in person was more than enough for me.

As Ringo banged on his drums, and the others played their guitars and sang, it looked like they too were enjoying themselves. After performing several songs, The Beatles' performance sadly came to an end. John, Paul, George and Ringo waved goodbye to the audience, and walked off of the stage. Instantly, the entire audience began to chant, "More, more, we want more!" But to everyone's disappointment, Alan Freeman came onto the stage, and announced, "Ladies and gentlemen, 'The Great Pop Prom' of 1963 has come to an end. I hope everyone enjoyed themselves." My sister and I sat back in our seats and watched as the crowds scurried out of The Royal Albert Hall. Now that I'd finally seen The Beatles, my only ambition was to see them again and again. After the crowd had dwindled, Angela and I decided that it was time to leave.

While we were walking by the main entrance, a chauffeur driven car came out of nowhere and almost plowed into me. This car had missed me by inches, and all of a sudden, the people in the back seat began screaming at me, "Hurry up, get out of the way!" I couldn't believe that these rowdy passengers were yelling at me. After all, I was the one who was almost killed. Too timid to yell back, I glanced over at them, and to my surprise the people who were hanging out of the car windows, and verbally abusing me were none other than that new group The Rolling Stones!

Trembling, I ran to the *pavement and grabbing my arm, Angela cried, "I got the fright of my life, that car came awfully close to running you over. What's their big rush anyway?" I whispered to her, "Can you believe The Rolling Stones were screaming at me like it was my bleedin' fault?" The two of us stood against the Royal Albert Hall and waited for my heart to stop thumping. Once I'd fully recovered, we continued walking down Kensington Gore.

All of a sudden, I heard a familiar voice, "Ursula, Angela, yoo-hoo, we're over here." The moment I heard that distinct Irish accent, I turned to Angela and said, "I'd recognize that voice anywhere, it's Mum." Laughing out loud, Angela replied, "What on earth would Mum be doing up the

West End? The shops aren't open on Sunday, and besides we're miles away from Oxford Street." Looking all around, I answered, "I'm telling you that was Mum's voice, I'd know it anywhere! She's probably terrified that we gonna forget the way home."

Suddenly Angela burst out laughing, and pointing down the street, she screeched, "Oh, bless her heart, there she is, and she's not alone." I turned to where Angela was pointing to, and there stood my mother, my father and our little sister Veronica. They were standing at the bus stop, and all three of them were frantically waving to us.

Grinning from ear to ear, I said to Angela, "There, what did I tell you?" We rushed over to them, and in unison said, "What are you doing here?" Smiling broadly, my Dad replied, "We thought we'd surprise you. So now you've had two surprises in one day, first the sweets, and now the pleasure of our company." Angela and I looked at each other and rolled our eyes!

At the bus stop, my parents began to chat with a little old lady who was also waiting for her bus. Making sure that we were out of earshot, I whispered to Angela, "Thank God, they hadn't seen The Rolling Stones' car incident. We'd never be allowed out of the house again, and our first pop concert would definitely be our last one. Giving me the thumbs up Angela replied, "I had such a lovely time and I'm determined to go to lots more rock and roll shows, so don't worry, your secret is completely safe with me."

On the bus ride home, barely able to control our excitement, Angela and I took turns telling our parents, and the other passengers all about The Great Pop Prom, and especially seeing The Beatles.

*<u>Cupboard</u>…Another word for closet.
*<u>Hook or by crook</u>…To do whatever is necessary.
*<u>Telly</u>…Another word for television.
*<u>Jumper</u>…Sweater or top.
*<u>Hush puppies</u>…Shoes.

*<u>Ta ta</u>...Goodbye.
*<u>Peckish</u>...Hungry.
*<u>Dolly mixtures</u>...Small soft, sugar-coated jellies.
*<u>Pavement</u>...Sidewalk.

CHAPTER 13
BEATLEMANIA IS NOW A WORD

In the early part of October, I read that Brian Epstein, The Beatles' manager had been making arrangements for The Beatles to perform on 'Sunday Night at the London Palladium.' This show was the most popular variety show on television, and every Sunday evening people all over England tuned in to watch singers, dancers, ventriloquists, comedians and many other talented acts. Bruce Forsyth was the host of the show, and everyone adored him.

Within days, my girlfriends and I managed to find out that John, Paul, George and Ringo's appearance was scheduled to take place on Sunday, October 13th, 1963. Reading an article about the upcoming performance, Valerie said, "I've got an idea, why don't we go to The Palladium and greet The Boys on their way in." The thought of seeing The Beatles close up made me squeal with delight, and seeing my girlfriends faces, it was obvious that they too felt the same way. With a gleam in her eye, Eileen cried, "What a *smashing idea. I've been to The Palladium and it's just a hop, skip and a jump away from here." Jumping up and down, Francis blurted, "It'll be so much fun. Let's do it!" Flushed with excitement, Rita threw her beret up in the air and squealed, "Yippee, I'm gonna see The Beatles."

The week before the show, our schoolwork was yet again put to one side.

For the West End trip, we had major plans that needed to be arranged. As we copied algebra problems from the blackboard, we chattered nonstop to each other. At the lunch table, our Palladium trip was the main topic of conversation. On our weekly excursion to Victoria Park, instead of continuously running around the field, we hid in the bushes, and finalized our plans. As we huddled in the tall grass, I whispered to my girlfriends, "Now here's what we're gonna do: At two o'clock sharp, we'll meet at the Newington Green bus stop." Turning to Rita, I added, "And we'll see you at The Angel bus stop. Be there no later than quarter past two, and the minute you see us, hop on board." Clicking her heels, and saluting, Rita replied, "Yes, sir, whatever you say, sir!" We all began to laugh at Rita's silly comment, and Eileen added, "I'm so excited, I think I'm going to burst!" When the outdoor meeting came to an end, we crawled out of the bushes and back onto the field, and once again the teachers were none the wiser!

On Sunday afternoon, at precisely two o clock, my girlfriends and I were gathered together at the bus stop. Laughing out loud, Valerie squealed, "It's a bleedin' miracle, this is the first time we've all stuck to the plan. Only The Beatles could have this kind of power over us." While we waited for the bus, our excitement grew. Peering anxiously down the road, Eileen cried out, "Come on bus, we haven't got all day, The Beatles are waiting for us."

Finally, the number 73 bus pulled up to the bus stop, and we broke into spontaneous cheering. Stumbling up the stairs with each step our laughter got louder. Giving Christina a little shove, I yelled, "Get up there." Dangling from the railing, she yelled, "Hey, watch it!" With glaring eyes, the downstairs passengers shot disapproving glances at us, but we were so happy we completely ignored them, and continued our rather loud behavior. As soon as we got to upper deck we ran to the front of the bus, and plunked ourselves down in the front seats.

Minutes later, the conductor came bounding upstairs to collect our bus fares. Reeling out our tickets, he asked, "You're a very cheery bunch, so where are you off to?" Eileen blurted out, "We're on our way to see The

Beatles. They're gonna be on 'Sunday Night at The London Palladium' tonight, and we're gonna wish them luck on their way in." Smiling broadly, the conductor said, "Cor blimey, it's a *good job I bumped into you girls. I'd completely forgotten about them being on the telly tonight. My wife would've been so disappointed if she had missed seeing them, and I'd never hear the end of it. Thanks girls, you've just saved me life!" Fifteen minutes later, the bus pulled into The Angel bus stop, and we immediately spotted Rita. She was leaning up against an ancient stone building, and even though she was wearing a thick, woolen scarf, she looked awfully cold, and quite miserable. To get her attention, we banged on the window, and waved to her. She finally looked up, and in a very cranky voice yelled up to us, "Well, it's about bleedin' time, I've been standing here for what seems like an eternity!"

Rita came upstairs, shuffled to the front of the bus, and plunked herself down next to Eileen. Sighing loudly, she groaned, "God, it feels so good to be sitting in a lovely warm bus. I didn't think you lot were coming, and I was just about to go home." The conductor never showed up to collect Rita's bus fare, and Valerie whispered to us, "Some people have all the bleedin' luck!" Five minutes later Rita had warmed up, and was back to her old bubbly self.

In what seemed like the longest bus ride ever, we finally reached our destination. As the bus pulled into Oxford Circus, we tumbled noisily down the stairs, and one by one jumped off the bus onto the pavement. The cheerful conductor gave us the thumbs up, and shouted out, "Have a lovely time girls, and be sure to give The Beatles a big kiss from my old lady!" Eileen yelled back, "Just for you, I'll give 'em two!"

Just knowing that we were around the corner from the London Palladium made us giddy with excitement. Combing her hair with her fingers, Valerie asked, "So how do I look? I've got to be perfect for Ringo." Giggling, I replied, "You always look gorgeous, but how many times do I have to tell you? Ringo only has eyes for me." Giving me a push, Valerie chirped, "Then we have no choice, we'll just have to share him?" Putting on a *posh voice, I purred, "I can't think of anyone I'd rather share him with."

My girlfriends and I couldn't contain our excitement any longer, so we began to run down Oxford Street. Eileen was ahead of us, and waving her arms and running sideways, she yelled, "Hold on Beatles, we're coming." People who noticed Eileen's silly walk stopped in their tracks and gawked at her. Seeing complete strangers staring at her made us laugh even more than we already were. From all the laughing, we were unable to keep up the running, and pointing a finger at Eileen, Valerie squealed, "Please, no more funny talk, I'm about to wet my *knickers."

After we regained our composure, we continued walking, but when we turned onto Argyll Street we came to an abrupt halt. Unable to comprehend what we were looking at, we stared in disbelief. Hundreds of girls were milling around the entrance to The Palladium, and the enormous crowd had spilled out onto the street.

Frustrated, Christina twirled around to face us, and cried, "Can you believe this? I thought we'd be the only ones here." Shaking her head in disbelief, Eileen mumbled, "How can so many people have the exact same idea as us?" Valerie moaned, "Now we know for sure we're definitely not the only Beatle fans in London." We somehow managed to find a tiny space among the noisy crowd and huddled together in the freezing cold.

Putting on a happy face, and trying to sound optimistic, I shouted, "Okay, get ready girls The Beatles will be here any minute now." Suddenly, a girl who was standing close by tapped me on the shoulder and said, "I couldn't help but overhear what you've just said, and I hate to be the one to give you the bad news, but The Beatles are already inside. They've been in there for hours." With a puzzled look, I turned to the girl and said, "That's impossible! The show doesn't go on until 8 o'clock, why on earth would they arrive so early?

In a sarcastic tone Valerie said, "Before appearing on the most popular show on telly, what's the one thing that every act, including The Beatles have to do?" Before I had a chance to think, Valerie snapped, "You silly cow, rehearse, the answer is rehearse!" Eileen chimed, "That's right, I'd completely forgotten about rehearsing, but then why are so many people standing around in the flipping cold?" Before anyone else answered I said, "The same reason we are." Always the optimistic, Rita chimed, "Hey, you never know, maybe The Beatles will pop out for a bite to eat." Through chattering teeth and barely able to speak, Eileen whimpered, "It's freezing cold, so how about we stay for one hour and see what happens?" We all shook our heads in total agreement.

Before long, we were enjoying the company of all the other fans that were around us, and despite the cold, we managed to have a really good time. Christina whispered, "These girls are like us, they love The Beatles almost as much as we do." Rita replied, "Yeah, well they just better stay away from my George!"

Two and a half hours later The Beatles still hadn't come out, and looking at her watch Eileen said, "I know we're having a lovely time, but if we leave now, we'll be home in plenty of time to see them on the telly, so what do you think?" Eileen was right, The Beatles were not about to come out, and we were all anxious to be home to watch them live on the telly.

While we were saying goodbye to our new friends, one of them named Susie came up and whispered in my ear, "Do you want to know a secret?" Giving her a curious look, I answered, "Yes, I know that song, isn't it fab?" Laughing out loud, she replied, "No, I have a real secret, and I'm positive that you and your friends will really like what I'm about to tell you."

She looked around, just to make sure that nobody was listening, and she whispered, "How would you and your mates like to know where The Beatles live?" Giggling, I replied, "Are you *having me on?" Everyone knew that John, Paul, George and Ringo had relocated to London, but their addresses were top secret, and nobody knew where any of them lived. Once again, Susie made sure that none of the other fans were eavesdropping. Then she continued, "Me and my friends practically live outside their houses.

If I tell you, you'll have to promise not to tell too many girls. The Beatles' neighbors wouldn't be very happy if their nice quiet streets were turned into madhouses just like this place is at the moment."

To me, Susie looked like an honest person, and besides, I had nothing to lose. So, I fumbled through my oversized bag, and somehow managed to find a tattered scrap of paper, and my trusty red *biro, and while Susie continued to whisper, I scribbled down the top secret addresses:

John ....13 Emperors Gate, Brompton.

Paul....57 Wimpole St. Marylebone.

George and Ringo....57 Green Street, Mayfair.

Writing down the addresses for the first time ever became real to me that The Beatles were now living in my city, and I couldn't ask for anything better. I thanked Susie at least a half a dozen times and placed the scrap of paper with the most sought after addresses in the whole of England into the bottom of my bag.

Walking down Argyll Street I turned to Valerie, and squealed "Can you believe it? This girl has given us the best present ever, and we now know where each and every one of The Beatles live!" Giving me a peculiar look, Valerie snapped, "Have you gone *balmy? She doesn't know where The Beatles live, she's making a complete fool out of you!" Annoyed at Valerie, I snapped back, "What a horrible thing to say, she seems like a very nice person, and I think she's telling the truth." Walking away, Valerie hissed, "God, you're so bleedin' gullible!"

Together, my girlfriends and I jumped on the 73 bus, and each of us got off at our appropriate stop and hurried home. When I got home, I walked in the front door and yelled, "Hey Mum, I'm home, what's for dinner?" Running from the kitchen, my mother cried, "Where have you been all afternoon? I was getting worried!" Taking off my coat, I answered, "I've been up the West End, standing in the freezing cold, and chatting with hundreds of strangers." Taking off her apron my mother sighed, "Well, it's a good job you're home, because dinner is just about ready."

White eating my favorite Sunday dinner which consisted of roast beef, *Yorkshire pudding, mounds of mashed potatoes, a couple of brussels sprouts, and all of it swimming in the best onion gravy on earth, I told my family about my wonderful afternoon standing in the bitter cold outside the London Palladium. My parents looked rather puzzled, but just nodded as I continued telling them all of the little details.

Later that evening, my family and I gathered around the television set to watch 'Sunday Night at The London Palladium.' Before it began my mother gave me one of her stern looks, and said, "The last time The Beatles were on the telly, you and your friends sang so loud, none of us heard a thing. So tonight, if you don't mind, we'd like to hear The Beatles instead of you." Laughing hysterically, I replied, I had no idea you were such a big Beatle fan!"

I grabbed my pillow off the bed and found the perfect spot on the living room floor.

As the clock struck eight the show began. The Beatles and Bruce Forsyth came out onto the stage, and pointing to them Bruce Forsyth announced, "If you want to see them again, they'll be back in forty-two minutes." Groaning loudly, I shrieked, "I don't believe this, now we're gonna have to watch the whole flipping show." In unison, my family shouted, "Shush!"

Resting my head on my pillow I laid on the floor and waited patiently for John, Paul, George and Ringo to come back on the screen. Precisely forty-two minutes later The Beatles came out onto the stage, and performed four songs: 'From Me To You', 'I'll Get You', their recent hit 'She Loves You' and ending with 'Twist and Shout.'

To watch them perform not one, but four fabulous songs, and to be able to stare at them for such a long time was without a doubt a teenage girl's dream come true. At the end of their performance The Beatles stood on the stage bowing and waving, and the camera zoomed in on the screaming audience, and my only thought was: "You lucky people, how did you managed to get tickets to this amazing show?"

At the end of 'Sunday Night at The London Palladium,' we watched The Beatles go around on the famous Palladium round about. Holding onto the giant, glittery letters, John, Paul, George and Ringo waved and smiled to the audience, and I was in heaven.

The following day it was reported that over 15 million viewers had tuned in to watch The Beatles on 'Sunday Night at The London Palladium.' Thanks to their amazing performance, and the chaos that had taken place that afternoon outside The Palladium, a new word was added to the British vocabulary.

And that new word was: 'Beatlemania'.

What a memorable day October 13th, 1963, had turned out to be. We may not have seen The Beatles in person, but on the very day that the word 'Beatlemania' was coined, my girlfriends and I had been part of the frenzy outside The Palladium. But for me the best thing that happened on that day was the fact that my girlfriends and I were now among the privileged few who actually knew where John, Paul, George and Ringo lived.

*_Smashing idea_...Great idea.
*_Good job_...Good thing.
*_Posh voice_...High class accent.
*_Knickers_...A woman's or girl's underpants.
*_Having me on_...Joking or lying.
*_Biro_...A ballpoint pen.
*_Balmy_...Crazy.
*_Yorkshire pudding_...An English food made from batter consisting of eggs, flour, milk or water. Especially delicious with roast beef.

CHAPTER 14
CLASSIFIED INFORMATION

The following week at school with our top-secret addresses, serious plans were put into place for the fast-approaching weekend. With so much planning there was very little time for schoolwork. The main problem that we had was deciding which house to visit first. Huddled together at the lunch table, Christina said, "I think Paul's house should be our first stop." Maroula quickly responded, "Oh no, definitely John's." Putting on her posh accent, Eileen joked, "Well I'd like to see George's current abode." I reminded everyone, "We have all of their addresses, so sooner or later we'll get to see all of them."

Standing up to leave, Valerie leaned over the lunch table and looking at us, hissed, "Don't forget, the whole thing could be a cruel joke, so let's not get our hopes up." We all knew that Valerie could be right, and even though we tried to remain optimistic, one by one our collective mood changed from excited to more than a little bit apprehensive.

The following Sunday afternoon, everyone but Rita, met at my house. Once again, Rita would be waiting for us at the Angel bus stop. We'd finally decided that our first trip should be to George and Ringo's flat on Green Street. By going to Green Street, we had the chance to see two Beatles on one visit. Plus, from all of the research that we'd done, George and Ringo were the two available Beatles.

Valerie teased, "Let's stick to the single Beatles, we don't want to be blamed for breaking up any happy families." Christina burst out laughing and replied, "I don't think we have to worry about that." Giggling, I turned to Christina and said, "Hey, you never know, we' might be young, but we're all quite gorgeous." After that comment we all had a good old laugh! Clapping her hands, Eileen shouted, "Okay, no more chit chat, let's get down to business."

We gathered around the dining table and unfolded my father's A to Z map of London.

Spreading it out across the table, we leaned over the map and studied the different areas and streets of London. We checked all three addresses: Green Street, Wimpole Street, and Emperor's Gate, and to our amazement we discovered that John, Paul, George and Ringo were practically living around the corner from us. Realizing this, each of us started to jump up and down, and began to scream.

Suddenly, we noticed that Francis looked rather quiet, and seemed to be deep in thought.

Valerie snapped, "What's the matter with you? You should be overjoyed!" With a tear in her eye, Francis answered, "I can't help but feel sorry for their fans back in Liverpool. They were the ones who helped make them famous, and now The Beatles are so far away from all of them. It just doesn't seem right." Valerie couldn't believe what she was hearing, and giving Frances a little push, she cried, "Oh for goodness's sake, wipe your bleedin tears. It's not our fault that The Beatles prefer our neck of the woods." Nodding my head in agreement, I added, "We're so lucky that we live in the capital where all the good, and important stuff happens." And in unison, everyone answered, "Yeah!"

I quickly finished writing down the directions to Green Street, and after a week of continuous talking about it we were finally ready to go. Sitting on the bus, Eileen peered out of the steamed-up window and sighed, "After all our planning, let's hope that The Beatles really do live at these addresses." I whispered, "Oh Eileen, please don't say that, now you've got me nervous!" The bus pulled into the Angel bus stop, and Rita was standing in her usual spot. She quickly jumped on board, came upstairs, and sat with us.

Thirty minutes later, we had arrived at Marble Arch, and one by one we hurried down the stars, and jumped off of the bus. We were now in the part of London that was known as Mayfair.

I fumbled through my messy bag and found the directions. Following the simple instructions, we made a left turn onto Park Lane, and a mere two blocks later we had reached our destination.

Green Street was in a very fashionable, residential area, and all along the street were red brick town houses with large, mullioned windows, and beautiful black wrought iron railings.

Walking down the street, Christina studied each house, and turning to face us, said, "Cor blimey, this is such a posh part of London, these houses are really nice." She was right, so we just nodded in agreement. As we continued our slow-paced walk, Eileen suddenly stopped in her tracks. With a smile on her face, she announced, "I think I know which house is number fifty- seven." And pointing down the street, she said, "I bet you a million pounds it's that one!"

Suddenly a group of girls came into view, and I noticed that most of them were sitting on the front steps of one of the elegant houses. Christina started to run, and waving her hands in the air, yelled, "Susie was telling us the truth." Valerie sighed, "But why did she have to tell so many other girls? Rita moaned, "Yeah, I thought it was supposed to be top secret. No matter where we go, there's always a gang of girls already there."

Laughing out loud, I reminded them, "After all, it is The Beatles, and we already know that we're not the only ones who like them." As soon as we got to number 57, the girls who were sitting on the steps moved over, and somehow, we managed to squeeze in. Rubbing one of the stone steps, Rita whispered, "Can you believe, we're sitting on George and Ringo's front steps. I wonder how many times they've walks on this very step?"

That afternoon, while we waited for George and Ringo to come home, my girlfriends and I had a really nice time chatting with all the other girls and listening to their stories about their numerous Beatle sightings. So, we decided right there and then that we'd rather be sitting outside a Beatle's home, than anywhere else in the world. Eileen chirped, "I can't think of a better way to spend my free time." Valerie chimed in, "But if The Beatles are away, we'll stay home, and give our families our undivided love and attention." We all started to laugh, and in unison chirped, "But of course!"

On our first visit to Green Street, we didn't see George or Ringo, and we soon found out that The Beatles had spent the day in Birmingham recording another 'Thank Your Lucky Stars' show. But sitting on George and Ringo's front steps we had such a good time, just chatting and laughing with all of our new friends. On other trips to Green Street, we had much better luck, and managed to see George and Ringo on quite a few occasions.

They were mostly getting in or out of taxis. Some days, they'd pose for a few photos or sign a couple of autographs, but they were usually in a bit of a rush, but we didn't mind, just to be able to see them in person was more than enough for all of us.

Some days, we'd travel to John's house on Emperors Gate, which was right off Cromwell Road. John, his wife Cynthia, and their little baby boy Julian lived in a flat on the top floor. It was an enormous white, shabby looking house, and it was obvious that there were several other flats in the building, because people were always dashing in and out of the front door. Each time we'd go to John's house, we'd see the same group of girls standing across the street, staring over at the house. One afternoon, we spotted Cynthia pushing little Julian in his *push chair. She was with another woman, and the moment she saw us, she lowered her head, and looked very uncomfortable. We didn't want to annoy her, so we stayed on the other side of the street.

With a tear in her eye, Rita sighed, "I feel so sorry for her, she looks quite lonely, and she's living in a strange city." I whispered, "I just wanted to have a little peek at baby Julian."

On other days, we traveled to Wimpole Street. Paul had moved into his girlfriend Jane Asher's family home. And someone had told us that Jane's parents had given Paul the entire attic, and that he had transformed it into his own private living space. There were always dozens of girls standing outside number 57, Wimpole Street, all eagerly waiting for a quick glimpse of Paul. On several occasions we saw Jane, and her brother Peter, but no matter how often we went to the Asher's house, we were never there at the right time, and never got to see Paul. But just standing around outside the house chatting with all the other fans was always great fun.

Whichever one of the Beatles' homes my girlfriends and I were at, we always had a good time. Whether we were standing among a huge crowd or a small group, it was always quite the social gathering, and before long we began to see the same girl's week after week. Some of the girls had travelled quite a distance to get to The Beatles' homes, and this made us even more grateful for living so close to them.

Unfortunately, none of us owned a camera, and we missed out on a lot of great photo opportunities. Quite a few times Valerie turned to me, and yelled, "You're the one with the bleedin' job, why don't you buy a camera?" Giving her a dirty look, I snapped back, "A pound can only go so far!" And Rita would always remind us, "There's no need to capture it on film, the memory will stay with us forever."

Rita was absolutely right. There were millions of girls all over the world who would give anything to see The Beatles just once, and here we were seeing them on a regular basis, or at least whenever they ventured out of their homes!

After living in the Green Street apartment for several months, George and Ringo moved into a new flat. Nobody had mentioned anything to us about the move, and on our usual Sunday afternoon visit, we were shocked to see the steps completely empty. Looking confused, and scratching her head, Eileen said, "What's going on here? It's awfully quiet, where is everyone?" Valerie turned to me, and asked, "Are you sure they're not away on tour?" I replied, "I would have read it in the Beatles' Book, no, I'm sure they're home."

My girlfriends and I sat on the steps, and tried to figure out where George, Ringo and the usual horde of fans had disappeared to. Suddenly, the young girl who was lucky enough to live next door came over to us and told us that George and Ringo had moved away. We couldn't believe what we were hearing! Nobody had said anything to us about them moving. Valerie asked the girl, "I don't suppose you know their new address?" "As a matter of fact, I do" she chirped. "Would you like me to give it to you?" With great big smiles on our faces, we yelled, "Yes please!"

I quickly found my trusty biro and a scrap of paper and handed them over to her. She told us that she had already given it out to quite a few of the other girls who had stopped by, and now she knew the address off by heart. She jotted it down and handed the piece of paper back to me. Getting up to leave, the young girl sighed, "I'm really going to miss all the excitement. It's going to be very dull around here without the two Beatles, and all of their fans."

Rita joked, "You'll just have to come and visit everyone at their new place. It's not like you don't know the address." Smiling sweetly, the young girl answered, "Maybe one day I will."

It was getting late so we left Green Street and headed home. Peering out of the bus window, Christina whispered, "I'd be heartbroken if I never saw George and Ringo again." Valerie sighed, "Yeah, me too."

I took the piece of paper out of my bag, and that's when I noticed that George and Ringo's former neighbor had scribbled down just three little words: William Mews, Knightsbridge. Rita moaned, "That's not gonna be much help to us. She hasn't even given us the house number. I hate to say this, but we may have lost George and Ringo forever." I looked over at Rita, and in a confident voice I declared, "*By hook or by crook, we'll find them again even if we have to knock on every single door on William Mews."

During the week, I had checked my father's map of London, and wrote down the directions to William Mews. This time we would have to take a bus to Kings Cross Station, and then the tube to Knightsbridge station. Once again luck was on our side, and George and Ringo's new place was just a short journey away.

The following Sunday, my girlfriends and I were all set to take our first excursion to another unfamiliar area of London. This time it was Knightsbridge. In what seemed like a flash, we were walking down George and Ringo's new street. All along the narrow mews were quaint little cottages, painted in lovely pastel colors. Valerie had recently read an article about mews homes, and now, whether we wanted it or not, she decided to give us a rather serious lecture. Pointing to the different houses, and sounding like one of our teachers, she informed us, "These compact houses had been constructed as either stables or staff quarters, and were built on the service road, and hidden away behind the grand town homes that were on the other side of the garden."

Laughing out loud, I cried, "Oh, would you listen to miss know it all." Looking all around, Maroula added, "It's hard to believe that this place is in central London. It feels like a different country." Pointing to a pale green cottage with pretty windows and a tiny Juliet balcony, I joked, "I've found my dream home, I'll take that one." Laughing hysterically, Rita chirped, "Yeah, when you marry Prince Charles." Still in lecture mode, Valerie continued, "Rita's absolutely right, these tiny houses are highly desirable, and these days they cost a small fortune." With wide eyes, Christina chirped, "They remind me of Steed's house on The Avengers." Nodding enthusiastically, we all agreed with Christina's keen observation.

At the end of the quiet mews, stood a modern five story apartment building. Valerie was horrified, and gasped, "Good gracious me, that building stands out like a sore thumb. It just doesn't belong among these beautiful little mews houses." At least a dozen girls were lolling about outside the entrance to the building. Rita shrieked, "I do believe we've found George and Ringo's new home!" Frances whispered, "The tenants in this building, must have been horrified when they found out that not one, but two of The Beatles were moving in." "Lucky them!" I replied.

We took our place among the other fans, and soon learned that the apartment building was named Whadden House. William Mews soon became our favorite Beatle place to be. Not only did George and Ringo live in Whadden House, but so did their manager Brian Epstein. Mal Evans, The Beatles' Road manager spent a lot of time at George and Ringo's new flat, and he often came outside to chat with the fans. He was such a friendly man, and all the fans loved him.

*<u>Push chair</u>…Stroller.

CHAPTER 15

OUR VERY SPECIAL MAGICAL MYSTERY TOUR

One very special and rare day, my girlfriends and I were the only fans standing outside Whadden House. Mal Evans came out of the building, and when he saw us standing there, he came right over to us, and in his usual cheerful manner, said, "Hello girls, how are you today?" Giggling, Rita joked, "We're okay, and how are George and Ringo today?" He stood chatting with us and looking all around he realized that we were the only fans there.

Grinning broadly, he said, "How would you girls like to take a spin in The Beatles' car?" In disbelief, I gasped, "Am I hearing things, or did Mal just invite us to take a ride in The Beatles' car?" Occasionally my girlfriends and I could be a little bit forward, but we would never have been *cheeky enough to actually ask him to give us a ride in their fabulous car. Unable to contain our excitement, we began jumping up and down, and together we screeched, "Yes please! Yes please!" Laughing out loud, Mal said, "Alright girls, hop in the back."

Before he could change his mind, we quickly piled into the backseat. I settled into the comfortable seat, and moving my hand over the soft leather, whispered to Rita, "This is the fanciest car I have ever been in." Inhaling deeply, Rita purred, "It even smells fancy." I would have been quite content to just sit in the car, but moments later the car pulled away from the curb, and my girlfriends and I were on our very own magical mystery tour.

Looking all around, Christina cried, "Can you believe we're sitting where The Beatles sit." The very thought made all of us squeal with delight. And with a twinkle in her eye, Maroula asked, "I wonder who's place I'm sitting in?" Maroula's comment immediately caused another round of high-pitched squealing. With my eyes closed, and still caressing the soft leather seat, I cried, "Pinch me, this can't be real, I must be dreaming!" With the biggest grin on her face, Christina replied, "Oh, it's real alright!" Before long, my girlfriends and I began to relax.

We rolled down the windows, and when our luxurious car stopped at a traffic light, we gave the strolling pedestrians the *Royal wave. At one of the stops, I yelled out to a boy on a bicycle, "Hello darling, we're on our way to Buckingham Palace for a spot of tea with the Queen, would you care to join us?" We were laughing so hard, that Mal looked back, and in a rather stern voice said, "Okay girls, now keep the noise down!" And together we chimed, "Sorry Mal." Ten minutes later, the car pulled up to the curb, and we were once again outside Whadden House.

Climbing out of the car, Rita moaned, "Looks like we're back in the real world again!" Even though our spectacular ride had come to an end, we all agreed that it was the most unexpected, and thrilling thing we had ever experienced. Rita waited for Mal to get out of the driver's seat, and running over to him, she cried, "Thank you Mal. If I live to be a hundred, I will never forget this day." I chimed, "That goes for me too, Mal." Smiling broadly, he replied, "It was my pleasure, I'm glad you all enjoyed yourselves."

We stood by the car and watched as Mal walked back into Whaddon House. Turning to my girlfriends, I chuckled, "If you can't have a Beatle, then riding in their car is probably the next best thing."

Good fortune was definitely with us that day. Not only did we get to have a ride in The Beatles' fabulous car, but we actually had a camera with us. So as soon as we were sure that Mal was out of sight, we climbed on the car, and someone took a photo for us.

Sitting on The Beatles' car.

Strolling down William Mews, my girlfriends and I couldn't believe what had just taken place, and we all wholeheartedly agreed that Mal Evans was indeed a very special person.

*<u>Cheeky</u>...Fresh.
*<u>Royal wave</u>...Gesture that conveys regality, class and control all in one succinct movement.

CHAPTER 16
A GLANCE AT PAUL AND GEORGE, AND A FUN DAY OFF FROM SCHOOL.

The Beatles had been invited to perform on The Royal Command Performance. To be chosen for this very special show was indeed a great honor. The show was scheduled to take place on Monday, November 4th.1963 at The Prince of Wales *Theatre in London. Eileen was lounging on the couch, reading an article about the upcoming show when suddenly she turned to us and said, "The Beatles and all of the other acts will have to rehearse, and according to what I've just read they're planning to be at the theatre early in the morning on the day of the show. I think we should be waiting for them when they arrive. We're bound to be able to see them, and you never know maybe they'll be able to get us in to see the show."

Looking at the article, I said, "I must admit, it's does sounds like fun, but there's one teeny weeny problem; it's on a Monday, so we would have to play the *hop from school!" Christina chimed, "We're always at school, taking one day off isn't gonna make a bit of a difference." We all nodded enthusiastically, and Valerie declared, "Well, that's it, we've made up our minds, we're going!" Excited by the possibility of seeing The Beatles, I ran over to the sideboard, dragged out the A-to-Z map, and searched for the theatre's location. And while I flicked from one page to the next, my girlfriends began to sing, "Yeah, yeah, yeah!"

Bright and early on the day of the show, someone was pounding frantically on my front door. As soon as I opened it, Christina came rushing in. Flushed and out of breath, she chirped, "I'm so excited, I can't believe the day is finally here." Heading for the kitchen, I said to Christina, "Before we leave, I have to give Angela her last-minute instructions". My sister was sitting at the kitchen table enjoying a bowl of hot *porridge. With a puzzled look, Christina stared at Angela's bowl, and blurted out, "Where's the porridge? All I can see is a giant puddle of *golden syrup." Angela was too busy enjoying it, so she just smiled!

I pulled up a chair, and said to Angela, "Now listen carefully, you have to tell Miss Goddard that I shan't be attending school today. I've broken out in a raging rash, and I'm almost positive it's highly contagious." Angela huffed, "You're so dramatic, nobody talks that way, and besides what are you gonna say tomorrow when your rash has completely disappeared?" Giving her a sideways look, I hissed, "Don't you worry about that, I'll just tell her it turned out to be one of those twenty- four-hour rashes!" Looking at me with admiration, Christina cried, "Cor, you're really good, I can never think up convincing excuses."

We left my house at the normal time for school, but instead of going to the bus stop, Christina and I went to Newington Green Park. As planned, our other girlfriends were waiting for us on a park bench. Our school mates were just yards away on the other side of the street, and thanks to the thick bushes, we were well hidden. We sat patiently waiting for their bus to whisk them off to school, and once they were gone, we jumped on a bus that was going in the opposite direction.

When our bus pulled up to the Angel bus stop, Rita was standing there. We banged on the window, and she jumped on board. I had written down the directions to the theatre, and following them, we got off the bus at Kings Cross Station, and from there, we took the tube to Piccadilly Circus. Twenty minutes later we were standing in front of The Prince of Wales Theatre.

Seeing the huge crowd of fans that were gathered outside, Rita moaned, "It's no different from the afternoon at The Palladium. There must be five hundred girls here." Valerie grunted, "Why aren't they in school? Where's a truant officer when you need one?"

It was still early in the morning, but because of all the fans walking in the road, plus the bumper-to-bumper rush hour traffic, everything was at a standstill. Horns were blasting, frustrated drivers were losing their tempers, and turmoil was swirling all around. Hanging out of his car window, a taxi driver screamed at us, "Come on you lot. Get off the bloody road!" Giving him a dirty look, Valerie barked back, "Oy, watch your language, there's no need to get nasty, and swearing isn't gonna help the situation." My girlfriends and I stood together on the crowded pavement on Coventry Street, and as each car drove by, we peeked into the windows.

At 10:30 a *coach rounded the corner, and from far away we heard someone scream, "Here they come!" In an instant, complete chaos broke out as hundreds of girls, including us stampeded through the congested traffic. We reached the coach just as The Beatles were coming out. They were immediately surrounded by several security men who rushed them into the theatre. I managed to get a brief glimpse of Paul and George, but within seconds all of the excitement was over.

This is not how we had envisioned their arrival, and instead of chatting with us, and giving us tickets to the show, they were gone! Leaning against the empty coach and holding her sides, Rita joked, "I don't know about you lot, but I've had more than enough exercise for one morning." In a dreamy voice, Valerie sighed, "Did you see Paul? Even in the wee hours of the morning he still looks absolutely smashing."

Once our breathing was back to normal, we walked away from the coach. The hordes of fans that only minutes earlier had caused such a commotion, had now scattered in various directions, and Piccadilly Circus had returned to its normal state. It was still quite early, and now we had the rest of the day to whatever we decided to do. We didn't have much money, so we took a nice long walk. Along the way, we stopped to admire the new buildings, and some of the ancient ones. At one o clock, we found a *Wimpey Bar and treated ourselves to hamburgers and chips.

Sitting in the cozy restaurant, I joked "We should do this every Monday, it's a lot more fun than being stuck in bleedin' school all day." Laughing our loud, Valerie said, "I'd much rather have a scrumptious hamburger than the dry beef and *pease pudding that we're forced to eat at school." Once again, we all nodded in total agreement. After lunch, we decided to go to The National Gallery. With free admission it was the perfect place for a bunch of poor schoolgirls.

For two hours, we walked around the gallery, and stared in awe at the magnificent paintings and sculptures.

Eileen was off in a faraway corner studying a Degas masterpiece. Pulling her away from the painting, Valerie said, "I do believe that's more than enough culture for one day. Now who wants to go to Trafalgar Square?"

Dodging the fast-moving traffic, my girlfriends and I ran across the bustling street, down the steps and into the crowded square. We ran to the nearest empty bench, plonked ourselves down and stared at a group of tourists who were taking dozens of photographs of Nelson's Column.

Ten minutes later we were bored, so we ran over to one of the famous lion statues that are in the center of the Trafalgar Square. We tried to climb onto it, but because we were laughing so hard, we kept sliding off. Suddenly, a policeman came out of nowhere, and ordered us to get down, "Oy, what do you think you're doing? You should be ashamed of yourselves acting like a bunch of hooligans, and with all these foreign visitors staring at you. Don't you realize you're giving the English a bad name? Now get down immediately!"

As we tumbled off of the giant wall that's underneath the lions, we yelled sarcastically, "Sorry constable." And as he walked away, he pointed his long spindly finger at us, and barked, "And don't you forget, I'll be keeping an eye on you lot!" Valerie waited until he was out of earshot and with praying hands, she begged, "Please, sir, we won't do it again sir. Please, sir, don't arrest us, sir." Eileen sighed, "Why do people always have to ruin our fun? Now what are we gonna do?" Checking to see how much money she had left, Rita said, "Let's feed the pigeons." We ran over to the birdseed vendor, and each of us bought a small cup of birdseeds.

After we had finished throwing our birdseeds, we sat on a bench and watched the pigeons land on the heads of unsuspecting tourists. Roaring with laughter, Valerie cried, "You must admit, this is even better than the circus!"

Our fun day off from school.

At four o'clock it was time to go home, and we had just enough money left for our bus fares.

And with a bit of luck, the conductor will forget to come upstairs to collect it. Later that night, while watching the evening news a segment came on about The Royal Performance Show. I stared in awe at the glamorous people who were entering the theatre. Then the news went to a clip that had been filmed earlier that day. It showed the huge crowd that had gathered outside the theatre, and to my surprise my girlfriends and I appeared on the television screen. We were running in the middle of the road, chasing after The Beatles' coach, with dozens of other girls.

My parents knew that I was taking the day off from school and when my father saw the clip, he laughed his head off. But my mother did not look happy, and turning to me she sighed, "I'm starting to get worried about the way you girls keep chasing after those Beatles."

The next morning, we were the talk of Cardinal Pole. On our way to the assembly hall, one of the boys yelled out, "Oy you lot, you're famous! Everyone saw you on the telly last night." Someone else laughed, "If only you knew how to run, you might have caught yourself a Beatle or two." With a worried frown, Rita whispered, "It looks like the whole school saw us." For the rest of the day, my girlfriends and I waited nervously to be summoned into the *headmaster's office.

Unable to concentrate, Eileen whispered to me, "If our classmates saw us then it's possible the teachers did too." When the school day finally came to an end, my girlfriends and I ran out of the gate and sang, "Yeah, Yeah, Yeah, we got away with it!"

The following Sunday, a small crowd of girls had gathered at my house to watch the televised highlights of The Royal Variety Show. Harry Secombe, Susan Maughn, Tommy Steele, Marlene Dietrich, and many other stars performed. Of course, we were waiting for just one act, and after what seemed like an eternity the moment had finally arrived. The audience, dressed in formal evening wear, clapped politely as The Beatles sang 'From Me To You.'

Francis jumped up and cried out, "Oh my God, I do believe I'm about to faint." In unison, we said, "Shush," so Francis sat back down. When 'From Me To You' ended, the camera scanned across the audience and Valerie laughed, "Cor blimey, look at the women in their fancy dresses, and the men in their silly *dicky bows!"

The camera went back to the stage, and Paul stepped up to the microphone. He thanked the audience for their applause and talked about the next song that they'd be performing. He also added a little joke about Sophie Tucker. Eileen seemed surprised, "I can't believe Paul actually looks quite nervous. I've never seen him like this before." Valerie snapped "You'd be nervous too, if you had to perform in front of royalty." After Paul's brief speech he began to sing, 'Till There Was You.' Together, my girlfriends and I moved closer to the television set and gazed up at him.

Next, it was John's turn to give a little speech and when he said: "Would the people in the cheaper seats clap your hands and the rest of you, if you'd just rattle your jewelry," John's comment had us all roaring with laughter. Eileen squealed, "He's so cheeky. I can't believe he said that, and in front of the Queen Mother too."

The Beatles' final song was 'Twist and Shout' and while they performed, my girlfriends and I swayed from side to side. As soon as the song ended, Ringo jumped down from behind his drums and joined the others in the center of the stage. Together, they bowed to the audience, and turning to face the royal box gave another bow. A close up of The Queen Mother came onto the television screen and from her smiles, it was obvious that she too had enjoyed The Beatles' performance.

The following day it was reported that a record breaking 26 million viewers had tuned in to watch 'The Royal Variety Show!' Laughing out loud, Valerie said, "See what happens when The Beatles are on the telly, everyone stays home to watch."

On November 22nd, 1963, The Beatles second Long-Playing album was released. The title of the new album was: 'With The Beatles.' Now that I was a working woman money was no object, and on the very day of its release I bought my second L.P. Before the record shop had even opened the line of people waiting to buy The Beatles' new L.P. went all the way around the corner. Lucky for me, I was one of the first people on the queue. The cover of the new album was simply breathtaking. It was the most beautiful black and white photo of the boys, and I truly believed that the cover alone was well worth one pound, ten shillings and eleven pence.

As soon as I got home, I read the back of the album cover and was thrilled to see that 'Till There Was You,' the beautiful song that Paul had sung at the Royal Command Performance was among the new songs. I was also really impressed that the majority of the songs were actually written by John and Paul. By playing each song over and over, and writing down all of the words, in time at all I knew all of the fabulous new songs.

One week later on November 29th, we were in for another wonderful treat! The Beatles next single, titled: 'I Wanna Hold Your Hand.' was released. This song was such a happy, upbeat song, and just as I'd predicted, just days after its release, the new single had taken over the number one spot on the hit parade, forcing 'She Loves You' down to the second spot.

*<u>Theatre</u>... The English spelling for theater.
*<u>The hop</u>...Another way of saying play truant.
*<u>Porridge</u>...Oatmeal.
*<u>Golden syrup</u>...Is a thick, amber-colored form of syrup.
*<u>Pavement</u>...Sidewalk.
*<u>Coach</u>...A bus.
*<u>Wimpey Bar</u>...A popular hamburger restaurant.
*<u>Pease pudding</u>... A savory pudding dish made of boiled legumes
*<u>Headmaster</u>... The principal.
*<u>Dicky bows</u>...Bow ties.

CHAPTER 17
TWO CHRISTMAS PRESENTS FROM THE BEATLES

During the month of November, The Beatles' fan club sent out a newsletter informing the members that for the Christmas season, The Beatles had two very special presents for their fans. The first was a record made exclusively for the fan club members, and that these records would be mailed out within the next two weeks. The second present was that two fan club Get Togethers were scheduled to take place during the month of December. One would be held in the South of England, and the other one in the north, and that John, Paul, George and Ringo will be attending both of the Get Togethers. But because of limited space only a certain number of fan club members would be able to attend. The newsletter informed us that a raffle will take place to determine the lucky winners, and that vouchers for both of the Get Together will also be mailed out within the next two weeks.

I was so excited, I couldn't wait to get my Beatle Christmas presents, and each day I'd rush home after school to see if they had arrived. Within a week, the postman delivered my Beatles' Christmas record, and I was thrilled. This little record was spectacular. The Beatles sang a very funny version of 'Good King Wenceslas' followed by John, Paul, George, and

Ringo each sending a personal Christmas message to their fans. The record ended with an amusing chorus of 'Rudolph the Red Nosed Ringo.'

The Beatles' Christmas record.

I played the floppy disc over and over and listening to The Beatles' lovely *Liverpudlian accents made me squeal with delight. Just to be able to hear the voices of John, Paul, George and Ringo was nothing short of a miracle.

My fan club 'Get Together' ticket still hadn't arrived, and I was getting worried. A week earlier, three girls that I knew had received their tickets, and I just couldn't imagine what the delay was with mine. By the second week I was forced to face the fact that maybe, just maybe, I wasn't one of the lucky winners. The thought of not winning a ticket hadn't entered my mind, and with each passing day I was getting more miserable.

Giving me a sympathetic hug Eileen sighed, "Don't take it so hard, it doesn't look like any of us got a ticket, so we're all in the same boat."

In October, my parents had sat me and my siblings down and out of the blue announced that sometime in the new year we'd all be immigrating to America. Over the years, practically all of my mother's family had

A Common Case of Beatlemania

moved to the United States and now we too would be relocating to the New World. This revelation had left me completely stunned, and for weeks I walked around in a bewildered daze.

I adored England and I loved running around London with my girlfriends, and best of all I loved living around the corner from John, Paul, George and Ringo. Even though I missed my relatives, I didn't need to see them on a regular basis. I was quite content to send them the occasional letter or to see them whenever they'd come for a visit.

Complaining to my girlfriends I cried, "You lot seem to forget, I'm about to move a million miles away, and if that isn't bad enough, now it looks like I'm not going to fan club 'Get Together.'"

December 14th, the date of the 'Southern Area Fan Club Get Together' was just five days away, and with each passing day, I was becoming more miserable.

A school friend of mine named Christine was one of the lucky three who had won a 'Get Together' ticket. Two weeks earlier she had started her dream job. She'd always wanted to work in a hairdresser's shop, and she had finally been given the opportunity to work on Saturdays in one of the better hair salons in Stoke Newington. Her duties included: washing heads, folding towels, scouring the sinks, and sweeping clumps of hair off of the floor. She knew that in time this could lead to a permanent position, where between her wages and tips she could be making a very comfortable living.

At lunch time Christine sat at the table next to mine and nibbling nervously on her sandwich I overheard her saying to her girlfriends, "I really don't know what I'm going to do. If I asked the boss for next Saturday off he's liable to *sack me on the spot. I've only had the job for a couple of weeks, and there's dozens of girls just dying to take my place." Poor Christine was in a difficult situation. We all knew how much she loved The Beatles, but she also wanted to hold onto her dream job.

This could be the perfect opportunity for me to get that precious ticket. She wouldn't just throw the ticket away, so she'd have to give it to someone, and I just had to be that lucky someone. I was willing to do whatever was necessary to get that ticket, even if it meant bribing her.

At the end of the school day, I stood in the playground, and paced back and forth, anxiously waiting for Christine to come out. When I finally saw her, I took a deep breath, and ran over to her. I didn't want everyone in the school yard to know about the ticket, so taking her to one side I whispered, "I have ten shillings at home, and I can bring it to school tomorrow. Please, just give me that ticket and the money is yours." Looking into her face, I reminded her, "You can buy a lot of stuff with ten shillings." It was plain to see that she liked the idea of getting a crisp *ten bob note for doing absolutely nothing, and I was confident that my worries were over.

But instead of agreeing to my very generous offer, she shrieked, "I don't know what to do, you're not the only one who loves The Beatles! I just need some time to think about it." I didn't want to antagonize her, so with my head hung low I slowly plodded away. As I walked through the school gate, I couldn't control myself, and cried out to her, "Please Christine, I beg of you don't give it to anyone else!"

The following day, as I entered the lunchroom, Christine immediately crouched down in her seat. Valerie noticed her odd behavior, and whispered in my ear, "Looks like someone's doing her very best to avoid you." For the next two days, which were the longest two days of my life, I stared at Christine who sat nervously pondering over her extremely upsetting situation, while I sat biting my nails to the quick.

On the third day she sent two of her friends to fetch me. Breathing a sigh of relief, I wiped my brow and followed her friends. I was so grateful that this harrowing episode, one way or another would finally be over. Standing together in the quiet hallway, Christine took a deep breath and began her heart-wrenching speech," This is the hardest thing that I've ever had to do, and if I didn't have my Saturday job you wouldn't stand a chance of getting my ticket." Her voice quivered with emotion, and then she continued, "But I have no choice I need that job, so give me the ten shillings, and the ticket is yours."

In a flash, I dumped the contents of my satchel onto the floor and frantically searched for the money. And before she had a chance to fully understand what she was about to give away, I stuck the crumpled ten *bob note into her hand. She immediately handed over the priceless ticket. My girlfriends stood at the far end of the hallway, and the moment the ticket was indeed mine I held it up and yelled, "I've got it!" While I jumped up and down, my girlfriends cheered loudly.

Christine folded the ten shilling note, placed it into her purse and turning to me said, "You do realize that it's not the actual ticket, it's a voucher to buy a ticket. You still have to pay three shillings and six pence on the day of the Get Together. Don't forget to bring the money or they won't let you in." Hugging Christine, I replied, "Don't worry, I won't forget."

For the total sum of thirteen shilling and six pence, I was about to spend the afternoon with The Beatles, and to me it was the bargain of a lifetime. That night, I tossed and turned and hardly slept at all. I couldn't believe that my impossible wish had been granted, and that I was now one of the lucky ones who in just two days will be attending 'The Southern Area Fan Club 'Get Together.' Without a doubt, I was the happiest girl in the whole of England.

My best friends were happy for me, but not so happy for themselves. They too had longed to be at the fan club 'Get Together' but none of them were lucky enough to win a voucher, or to have the opportunity to buy one. Staring at my ticket Valerie cried, "It's not fair, we want to go too."

I quickly reminded her, "You seem to forget that this time next year I'll be more than three thousand miles away, and where I'm going, there will be no John, Paul, George or Ringo. You lot will still be here, and can pop round to their houses, and see them anytime you feel like it." Smiling broadly, Rita chirped, "I just knew that if one of us would end up with a ticket, it would be you!"

Kissing my ticket, I continued, "The clock is ticking so if I want to see

The Beatles I have to do whatever it takes while I've still got the chance." Sighing deeply Valerie snapped, "In all my life, I've never heard anyone feel so sorry for themselves. You act as if you're being shipped off to bleedin' Siberia." And with tears in my eyes, all I could say was, "Well that's what it feels like to me."

*<u>Liverpudlian accent</u>… The dialect of people from Liverpool.
*<u>Sack</u>… Fired (dismissed)
*<u>Ten bob note</u>… Ten shilling note.

CHAPTER 18
THE FAN CLUB GET TOGETHER.

On Saturday, December 14th, 1963, for the first time in my life, I was wide awake at 6 o'clock in the morning. I was so excited I just couldn't lie in bed a minute longer. I drank two cups of tea, nibbled on a couple of buttered digestive biscuit, and stared at the ticking clock that hardly moved. After what seemed like an eternity, 8 o'clock finally came. I put on my comfortable *plimsoles, and walked around the corner to the telephone box to make my sick call to Boots The Chemist.

With a sympathetic ear, the manager listened as I rattled off my long list of highly contagious symptoms. In a fatherly tone he gave me his professional advice, "Young lady, I do believe you have a touch of the common cold. Go straight back to bed, take two aspirins every four hours, and be sure to drink plenty of fluids." Coughing loudly into the phone, I answered in a raspy voice, "Thank you, Mr. Jones, I'll be sure to do that." I felt so ashamed for lying, but at the same time just knowing that later today I'd be seeing The Fab Four made me giddy with excitement.

Poor Mr. Jones giving me his medical advice when the condition that I have is called "Beatlemania", and I know for a fact there is no cure!

Now that I'd taken care of my obligation, I was feeling as light as a feather, and I skipped all the way home. At 10 am, I met up with Pat and Catherine, the two lucky cousins who had both won tickets to the Get Together, and the three of us somehow managed to find our way to Wimbledon Palais.

The 'Southern Fan Club Get Together' was an afternoon function, and printed on my voucher was the statement: The doors will open promptly at 12.45 p.m. By twelve o 'clock we had made it to the venue and got on the end of a very long queue which went all the way around the building. After what seemed like an eternity, we finally reached the main entrance. We handed our money, and our vouchers over to a lady who was seated at a table. I watched as she put the money in a tin box, and the vouchers in separate pile. Looking up, the lady smiled and pointing to the door, said, "Alright girls, go straight through and find yourself a spot in the ballroom."

We immediately ran through the doorway, and into a huge hall. I was expecting the ballroom to be a bright, cheery place, but instead the wooden floor planks were old and creaky, and the hall was dimly lit and rather dark. Hundreds of fans were already inside, and carefully scanning the ballroom the three of us searched for the perfect spot. As soon as we found a quiet corner, we ran to claim it.

We watched as the excited fans kept piling into the hall. And with a disgusted look, Catherine cried, "I didn't expect this many girls to be here." Giving her a little shove, I teased, "What were you expecting? A private party for just us, and The Boys?" Giggling, she sighed, "Yes, wouldn't that be nice?" Pat whispered, "I wonder if they've arrived yet?" The very thought of seeing The Beatles again made me weak at the knees.

Suddenly, a powerful voice came over the loudspeakers, and instantly a hush descended over the crowd. The voice continued, "Soon everyone will be going into the bar area to meet The Beatles. They want to personally greet each and every person that's here today."

Every girl in the ballroom squealed with delight, and then the announcer instructed us to form a single line. Everyone happily obeyed, and in record time a single line went right around the enormous hall. In a loud voice a security guard barked, "To keep the line moving, photograph taking, and giving of autographs is strictly forbidden."

The queue started moving towards the bar area, and Catherine, Pat and I cheerfully shuffled along. I realized that with each tiny step I was getting closer to where The Beatles were, and I could barely contain my excitement. An hour and a half later we had reached the bar area, and standing on our tippy toes, The Beatles finally came into view. Jumping up and down Pat screeched, "Oh my God, it's them!" Catherine and I were speechless, and just gazed lovingly at The Fab Four.

The Beatles were sitting at a very long, narrow table, and behind them were glasses, bottles and all sorts of bar accessories. John was at the head of the table, Paul sat next to him, followed by Ringo, and at the far end of the table sat George. In their perfectly tailored suits and dark ties they looked extremely smart, and as gorgeous as ever. Paul and George both wore white shirts, while John and Ringo opted for blue ones.

The queue kept moving along, and we were getting closer to the table where they were sitting. I noticed that in between greeting the fans John and Paul were drinking cups of steaming hot tea. Smiling, laughing, and shaking hands with one fan after another it was obvious that they were thoroughly enjoying themselves.

Suddenly a cheeky girl tried to grab Paul's hair. Paul automatically flung himself to the back of his chair, while the other Beatles laughed hysterically. I was now close enough to be able to hear them, and in their lovely Liverpudlian accents I could hear them greeting the fans. Some of the girls looked as though they were about to faint, but most were thrilled to not only be seeing John, Paul, George, and Ringo up close, but to be allowed to actually touch them was something none of us had been prepared to do.

As we shuffled along getting closer to them, I became quite nervous. Suddenly, I remembered an article that was published in my mum's Woman's Own magazines. The article stated: "To relieve tension, just close your eyes, breathe deeply, and your anxiety will simply fade away." I had nothing to lose, so I decided to give it a try. I closed my eyes, inhaled deeply, and continued to tiptoe along the bar area.

Suddenly, Catherine nudged me back to reality, and when I opened my eyes, John Lennon was sitting right in front of me. He was grinning from ear to ear and waiting for me to shake his hand. I held out my trembling hand, and he grabbed it and smiled. My mouth was as dry as the Sahara, and I knew that nothing would come out, so I gave him a feeble smile, let go of his hand, and shaking all over managed to walk away. While I waited for the fans in front of me to move along, I continued my deep breathing, and to my surprise by the time I had reached Paul, I was feeling a little bit better. Standing so close to Paul, and not having a crowd of girls slobbering all over him made me feel as if we were the only two people on earth.

Paul smiled at me, and turning his head to one side he gave me a little wink, and said, "How are ya?" With a bashful smile while ever so slightly batting my eyelashes, I answered, "I'm really good now." (Did I just flirt with Paul McCartney? I couldn't believe how cheeky I was becoming.) While shaking his hand I peered into his face, and my only thought was " he truly is the most gorgeous man I have ever laid eyes on". Thirty seconds later, it dawned on me that I was still clutching his hand. I instantly released him, and I noticed that Paul looked quite relieved.

As I moved on down the table, Ringo came into view. He and the girl ahead of me were deep in conversation, and while I was waiting for my turn I stood back and admired Ringo from afar. The girl was chatting away, and Ringo seemed to be fascinated with whatever she was telling him. Then it dawned on me that I was about to shake hands with Ringo, who had always been my favorite Beatle. So once again my nerves got the better of me. I'd been this close to Ringo a couple of times at Green Street, but there had always been dozens of other fans too. This time it was just the two of us- Ringo and me - face to face. Finally, the chatty girl moved away, and Ringo Starr was sitting quietly waiting for me. My heart was pounding, my legs felt wobbly, and I felt as though I could faint at any moment. I tiptoed over to the table and praying that he wouldn't notice my trembling, I shook

Ringo's hand. Ringo smiled, and in his lovely accent said, "Hello." I was so nervous all I could do was give him a pathetic, quivering little smile, and I quickly moved away.

George was next. The girl ahead of me had just waved goodbye to him, and now he was sitting alone. As I came towards him, he smiled broadly, and held out his hand to greet me. We shook hands, and in unison said, "Hello" and then we both started to laugh. Being so close to George I could see how young, and handsome he was. Compared to the others he seemed a little bashful, and now I totally understood why so many people called him the quiet Beatle. By this time my trembling had completely stopped, and I was quite eager to have a nice chit chat with George. Suddenly someone in the queue shouted, "Hurry up!" So reluctantly I said goodbye to George, and slowly walked back into the ballroom. The two cousins came following close behind me.

Looking down at my right hand, I thought, "This hand has just shaken hands with John, Paul, George and Ringo, and this alone was well worth the ten bob that I'd given to Christine!" Standing in a corner with Pat and Catherine I turned to them and said, "That was the most exciting thing I've ever done." The cousins nodded in total agreement, and all around us were hundreds of other girls all reliving their special moments with The Beatles.

I noticed that the queue waiting to go in to meet The Beatles was now much shorter. I looked around the huge ballroom searching for the security guard, and I finally spotted him on the other side of the hall. He was chatting with a group of girls and seemed to be thoroughly enjoying himself. And that's when I decided to risk everything and go back into the bar area to meet The Beatles just one more time.

I whispered my intentions to Pat and Catherine, "Nobody's watching, so I'm going in again. Do you want to come with me?" The cousins were horrified, and they pleaded with me not to do it. In unison they cried, "You're gonna get *chucked out! Please, don't do it!" Whispering to the cousins, I said, "Shush, keep your voices down. If you get any louder, you'll be the ones who'll be getting chucked out."

I had no doubt that I could get away with what I was about to do, and turning to the cousins, I cried, "If you two don't want to come, then suit yourselves, I'm off." I tiptoed over to the end of the line, and casually took my place with the other waiting fans. I only had to wait about twenty minutes, and I was once again back in the bar area. This time, I was not going to be a timid little schoolgirl. I was determined to come across as a friendly, outgoing, and confident young woman.

I knew that what I was about to do millions of girls all over the world could only dream of. I was meeting The Beatles for the second time in one day, and if that wasn't enough, I was about to touch all four of them again! *By hook or by crook, I was going to make the most of this very special occasion! Minutes later, I was once again shaking hands with John Lennon but this time I leaned over the table and chirped, "So nice to meet you, John." Grinning cheerfully, he replied, "Nice to meet you too."

The difference between this meeting and the last one was astonishing. The stress, the tension and all of the anxiety had completely disappeared, and I was thoroughly enjoying myself. As I slowly walked away I waved goodbye to John, and moved on down the table. As I approached Paul, he gave me another little wink, and that's when I realized that he had probably given every single girl in the ballroom their very own personal wink. Oh well, I wasn't the jealous type, so I didn't mind! Shaking his hand, I stared into his beautiful hazel eyes, and totally understood why so many girls simply adored him. Not only was he the most attractive man I had ever seen, but he was also such a nice down to earth person.

I was just about to walk away when someone handed Paul another cup of steaming hot tea, and taking the cup he sighed, "Oh lovely!" Leaving Paul, I shuffled on down to Ringo, and once again in his beautiful Liverpudlian accent, he chirped, "Hello." I leaned over the table, grabbed his hand and purred, "Hello Ringo." Ringo sat there smiling, and as I lovingly held onto his hand, I gazed into his cheery face, and my only thought was: "I could stand here forever."

Suddenly, I was brought back to reality. The girl behind me gave me a powerful push, and hissed impatiently, "C'mon, you've been there long enough, it's my turn now!" I released Ringo's hand, and twirling around to face the nasty girl, I shouted, "I was just about to leave there's no need to be so bloody rude!" Ringo sat there, staring at both of us, but I refused to let this horrible girl ruin my perfect day. So, I gave Ringo a little wave, and moved on down the table.

Before I had even reached George, I had already made up my mind to go around and meet The Beatles just one more time. This was so easy, nobody was watching me, and with my innocent looking face, I knew without a doubt that I could get away with it. There were hundreds of fans standing in the ballroom, but none of them were brazen enough to attempt what I was doing, and that made it so much easier for me to do.

When I reached the end of the table, I shook George's hand and said what a pleasure it was to meet him. He smiled broadly, and on my way out I waved goodbye to him, knowing that I'd be seeing him again shortly.

The moment I was back in the ballroom, I walked straight over to the very short queue, and stood quietly with the few remaining fans who were waiting to meet The Beatles. In less than ten minutes I was once again back in the bar area. When I reached the table, I held out my hand to John. Giving me a puzzled look, and sounding just a little bit sarcastic, he asked, "Haven't we met before?"

I was about to panic, but I noticed that he was actually smiling. I didn't know what to say so I just shrugged my shoulders. He sat there waiting for an answer, so I leaned over the table, and whispered in his ear, "I promise, I won't do it again." John burst out laughing, and as I walked away, I could still hear him laughing. Now that John had recognized me, I was terrified that the others would too, and so I rushed on down the table. This time I kept my head low and hid my face. Without looking at them I somehow managed to shake hands with Paul, then Ringo, and finally

George. I didn't even look up to see if Paul had given me another one of his endearing little winks.

I hurried out of the bar area, and back into the noisy ballroom. Knowing that I had managed to get away with it, I breathed a deep sigh of relief, and keeping my promise to John I didn't go back to meet The Beatles for a fourth time. I somehow managed to find Pat and Catherine among the rowdy crowd. As I pushed and shoved to get to them, I noticed that the cousins were laughing. Shaking a finger at me Pat said, "I can't believe you didn't get chucked out." Giggling, I whispered, "I told you to come with me. After meeting The Beatles three times I'm beginning to feel like one of their friends." Catherine whispered, "You're so daring."

With an exaggerated sigh, I huffed, "You'd be bold too if in a few months you were going to be forced to move to some far-off country, and probably never have the chance to see The Beatles again." Both of the cousins gave me a sympathetic look.

The last of the fans had finally met The Beatles, and now all the fans in the ballroom were anxiously waiting for John, Paul, George and Ringo to come out and perform. We gathered around the stage, and the cousins and I could barely contain our excitement. The stage was very unusual. It was quite a few feet off the ground and was surrounded by steel barriers and a wired fence. It looked more like an animal enclosure at The London Zoo. I whispered to Pat and Catherine, "The organizers have made a cage for The Beatles. We can look, but no touching allowed." A girl who was standing next to me, replied, "It's a bit late for that, everyone here has already touched them today." And giggling, I thought to myself, "And some of us have managed to touch them three, yes three times!"

Finally, John, Paul, George and Ringo came out onto the stage. There were no seats in the ballroom, so we stood gazing up at them. The Beatles treated us to a wonderful show, and they sang several of their hit songs. Even though the ballroom was jam packed with fans, we somehow managed to dance in place, and it was plain to see that everyone at The Wimbledon

Palais thoroughly enjoyed The Beatles' performance. All too soon, The Southern Area Fan Club 'Get Together' came to an end.

Walking to the underground station I turned to the cousins, and sighed, "This has been the best Saturday of my entire life." And it was plain to see that they too had had a wonderful time. Later that evening, I was still reeling from the excitement of the 'Get Together.' I'd already recounted the entire event to my family and some of my girlfriends, but I couldn't stop thinking about how fortunate I was.

And in the middle of the night, I decided to write a letter to the fan club secretaries; Anne Collingham and Bettina Rose. I just wanted to say thank you, and to tell them how grateful I was for being one of the lucky fans who'd spent that very special afternoon with The Beatles. Of course, in my letter I didn't mention anything about going around to meet John, Paul, George, and Ringo three times. That would give the impression that I was cheeky, and I wouldn't want that!

<u>Chucked out</u>...Forced to leave.

CHAPTER 19
LETTERS GALORE

On a rainy Saturday afternoon, while tidying up the counter at 'Boots The Chemist', my girlfriend Cecilia came rushing into the shop. She immediately spotted me and pointing to the door motioned for me to come outside. The rain was pelting down so we stood in the doorway under the awning. Cecilia was normally a very quiet, reserved girl, but on this particular day she seemed unusually excited, and her face was quite flushed.

Giggling, I said to her, "Cecilia, you look like you're about to burst, it's obvious that you've got something to tell me, so come on let's have it." Taking a deep breath, she grabbed hold of my arm, and cried, "Oh Ursula, you're not going to believe this. Half an hour ago I bought the new Beatles' Monthly Book, and because of the lousy weather, I decided to get out of the rain. I went into that nice little cafe next door to Sainsbury's and treated myself to a scrumptious buttered roll and a nice cup of tea, and then I began to flip through my new magazine."

Trying not to yawn I sighed, "How nice! It sounds like you've had a lovely time, I wish I could have joined you." Noticing my sarcasm, she cried, "Hold on a minute, I didn't get to the good part yet. Are you ready for this?" I gave a little nod, and Cecilia squealed, "Your letter has been published in this month's Beatles' Book. The letter is all about your afternoon with The Beatles at the fan club Get Together." Laughing, I asked, "*Are you pulling my leg?"

Cecilia dragged her damp copy of The Beatles' Book out of her raincoat pocket and began to read aloud. I instantly recognized the familiar words, and when she had finish reading I sighed, "Oh dear, that's mine alright!" I'd read that The Beatles' fan club received thousands of letters every day from fans all over the world. Scratching my head I sighed, "I'm really confused, that letter's nothing special, and I certainly never expected to see it in The Beatles' Book." Smiling, Cecilia turned to me and said, "Well somebody at the fan club thought it was good enough to be published, and I think it's a lovely letter."

Cecilia handed me her Beatles' Book, and I noticed that right under the letter my name and address had also been published. Suddenly, I remembered the call that I'd made to my manager, and the multiple lies that I'd told him that day. Waving the magazine, I whispered nervously, "Let's hope my boss never sees this, I'll be sacked on the spot, and I really don't fancy traipsing all over Dalston with my Mum looking for another bleedin' Saturday job!"

I gave Cecilia a big hug and said, "Thanks for showing me the letter, and for coming all the way to the shop in this dreadful weather." Cecilia stuffed her soggy Beatles' Book back into her pocket, covered her head with her plastic rain bonnet, and said, "You should be very proud of yourself. After all, it's not everyone that gets their letter picked to be published in The Beatles' Book. Well, I'm off, see you on Monday." Cecilia ran into the pouring rain, and I crept back into the shop. Climbing up the creaky old stairs, I spent the rest of the day weighing, packing and munching on the assorted flavored cough drops, and reliving that wonderful afternoon with The Beatles.

A Common Case of Beatlemania

LETTERS from BEATLE PEOPLE

BEATLEMANIA

The group that makes the girls all scream,
(Especially Paul, 'cos he's a dream)
When they're singing "From Me To You,"
"Twist and Shout," and "Love Me Do,"
The girls are screaming; fainting; mad . . .
Funny; 'cos they're not THAT bad.

On his drums Ringo is banging,
On his guitar George is twanging,
John is singing "Thank You Girl"
While Paul has sent us in a whirl.

In the papers we always read
About the girls when they stampede,
To see the BEATLES, face to face,
Means queueing all night in a certain place,
Waiting for Ringo, John, George and Paul;
We dig this group the most of all.

              Lots of love from
             two Beatle crazy people,
Jennifer Troops and Jennifer Bishop (13-13).
10 Chestnut Ave., Ordsall, Retford, Notts.

Dear Tina and Anne,
    Thank you for making my dream come true—in other words thank you for inviting me to attend the Southern Area Fan Club Convention at Wimbledon Palais in December! I shall never forget that day as long as I live—it was the happiest of my life. I not only saw the boys performing—I actually touched John, Paul, George and Ringo after queueing up to meet them all for two hours.
    Thank you for making it possible for me and for everyone else who was present on that fab afternoon at Wimbledon.
              Lots of love,
              Ursula Fuery,
6 Emerson House, Matthias Road, London, N.16.

Tina and Anne write:—
We've been receiving hundreds of letters like this one from Fan Club members since the middle of December and we're more than pleased everybody had such a good time at the Get Together. We'd like to take this opportunity of thanking The Beatles for giving up a free afternoon at the end of a very busy tour to attend.

Dear Anne,
    Thank you very much for my copy of The Beatles Christmas Record. It is really fabulous—I have played it over and over again and I can just picture the four boys singing round Christmas tree. I like the way the recording starts off with that off-beat version of "Good King Wenceslas" before each of the boys talks to us all. Paul is absolutely terrific and George, Ringo and John are just as cute.
              Yours sincerely,
              Dawn Ratcliffe,
    16 Glenhills Boulevard, Leicester

Anne Collingham replies:—
Not a single copy of the Fan Club record remains undistributed—a final total of 28,000 discs went into the post to members just before Christmas. We were asked by some of the big newspapers to sell them copies for competition prizes but we said "No" to preserve the true souvenir value of this recording—free copies went ONLY to club members and the disc will NOT be available to the public.

Dear Beatles,
    Lately in our American newspapers and magazines there have been lots of articles about the Mersey Beat and photographs of you four. I was particularly interested in all this because I was lucky enough to see one of your shows at Weston-super-Mare when I was over in England last summer.
    I simply fell in love with your sound and bought your "Please, Please Me" LP album and your current singles. At home I have been playing them to all my friends. All of them think you have a "tuff sound" as we say here.
    I hope I'll have a chance of seeing you on television when you come to America in February and, in the meantime, we're all keeping our fingers crossed for your success.
              Your faithful fan,
              Louise Hauser,
907 Granard Parkway, Steubenville, Ohio

Paul writes:—
We've just read your letter in our dressing room at the Olympia in Paris, Louise, and I can tell you we're all very, very excited about our

My letter that was published in The Beatles' Monthly.

One week after my letter appeared in the Beatles' Monthly Book, the most astonishing thing happened: Every day dozens of letters came pouring through our *letter-box, and to my amazement these letters came from all over the world, and they were all addressed to me. My brother John was an avid stamp collector and now, thanks to these totally unexpected letters, his foreign stamp collection tripled overnight. I handed him the empty envelopes, and he carefully peeled off each and every colorful stamp, and placed them neatly into his stamp album.

All of the letters were written by girls who had read my letter in the Beatles' Monthly Book. Each of them wanted me to write back and give them all the details about that special afternoon at 'The Southern Area Fan Club Get Together.' Some of the letters were written in strange, foreign languages, and I didn't have a clue as to what they said. But by carefully studying the stamps, I could usually tell which countries the letters came from.

One afternoon, while walking home from school with some of my girlfriends, I bumped into our postman. He immediately plonked down his overstuffed postman's sack onto the ground, and taking me to one side said, "I've been dying to know what's going on with all these foreign letters you've been receiving? Why are so many people writing to you?
What's it all about Ursula?" Noticing the postman's puzzled look on his face, my girlfriends and I couldn't stop laughing. So, in my poshest accent, I replied, "What can I say? I'm a very popular girl." As we walked away, the postman just stood there scratching his head, and it was obvious that now he was even more confused.

Most of the writers asked if I'd like to be their pen-pal, and so I choose three girls each from a different part of the world. One was from Budapest, Hungary, another was from Sweden, and the third one lived in America.

My Swedish pen pal Lize Lottie

I'd always loved writing letters but up until now, my only pen-pal had been my grandmother in Ireland. I loved writing to my Nana, but no matter how hard I tried to convince her, she just didn't share my passion when it came to The Beatles. Now, I had three pen-pals and we all had the exact same feelings for John, Paul, George and Ringo.

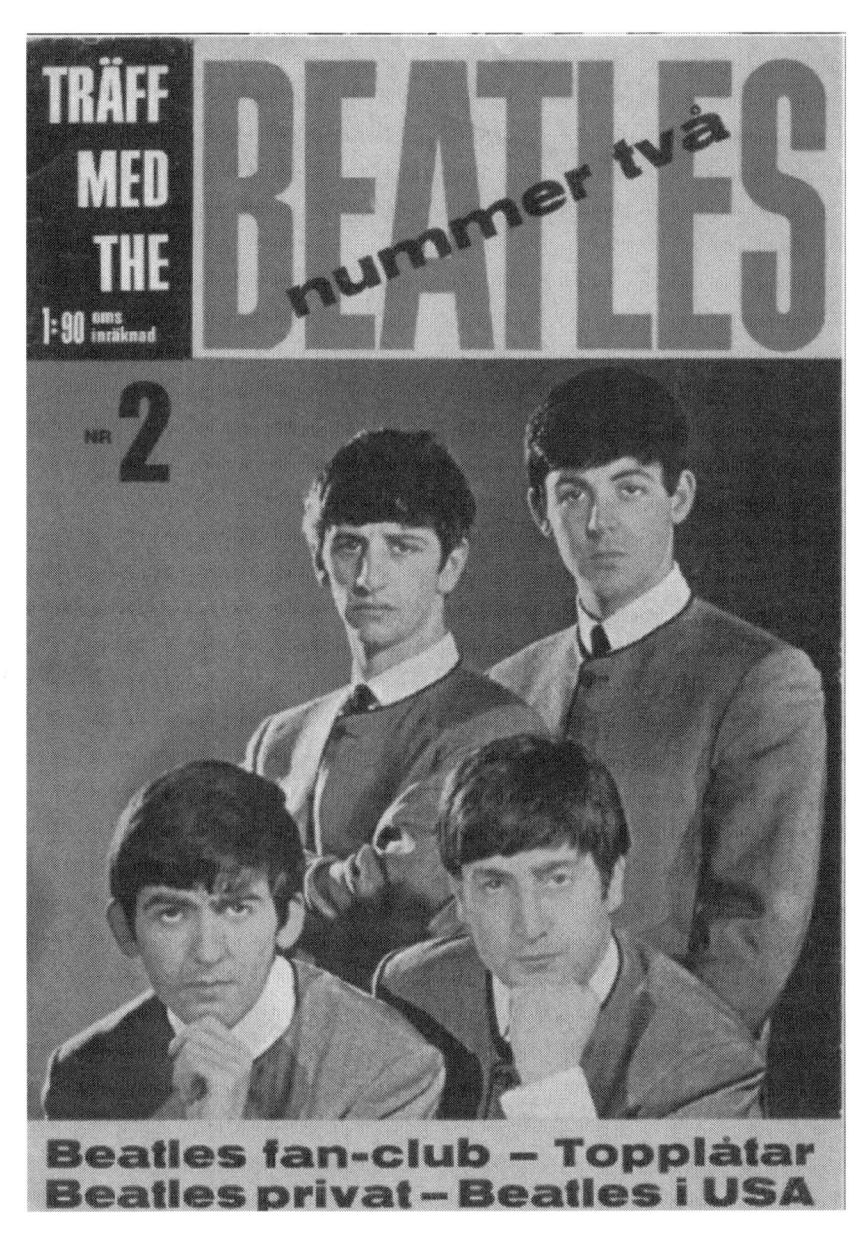

One of the many Swedish magazines from Lize Lottie

A Common Case of Beatlemania

Lize Lottie, my Swedish pen pal, wrote and asked if any of my girlfriends would like to become pen pals with her girlfriends. Maroula and Rita were happy to oblige, and within days they were exchanging letters with their very own Swedish pen-pals. I knew that between my schoolwork, my social life, and my Saturday job, I couldn't possibly answer all of the letters.

Holding a newly arrived batch I complained to my sister Angela, "To answer all of these letters, I'll need a stack of paper, a ton of envelopes, and hundreds of air mail stamps. I'll have to quit school and get a full-time job just to be able to pay for all the stamps I'd need." I placed the new letters into the wicker basket on top of the ever-growing pile of unopened letters.

With a worried look, Angela sighed, "You're right, the stamps alone will cost a small fortune, so what are you gonna do?" I didn't know what I was going to do, but I knew that I couldn't ignore these letters that came from girls who were just like my girlfriends and me and loved The Beatle almost as much as we did. With each passing day, more letters arrived, and the stack continued to grow. One night, while lying in my bed and worrying about the ever-growing heap of unopened letters, the solution suddenly popped into my head. The following morning, I stuffed a bundle of letters into my satchel, and took them with me to school.

In the playground, I stood on a bench and pretended to be at *Speakers Corner. I held up a handful of letters, and at the top of my lungs I screamed for everyone's attention. Immediately, dozens of curious girls gathered around to hear what I was ranting about. I told them about my dilemma, and to my surprise, practically every girl listening wanted a letter. From that day on, each morning as I walked through the school gate, a crowd of girls were waiting for me. Each of them hoping that today would be their lucky day, and that a letter from a faraway country would be handed over to them.

By the time the letters stopped coming, dozens of girls at Cardinal Pole Secondary School had their very own foreign pen-pals. And all thanks to that one letter that I wrote to The Beatles' fan club secretaries!

*<u>Pulling my leg</u>...Joking
*<u>Letterbox</u>...mail slot or mailbox
*<u>Speakers Corner</u>...An area in Hyde Park, London where people discuss and debate all sorts of issues.

CHAPTER 20
FOUR CHRISTMAS SHOWS

Ten days after The Beatles' Fan Club Get Together, good fortune came my yet again. The Beatles' Christmas show opened at The Finsbury Park Astoria. This *theatre was practically around the corner from where my girlfriends and I lived. If someone had asked me to pick a local theater for The Beatles' Christmas Show, The Finsbury Park Astoria would have been my first choice.

From the moment we found out about the upcoming Christmas show, my girlfriends and I vowed to save every penny that we could scrape together. We didn't want to go to one show, the goal was to attend as many shows as we could possibly afford. Not only did I want to buy tickets for The Beatles' Christmas show, but now that I had a Saturday job, for the first time ever I would be able to buy presents for my entire family, and I wanted to buy each of them something really expensive. So, before I had the chance to squander my hard earned pound note, I went straight to the post office and bought *national saving stamps.

The advertisement for The Beatles' Christmas show

Rita watched, as I carefully licked the stamps, and placed the half a crown 'Prince Charles' stamps in one savings book, and the sixpenny 'Princess Anne' stamps into my other book. I said to Rita, "As long as I don't have the cash lying around, I can't be tempted to spend it." With a smile on her face, she asked, "But what about all the little luxuries you've grown accustomed to?" Laughing out loud, I said, "It's not going to be forever, and besides I'd much rather have one more ticket to one more Beatles' Christmas show than another twin set from *Marks and Spencer's." Nodding in agreement, she said, "You're absolutely right. After all how many twin sets can one girl possibly need? But to have the chance to see The Beatles night after night, now that's special."

It didn't take my girlfriends and I too long to come up with some rather unique ways to save a penny here, and a *ha'penny there. Now, dodging the bus conductor had new meaning. It was no longer a silly schoolgirl's game; it was now serious business. We needed our precious *thrupenny bits, and by hook or by crook we were determined to hold onto them. In no time at all, we became quite skillful at avoiding the bus conductor, and on most days, we still had our money when we jumped off of the bus.

Occasionally, Frances' mother invited us over to their house for lunch. We loved going there for two reasons: She always made a scrumptious fry up, that included sausages, chips, fried tomatoes and a heaping serving of Heinz baked beans. After eating this enormous meal, the thought of going back to school was the last thing any of us wanted to do.

Walking out the door, I'd always remember to complement the chef, "Mrs. Warren, that was the best lunch I have ever eaten." Laughing out loud, she'd reply, "Oh Ursula, flattery will get you everywhere, but don't let your mother hear you talking that way." The second reason was, as Valerie reminded us, "Not only did we have the most delicious lunch, but that's another shilling in the *kitty."

I still needed to find other ways to add to my savings, so I asked my parents to give me cash for my Christmas present. With a puzzled look, my mother cried, "But we've never done anything like that before, and besides, I haven't even thought about Christmas, it's still months away." Taking a deep breath, I tried to explain, "But the tickets go on sale for the Beatles' Christmas show on October 21st., and if my girlfriends and I don't buy them on the very first day, they'll be completely sold out. My parents looked completely baffled.

Not knowing how to respond, my father just shrugged his shoulders (which meant that he was leaving this sticky situation up to my mother). I continued my emotional appeal, "You must understand, there's only one thing that I want for Christmas, and that's to see The Beatles' show at least a dozen times." After listening to my plea, it was obvious that my mother was now totally confused! Scratching her head, she cried, "But aren't they going to be singing the same songs night after night? How could that be enjoyable? Are you sure you wouldn't prefer a nice new *jumper, and a pair of those fluffy slippers that everyone's wearing?" Hearing her response, I almost burst out laughing, but I knew better so I continued my begging, "Oh please Mum and Dad, just give me the money, and please be as generous as possible!"

The begging and pleading went on for three nights without any success, but on the fourth night just as I was about to begin my usual plea, my mother groaned, "Your father and I have talked it over, and whatever you want is fine with us."

It was obvious that my parents had had enough of my ranting, and they knew that if they wanted to restore tranquility back into their lives, they had no choice but to give in to my very reasonable request. I thanked my parents over and over, and as I was leaving the room, I overheard my mother say, "Finally, we'll be able to watch *Coronation Street in peace again!" And my father's answer was an enormous sigh.

By the time the tickets went on sale all of my scrimping and saving had paid off. I had enough money to buy four tickets to four separate Christmas shows, and still had enough money left to buy each member of my family a really nice present.

As I left The Finsbury Park Astoria box office I kissed my precious tickets, and said to myself, "I might not be going to a dozen shows, but for a poor schoolgirl four shows is still jolly good."

*<u>National saving stamps</u>…Stamps issued by the government to enable small amounts of money to be saved over time.
*<u>Ha'penny</u>…A former British coin equal to half a penny.
*<u>Marks and Spencer's</u>…A major British retailer
*<u>Kitty</u>…An amount of money that's being saved for a particular purpose.
*<u>Jumper</u>…Sweater.
*<u>Coronation Street</u>…A British evening soap opera that began in 1960 (and is still on today)

CHAPTER 21
SWEETS FOR THE BEATLES

The Beatles' Christmas Show opened on Christmas Eve and for that first performance my girlfriends and I took up an entire row. On our way to the theatre, we stopped at a nearby sweetshop, and each of us bought a sixpenny bag of *jelly babies. For months, we'd been reading about The Beatles' love for the soft and chewy sweets, and because of all the publicity a new tradition had sprung up among Beatle fans. While John, Paul, George and Ringo performed, the fans threw handfuls of colorful jelly babies onto the stage and my girlfriends, and I were determined to keep this new tradition alive.

The tiny sweetshop was overflowing with teenage girls who were all buying jelly babies. The flustered shopkeeper was running from the counter to the weighing scale, and back to the counter. It was plain to see that he was having a difficult time keeping up with the massive influx of customers. As he carefully weighed my sweets, I overheard him whispering to his wife, "First thing in the morning remind me to put in a large order for more of these jelly babies." And with a little chuckle, he added, "I don't know what's going on, but if this keeps up we'll be millionaires in no time!" As Valerie watched all the other customers carrying their bags of jelly babies, she shook her head in disbelief, and cried out, "Cor blimey, these days it's just impossible to be original."

The Beatles' favorite sweets

As soon as we were finished in the sweet shop, we headed off to The Finsbury Park Astoria. With tickets in hand, we ran into the theatre and quickly found our seats. We were in the fifth row and could barely contain our excitement when we saw how close we were to the stage.

While we waited for the show to begin, we chatted among ourselves, and nibbled on our jelly babies.

Brian Epstein was the manager of all of the acts that were taking part in the Christmas Show. In addition to The Beatles, Billy J. Kramer, The Fourmost, Tommy Quickly, The Barron Knights and Cilla Black were also performing, and the host of the show was the popular Australian comic, Rolf Harris.

After what seemed like an eternity it was finally time for the show to begin. As the curtains opened a gigantic cardboard helicopter slowly descended onto the stage, and one by one each of the performers came out of the helicopter, and Rolf Harris introduced them to the audience. The performers bowed and waved, and the audience clapped and cheered loudly.

With bated breath we and everyone in the theatre sat there anxiously waiting for John, Paul, George and Ringo to make their grand entrance. The anticipation was sheer agony, and after a while a group of girls in the back of the theatre started shouting at the top of their lungs, "We want The Beatles!" After hearing that, the entire audience started stamping their feet, and screaming, "We want the Beatles, we want The Beatles!"

Rolf Harris stood on the stage and looked confused. He shrugged his shoulders, scratched his head, and just couldn't understand what all the fuss was about. Suddenly, the helicopter glided up to the top of the stage, and the audience gave a collective gasp. Then the chanting began all over again: "We want The Beatles! We want The Beatles!" For the second time the helicopter landed on the stage, but this time, to everyone's delight, John, Paul, George and Ringo came marching out of the cardboard aircraft. Immediately, every person in the theatre jumped to their feet. And as The Beatles stood waving and smiling, everyone in the audience screamed at the top of their lungs.

As soon as The Beatles left the stage a hush fell over the audience, and everyone sat back down. The Barron Knights were the first to perform, followed by some of the other performers that were on the bill. To our delight, in between the various performers The Beatles came out and did little comedy sketches. The moment John, Paul, George and Ringo appeared on the stage; the audience went completely wild. The Beatles wore silly costumes and performed short skits that reminded me of a Christmas *pantomime.

Whispering into my ear, Valerie said, "These skits are so bleedin' corny, if anyone other than The Beatles were up there, I'd be yelling, 'Chuck 'em off!'" Giggling, I replied, "Yeah, me too!" Eileen added, "They could bring a couch out onto the stage, and as long as it was The Beatles sitting there, I'd be quite content!" With a dreamy smile, Valerie sighed, "Just to be able to look at them is more than enough for me." We all nodded in total agreement.

In between The Beatles' comedy sketches, the other performers came on stage, and did their very best to entertain us. They were all very good, but we were there to see The Beatles, so we couldn't wait for the other acts to be finished. Finally, the moment had arrived, and it was time for The Beatles to perform. As soon as the curtains opened the screaming began all over again.

As if on cue, my girlfriends and I jumped out of our seats, ran up the aisle and threw the remainder of our jelly babies onto the stage. (Fortunately for The Beatles, by this time we had eaten most of the jelly babies.)

The Beatles started off the set by performing 'Roll Over Beethoven', but because of the screaming, we really didn't hear it. After 'Roll Over Beethoven', they performed, 'All My Loving', followed by 'This Boy' and continued the set by performing several of their other songs. Before each song, a hush would come over the audience which was just long enough to hear which song they were about to perform, and as soon as everyone recognized the first few bars, the screaming began all over again. My girlfriends and I screamed at the top of our lungs, and by the second song we, along with everyone in the theatre, were standing up and dancing in place.

In what seemed like a flash, thirty minutes had gone by, and to our disappointment, The Beatles' performance came to an end. John, Paul, George and Ringo bowed to the screaming audience, and quickly walked off the stage. We waited in anticipation for them to come back out, to give us an encore performance, but suddenly the national anthem began to play. Everyone rose to their feet, and enthusiastically sang a very loud rendition of 'God Save The Queen'

After the national anthem we knew that The Beatles were long gone, so along with everyone else we piled out of the theatre. From all of the screaming, and excitement we were totally *knackered, so instead of looking for a Wimpey Bar or somewhere to sit, we decided to go straight home.

On Christmas day, because I didn't have too many presents under the tree, my parents both had the same guilty look on their faces. Sipping my steaming hot cocoa, I said, "Don't be silly, last night I was at The Beatles' Christmas show, and I had the time of my life. And if that wasn't enough, I still have three more tickets to three more shows. I'll be getting Christmas presents right up until their last performance on January 11th., so what more could I possibly want?"

Hearing that, my mother looked relieved and with a contented smile she went back to basting the turkey.

My girlfriends and I made sure that the tickets that we had bought were for the second performance of the day, and after each of the shows we felt exactly the same: completely exhausted and not to mention, quite hoarse from all the screaming. On many of the nights that we didn't have tickets to get into the show, we still went along to The Finsbury Park Astoria. It was so close to where we lived, and just knowing that The Beatles were going to be there was exciting enough for us.

Walking down Seven Sisters Road and seeing the streets overflowing with fans who were on their way to see the show was so exhilarating, and the closer we got to the theater, the more excited we became. The atmosphere outside the theatre was unlike anything we had ever experienced, and just to be in the middle of all that excitement was more than enough for us.

Most nights we got to the Astoria just in time to see The Beatles rushing in through the side entrance. As soon as The Beatles' car pulled up, everyone standing in the orderly queue ran to catch a glimpse of John, Paul, George and Ringo, and instant turmoil broke out. Within minutes The Beatles were inside, the people got back on the line, and my girlfriends and I headed home. Limping along, Valerie chirped, "Cold feet and chilblains are a small price to pay for seeing The Beatles practically every night." Eileen added, "I'm having such a smashing time I'd completely forgotten about the awful weather." Two of the shows that we attended were in January and gushing with enthusiasm, Rita chirped, "I can't think of a better way to start the new year. 1964 is definitely off to a fab start!" Eileen sighed, "I'd like to start every new year with The Beatles."

Just like my mother had predicted, each of the Christmas shows were similar to the previous ones, but we didn't mind, and we thoroughly enjoyed every one of them. The screaming continued at every show, and of course, our screaming continued too! We were there to see the Beatles, and to be breathing the same air that John, Paul, George and Ringo were breathing! We had all of their records so we could listen to their songs any time. We were at the shows to be part of the frenzy that was now widely known as Beatlemania. We made sure that we had tickets for the final Christmas show, and just knowing that this was the last performance was quite emotional for all of us.

As soon as the show was over, and we were back outside in the freezing cold, we realized that our thrilling evenings with The Beatles had come to an end. Walking to the bus stop, we shuffled along and nobody said a single word. Waiting for the bus, Eileen finally broke the silence, "Now, what are we gonna do with ourselves? I was getting used to seeing John, Paul, George and Ringo on a nightly basis." With a tear in her eye, Christina sighed, "It's not gonna be easy to top this!"

*<u>Jelly babies</u>… A type of soft sugar jelly sweets shaped as plump babies in a variety of colors.
*<u>Christmas pantomime</u>…A traditional British play that includes dancing, singing and comedy.
*<u>Knackered</u>…Exhausted.

CHAPTER 22
THEY'RE OFF TO FRANCE

On January 14th, 1964, just three days after The Christmas show had ended, The Beatles flew to France. Arrangements had been made for them to perform a three-week session at The L'Olympia Theatre. We'd read several articles about the upcoming French tour, and one of the newspapers had published the name of the hotel where The Beatles were staying. It was The George V Hotel in the center of Paris.

One afternoon, my friends and I were sitting in my living room, drinking cups of tea and reminiscing about the Christmas show. We missed seeing The Beatles and all the excitement that went along with the nightly shows. Now, our evenings were dull and rather boring.

Dipping another *biscuit into her tea, Valerie moaned, "And because they're all the way over in bleedin' France, we can't even pop round to their houses to see them." While Valerie continued her moaning, I suddenly remembered the article that had published the name of the hotel where the Boys were staying. I kept everything that was written about The Beatles, so I knew that it had to be somewhere in my chest of drawers. I ran to my bedroom, rummaged through my messy drawers, and somehow managed to find it.

Rushing back to the living room, I said to my girlfriends, "I've got an idea, why don't we call The Beatles on the telephone. I know it's not the same as seeing them, but it's the next best thing." In a sarcastic tone, Valerie snapped, "Oh yeah, and who do you know that owns a telephone?" Smiling broadly, I told my girlfriends all about the public telephone box that was right around the corner, and lucky for us, it had been broken for weeks. The great thing about it was that you could call anywhere in the world, and no coins were necessary! The entire neighborhood, not to mention their friends and family members had been enjoying this unexpected gift from British Telecom for quite a few weeks. Other than a couple of friends, I didn't know anyone who actually owned a telephone, so up until now, I had no one to call.

It was plain to see that my girlfriends didn't believe a single word that I had said. So walking to the front door I held it open, and yelled, "Come and see for yourselves." We quickly threw on our coats and scarves, and ran all the way to the telephone box. When we reached it, the five of us somehow managed to squeeze into the tiny space, and I volunteered to do the speaking. I dialed O and within seconds, a cheery telephone operator came on the other end, and chirped, "How may I help you?"

In my poshest accent, I replied, "Could you please put me through to The George the Fifth Hotel, in Paris, France." The operator asked, "And what number are you calling from?" Panicking, I glanced over at my girlfriends. They were doubled up with laughter, and I immediately knew that none of them were going to help me.

Ignoring my silly friends, I gave the operator my neighbor's telephone number and the operator relied, "Thank you, madame" She immediately connected me to the far away hotel. The phone began to ring on the other end, and I instructed my girlfriends to, "Keep the noise down!" Suddenly, a man with *Maurice Chevalier's voice answered the phone, "George za Fifth Hotel, can I help you?" Everything was happening so fast, and that's when I realized that I hadn't planned any of this. With a charming French man on the other end of the line, I was about to panic.

I knew that this was a great opportunity to speak to one, if not all of The Beatles, so I cleared my throat and in an even posher accent I replied, "I say old chap, would you be a dear, and put me through to George." Pausing ever so slightly, I continued, "Of course, I'm referring to George Harrison of The Beatles". To stop myself from laughing I held my nose, and refused to look at my four hysterical girlfriends. I could hear paper rustling on the other end of the line, and then the very polite Frenchman came back on the phone, "I'm afraid Za Beatles are not in at za moment. May I take a message?" Relieved, that he hadn't put me through, I chirped, "Thank you so much darling, I'll try again later."

I quickly hung up the phone, and the five of us tumbled out of the telephone box. For the next ten minutes, we stood on the pavement and couldn't stop laughing. The people walking by gave us peculiar looks, but we just continued laughing. After regaining her composure Eileen chirped, "Ursula, we had no idea you were such a great actress. The minute you get to America, you've got to go straight out to Hollywood, because you're a natural." Giggling, I replied, "Why thank you my dear! I'm ever so pleased that he didn't put me through. If one of The Beatles had actually answered, I'd have fainted on the spot."

Laughing out loud, Valerie said, "Even if you had fainted, with so many of us in the telephone box there's no way you'd have touched the floor." Eileen asked, "By the way, where did you get the telephone number that you rattled off to the operator?" I replied, "I gave the operator my neighbor's telephone number. It was the only number that I knew off by heart. God, if she ever finds out she'll kill me!" Valerie whispered, "Don't worry, your secret is safe with us!"

Months later, Rita took me to one side and whispered, "I've been meaning to ask you, did your neighbor mention anything to you about getting an enormous telephone bill for a certain long-distance call?" I turned to face her, and once again in my poshest accent, answered, "Darling, I've no idea what you're talking about." And together the two of us roared with laughter.

*_Maurice Chevalier_…A French singer, actor, and entertainer.
*_Poshest accent_…Upper class English accent.

CHAPTER 23
THE BEATLES IN AMERICA

On December 26th, 1963, 'I Wanna Hold Your Hand' was released in America. The song entered the American charts on January 18th at number 45 and climbed all the way to the number one position where it remained for seven consecutive weeks! People all over America were listening to this new song, and with each passing day The Beatles were getting more popular.

Now that they had a number one hit in America, we knew that it was only a matter of time before our boys would be crossing the pond to meet their new American fans. As predicted, on February 7th 1964 The Beatles flew off on their first American Tour. On the nightly news we'd watch the film footage of The Beatles being mobbed by their new American fans.

One evening Christina and I watched in awe as thousands of girls stood behind the barriers outside The Plaza Hotel in New York City. Looking over at Christina, I joked, "Maybe they'll decide to move to New York, and that would certainly make my move a lot more pleasant. With John, Paul, George and Ringo once again living so close to me, I do believe I could get used to living in a foreign country!" Laughing her head off, Christina shouted, "No such bleedin' luck, they're staying right here where they belong!"

On Sunday February 9th, The Beatles appeared on 'The Ed Sullivan

Show.' This show was the American version of 'Sunday Night at The London Palladium' and it was the most popular variety show on American television. The Beatles had two segments on that first appearance. For the first segment they sang: 'All My Loving' 'Till There Was You' and 'She Loves You.' The greater part of audience was made up of teenage girls and from the moment The Beatles came out onto the stage the girls screamed and applauded.

Thirty-five minutes later The Beatles were back for their second segment. This time they performed: 'I Saw Her Standing There' and their number one hit, 'I Wanna Hold your Hand.' Once again, pandemonium broke out in the studio audience.

It was reported that over 73 million people had tuned in to watch them, and after that one performance Beatlemania had officially arrived in America.

The following Sunday, The Beatles made a second appearance on the Ed Sullivan Show.

This time, it was a live broadcast from their hotel in Miami, Florida. For this second appearance, The Beatles sang six songs: "She Loves You' 'This Boy' 'All My Loving' 'I Saw Her Standing There' 'From Me To You' and once again, 'I Wanna Hold Your Hand'.

On their first American tour The Beatles also did three live shows: one at The Coliseum in Washington D.C. and two shows at Carnegie Hall in New York City.

While The Beatles were in America, dozens of magazines were published, all reporting on their amazing tour. Every time I walked into the paper shop, yet another magazine would be on display. The magazine covers were absolutely fab, and even though the magazines cost a small fortune, thanks to my Saturday job I could afford to buy them.

A Common Case of Beatlemania

*One of the many magazines that were published while
The Beatles were in America*

I thoroughly enjoyed reading about the different places that the boys were visiting and knowing that I would be moving to America before the end of the year, I imagined myself going to some of these fascinating places. I found it very strange that one day The Beatles were in heavy winter coats, looking extremely cold, while posing on a snow-covered road in Washington D.C., and less than a week later they were in a place that had clear blue skies, palm trees, and they were wearing *swimming trunks. I couldn't believe how big America was.

As soon as I'd finished reading the articles, I'd carefully remove the never-before-seen pictures and taped them onto my bedroom wall. With more than a twinge of jealousy we continued to watch John, Paul, George and Ringo on the evening news. They certainly looked like they were enjoying themselves in America, and we were not happy.

The Beatles were due to return to England on Saturday, February 22nd.

My girlfriends and I talked endlessly about them coming home, and we couldn't wait for our boys to get back to where they belonged.

While sitting together at the table in the school lunchroom, Eileen came up with a brilliant idea, "I think we should all go to the airport to welcome our boys home. It's on a Saturday so we won't have to worry about taking another day off from school, and we'll have a great day out.

They're arriving early in the morning, so we'll probably be the only ones at the airport." None of us had ever been to London Airport and we all agreed that this could be an exciting adventure.

Several of the girls in our class wanted to come along, so we decided to have a meeting. Betty said that her house would be the perfect place to hold the meeting, and that her mother would be *thrilled to bits to have so much company. The following evening twelve girls showed up for the first meeting. Lounging on her soft velvet couches, we decided that being as it was Betty's house, Betty should be the one in charge.

Delighted that she had been chosen to be the leader, Betty proudly stood up and asked, "Does anyone know the way to Heathrow Airport?" I immediately raised my hand, and said, "Leave it to me Betty; I've got the A to Z map. I'll study it, and by the next meeting I'll have the directions written down." That was one less thing for her Betty to worry about, and she looked relieved. She continued, "Now, I suggest we do something really special to welcome our boys' home."

Valerie chuckled, "And what do you have in mind Betty?" In a serious tone, Betty replied, "A giant banner would be rather nice." Everyone smiled and nodded enthusiastically. Seeing our eager faces, Betty could no longer contain her excitement. Jumping to her feet and waving her arms, she continued, "This amazing banner will have bold lettering splashed across it. And the lettering will be so enormous, The Beatles will be able to read it while they're still up in the air!"

Betty's enthusiasm had rubbed off on Rita, and flushed with excitement, Rita chirped, "Sounds like a great project! I've never made anything out of wood, but I'm more than willing to *give it a bash!" Putting on an upper-class accent, Eileen patted Rita on the back, and cried, "That's the spirit old chum!" Betty was in no mood for silly comments, and got right back to business, "Does anyone have a white sheet that they'd be willing to donate to the cause?"

Christina raised her hand, "My mum's bound to have an old sheet that she wants to get rid of, so I'll take care of that." Once again, Betty looked relieved. A few more things were discussed, and our first meeting came to an end.

Betty's mother who'd been listening to all of our plans, immediately ran to put the kettle on. Ten minutes later we each had a nice cup of tea and a huge slice of Victoria sponge cake. As we were leaving, Betty yelled from the balcony, "At the next meeting, be prepared to roll up your sleeves, because we have a lot of work to do."

Two days later, ten of us were back at Betty's house. With scissors in hand, Betty cut Christina's old sheet, and together Mary and Eileen hand stitched a perfectly straight hem. Wearing her brother's enormous workman's gloves, Rita carefully stapled two pieces of wood to either side of the sheet. Once the sheet was tight and secure, we were ready to add our message. Holding a paintbrush and a tin of black paint, Betty stepped forward to create her masterpiece, and in big bold letters she wrote: "Welcome Home Boys."

Looking at the perfect lettering, Valerie grumbled, "It looks very nice, but I've seen that message before." Turning to Valerie, Eileen cried, "I think it's absolutely *smashing, and who cares if someone else's banner says the same thing. After all, you're the one who keeps reminding us that these days it's almost impossible to be original!"

Beaming with pride, Betty added, "If I do say so myself, we've done a first-class job. Now, who's ready for a nice cup of tea, and some of my mum's delicious *fairy cakes?" In unison, we all yelled, "Yes please."

As we were leaving Betty's building she yelled from her balcony, "We're going to be out bright and early on Saturday morning, and the weatherman said it's going to be bitter cold, so please make sure you wear your winter coats, scarves, and hats". Laughing out loud, Valerie shouted back, "Yes Mummy!"

*<u>Swimming trunks</u>...Swim suites
*<u>Thrilled to bits</u>...Very excited, and pleased.
*<u>Give it a bash</u>...Give it a try.
*<u>Smashing</u>...Very good, impressive, perfect.

CHAPTER 24
LONDON AIRPORT

On the morning of February 22nd. I was *up with the birds. It was still dark outside and for the first time in my life my father was still asleep. I made myself a cup of tea and toasted a crumpet and covered it in butter. Sitting alone at the table I realized that without my father's company, the kitchen seemed strangely odd. Getting dressed, I remembered Betty's continuous weather warnings and so I added an extra layer of clothing. I'd taken a personal day off from Boots The Chemist, so this time I didn't have to tell any lies.

Walking through the deserted Mayville Estates, my familiar neighborhood seemed more than a bit scary, and so I began to run. As planned, my girlfriends were waiting for me on the corner of Matthias Road, next to the Mildmay Club. Rushing over to them, I cried, "I'm ever so glad to see you, being as it's still dark this place is giving me the *willies."

Laughing hysterically, Eileen said, "You're with us now, so there's no need to worry about the Stoke Newington ghost." Yawning loudly, Valerie moaned, "I've never been up this early and I'm bloody exhausted." Pulling at Valerie's coat sleeve, Eileen said, "Come on lazybones you can do it." Looking at my watch I cried, "We'd better get a move on. The Beatles' plane is arriving at eight o' clock sharp. I'd hate to go all the way there and miss

143

them." Yawning again, Valerie mumbled, "With it being Saturday, and so bleedin' early I'm sure we'll have the bus and the train all to ourselves."

Some of us girls who were at The London Airport.

As promised, I had studied the London underground map and written down all the directions. So, while we waited for the bus, I read the simple directions to my girlfriends: "We take the 73 bus to Kings Cross station, and then we have to find the Piccadilly line. Once we're on the tube, we'll be at Heathrow Airport in no time at all." Frowning again, Valerie cried, "Just thinking about all the traveling that's involved is making me exhausted." Looking straight at Valerie, I snapped, "Oh for God's sake stop all that grumbling, you lazy cow!"

Everything was going according to plan: the number 73 bus was completely empty and instead of sitting together, we each had our own double seat. Once the conductor was out of sight, we put our feet up and made ourselves comfortable. For the umpteenth time, Valerie moaned, "Nobody in their right mind is gonna be taking a bus ride at this ungodly hour."

At King's Cross Station, we found the Piccadilly line and I was surprised to see a few Beatle looking fans standing on the platform. Before long we heard the approaching train, and, Valerie moaned, 'This early morning stuff just *isn't my cup of tea. Thank God it's a long ride because I'm ready for a nice, relaxing sit down."

As the train pulled into the station, I immediately noticed that all of the windows on the train were fogged up, and you couldn't see inside the train. Rita noticed it too and looking confused, she sighed, "There's something dodgy going on here!" Finally, the doors opened, and we could finally see into the train compartment. We were so disappointed because the train was overflowing with hundreds of half asleep Beatle fans. As she forced her way into the overcrowded compartment, Valerie screamed, "I don't believe this!"

Maroula grumbled, "Just like every other time, all these people had the same idea as us, and now it looks like we're gonna have to stand for the entire train ride." Betty was squashed between two rather plump girls and from the look on her face it obvious that she was not happy. The train ride was at least twenty stops, and at every station more Beatle fans squeezed into the jammed packed compartment.

Chugging along, the train got closer and closer to the airport and the excitement in the crowded compartment grew to a fever pitch. Suddenly a voice yelled out, "Hold on tight everyone, we'll be there in a few more minutes!" Hearing this, everyone began to cheer loudly. We later learned that London Transportation had anticipated a huge fan turnout, and in order to be prepared for the crowds had actually added more trains to the Saturday schedule: Good thing they had, or we would never had made it to the airport.

Once we arrived at Heathrow, we just followed the crowd. A friendly policeman directed all of us onto the roof of The Queens Building. Thousands of fans were already on the rooftop, and so our first task was to find a decent spot where we could stand together and still be able to see the runway. Scanning the rooftop, my girlfriends and I saw the perfect vantage point near a guardrail, and quickly ran to claim the space. With a worried look, Valerie sighed, "What happens if we need to use the *loo?" Instead of answering, we all stood there looking at each other, and it was obvious that not one of us had even thought about that.

Standing on the open rooftop, exposed to the frigid February air, my girlfriends and I were very pleased that we'd taken Betty's advice, and dressed appropriately. We each wore our identical black and white speckled coats with the black leather collars. These coats were the height of fashion, and looking around the rooftop I noticed that dozens of other girls were wearing the exact same coats. My girlfriends and I also had on hats, scarves and gloves.

Checking my watch, I realized that we still had two hours to wait before The Beatles' plane was due to arrive, and I wondered how we'd manage to while away the time.

Suddenly, 'I Wanna Hold Your Hand' came blasting out of the public address system.

Immediately, a hush descended over the noisy crowd, and then everyone began to cheer. Wiping away a tear, Francis cried, "None of us expected this, what a lovely thing to do for the fans." Valerie chirped, "That's it, from now on I'm only taking flights that leave from Heathrow Airport." Laughing loudly, Francis reminded her, "You've never even been on a blooming plane." Giving her a funny look, Valerie replied, "Well, I'm thinking of the future."

Over the loud speakers came one Beatle song after another, and it was plain to see that everyone's mood instantly changed from being fidgety to being calm and extremely happy. Swaying to the beat and grinning from ear to ear, Francis cried, "Twenty minutes ago I was freezing my*arse off, and now thanks to The Beatles' amazing music I could stand here all day."

Every once in a while the music stopped, and a spokesperson made an announcement letting us the latest information on The Beatles' time of arrival. After each announcement, loud cheers erupted and then The Beatles' music resumed. Finally, the announcement that everyone had been waiting to hear: "The Beatles will be home in ten more minutes." We, along with the thousands of other fans cheered loudly, and peered up to the cloudy sky. Within minutes The Beatles' airplane came into view.

Just as the plane was approaching the runway, over the loud speakers came The Beatles' song: 'It Won't Be Long' and everyone on the roof began to sing along with the record. It was the perfect song to be playing as our boys were about to arrive home.

At last, The Beatles' plane landed and after what seemed like an eternity a metal passenger stairway was wheeled over to the plane. The crowd gave a collective gasp, and silence took over the once noisy rooftop. Finally, the moment that everyone had been waiting for: The plane's door swung open, and out stepped Paul followed by George, then John, and finally Ringo.

The roar from the crowd was deafening, and at the same time quite thrilling. After standing in the freezing cold for so long, and finally being able to see our boys in the misty morning light was quite an emotional event for all of us. Standing on the metal airplane steps, The Beatles waved enthusiastically to all of the cheering fans. We, along with everyone else on the roof waved back, and of course, continued to scream.

Dressed in dark overcoats, with white shirts and dark ties, The Beatles looked extremely smart, and very fashionable. As they slowly descended the steps, each of them continued to smile and wave. Suddenly, my girlfriends and I heard Betty's high pitched wail, "Come on you lot, give me a hand with the banner!"

We quickly unfolded our banner, hoisted it up high above the other fans' heads, and continued waving to The Beatles. With so much excitement swirling all around, and so many of the fans jumping up and down I thought that the entire roof was about to collapse at any minute. In what seemed like a flash, The Beatles were whisked away by several policemen.

Unable to comprehend that the homecoming had come to an abrupt ending, my girlfriends and I stood on the roof dumbfounded. In the blink of an eye, the excitement and the chaos was over, and everyone on the rooftop began to leave. My girlfriends and I had done our bit to give The Beatles the best homecoming they'd ever had, and now that it was over, the nasty weather quickly became a reality. Plodding along the train station with hundreds of others exhausted fans, we were more than ready to go home.

With a long weary sigh, Valerie mumbled, "All I want is a nice cup of tea, and some beans on toast." Rita purred, "Mmm, that sounds wonderful." Walking along the platform, Betty turned to face us and shaking the banner, cried, "I've been carrying this thing all day, it's time for someone else to have a go." Valerie snapped, "Oh for God's sake just chuck the bleedin' thing in the *rubbish bin, we'll make an even bigger and better one for the next homecoming." Through chattering teeth, Eileen cried, "Well let's hope the next homecoming will be in the summertime, because I really don't fancy standing outside in the bitter cold again!"

Now that Betty had our permission, she immediately threw the tattered banner into an overflowing rubbish bin, and from the smile on her face, it was plain to see that she was quite relieved to be rid of it. As soon as the train door opened we ran into the compartment, and collapsed into the first available seats. Rubbing her swollen ankles, Francis gave a contented smile and purred, "Ah, just to be sitting in a lovely warm train feels like heaven."

Giggling, Eileen reminded us, "We'll be on this train for quite a long time, so we better not conk out, cos we're liable to wake up somewhere in the Scottish Highlands, and it's even colder up there!" Closing my eyes, and barely able to speak, I quietly mumbled, "I'd give anything for a nice *cuppa and a buttered scone. Being a loyal Beatle fan can be exhausting work." Resting her head on Valerie's shoulder, Christina slurred, "I don't know about you lot, but I've had a smashing time." We didn't have the energy to answer, so we just shook our heads in total agreement.

*<u>Up with the birds</u>…Very early in the morning.
*<u>The Willies</u>…A feeling one gets when he or she is nervous.

*_Done me in_...Made me exhausted.
*_My cup of tea_...Something you don't like or care to do.
*_The loo_...The bathroom.
*_Arse_...British word for ass.
*_Rubbish bin_...Garbage can.
*_Cuppa_...Cup of tea (or coffee)

CHAPTER 25
A TINY FIB

By the spring of 1964 The Beatles had appeared on 'Ready Steady Go' on at least on two occasions. Ready Steady Go' was the number one pop music program on television, and every Friday evening millions of teenagers all over Great Britain tuned in to watch the show. Ready, Steady, Go featured all of the popular acts of the day. While the artists performed their latest hits, the studio audience danced around them. After each performance, the artists would have an informal interview with one of the hosts of the show.

There were two presenters on the show: Keith Fordyce who, because of his easy-going personality was loved by everyone, and the second presenter was Cathy McGowan. Cathy wore the most amazing clothes, and because of her unique fashion sense she became known as: 'The Queen of the Mods.' Cathy always came out onto the dance floor wearing the most up to date fabulous clothes, and whatever she wore became an instant 'must have' item for fashion conscious teenage girls all around the country.

One Friday evening, as I was watching Ready Steady Go, and drooling over Cathy's fabulous crocheted *frock, she informed the television audience that the following Friday a very special raffle will take place. In her usual enthusiastic manner, she looked straight into the camera and announced,

"All the days and months of the year will be placed into a drum, and one lucky date will be drawn. Any teenager born on the chosen date will have the opportunity to write to the television company and request tickets for a very special show. If their letter is picked, not one, not two, but three tickets will be sent to them: one for the winner, and two for their best friends This show will be an hour long, televised show featuring none other than The Beatles.

The moment I heard: 'The Beatles,' I jumped up, rushed over to the television set and turned the volume all the way up. Cathy continued to tell the audience at home about the upcoming show. And the more I heard, the more excited I became, and I knew that I just had to be one of the lucky winners.

After all, my days of popping round to John, Paul, George and Ringo's homes were quickly coming to an end. I wasn't going to be living in England much longer, and I was fully aware of the harsh reality that once I had left England my chances of ever seeing The Beatles again were practically nil. But I had two problems: how would I get these highly desirable tickets? Which two special friends would I take with me? I didn't want to leave any of my friends out, but with only three tickets, I knew that someone's feeling were about to get hurt!

That night, with so much on my mind, I just couldn't sleep. I tossed and turned, and kept hearing Cathy McGowan's excited voice telling us all about The Beatles' upcoming show. I stumbled out of bed, and for what seemed like hours on end, I paced back and forth. In the wee hours of the morning, as the sun began to rise and the birds began to chirp, the answer suddenly popped into my head.

I immediately began to search for the unopened box of pastel colored, checkered writing paper with the matching envelopes. This stationary set was a present from Lize Lottie my Swedish pen pal, and because it was so beautiful, I was saving it for very special letters. Finally, the perfect occasion had arrived. After all, what could be more special than requesting tickets to see The Beatles? It didn't take me too long to find the box of stationary, and inside the box I had placed my brand-new fountain pen. I quickly filled the pen with my favorite Parker royal blue ink and began my emotional plea to the people at the television company. I wrote that my twin sister and I were born on the chosen date. (I left a blank space, which I would fill in after the date was revealed on the night of the drawing) I wrote that we were both loyal, longtime fans of The Beatles, and that our four best friends who we were hoping to bring along to the show, were even bigger fans than us. "So please may we have six tickets? Please, please. please!"

If I were one of the lucky winners, I'd still have to choose which of my girlfriends would be coming to the show with me, and no matter who I picked, there'd still be some very disappointed girlfriends left behind. I had thought about saying that I was a triplet, so that I'd get nine tickets, but I didn't want to push my luck!

The following Friday evening the live drawing was held, and the lucky date revealed. My letter was laid out on the coffee table, and in one swift motion I filled in the blank space with the winning date that had just been announced. I carefully folded my letter with the perfect penmanship, and together with my return self-addressed, stamped envelope, stuffed both of them into an enormous brown, official looking envelope. I couldn't take the chance that the letter would be returned for insufficient postage, so I covered the entire front of the envelope with dozens of stamps. Then to make sure that everything stayed inside the envelope, I plastered the back of the envelope with yards of *cella tape, and I ran out of the door, down the stairs, and across the street. Before I had the chance to examine my conscience, I dropped the envelope into the shiny red post box. Wiping the sweat from my brow, I leaned against a building, and said a quick act of contrition. I'd never done anything like this before, and I was more than a little bit ashamed of my dishonesty. But I had to be at that show, I needed to see The Beatles perform just one more time before I'd be whisked away to some far away, unfamiliar country. The more I thought about it, the more I realized that anyone in my position would have done the exact same thing. After all, it was only a little white lie, and besides, what harm could it possibly do?

Less than a week later, when I arrived home from school, my self-addressed stamped envelope was lying on the kitchen table. Clinging to the edge of the table, I stared down at the envelope. My heart was beating so fast, my head was spinning, and I began to shake uncontrollably. What if it's a 'So Sorry' form letter, or worse, what if it's a letter stating that I was greedy for asking for so many tickets. Oh God, why couldn't I be like a normal teenager, and be satisfied with getting three free tickets?

After staring at the envelope for fifteen minutes I finally bucked up the courage and grabbed it off of the table. I drew in a quick breath and in one swift motion, ripped open the envelope.

To my complete surprise, a bunch of tickets came tumbling out onto the kitchen floor. Gathering them up, I was overjoyed to see that the television company had sent me six tickets: three for me, and three for my twin sister.

Breathing a sigh of relief, I knew without a doubt that I was the luckiest girl in the whole of London. I was going to 'Around The Beatles' and so were five of my best friends. There was one small catch: Printed on the front of the tickets, in big bold letters was the statement: 'No admission without a Birth Certificate'. With a nervous twitch I said to myself, "Oh dear, that could be a problem. But right now, I'm so happy, I'm not even gonna think about it!"

*<u>Frock</u>…Dress.
*<u>Cella tape</u>…Scotch tape.

A Common Case of Beatlemania

REDIFFUSION
LONDON

Invites you to see

AROUND THE BEATLES

in STUDIO 5

WEMBLEY TELEVISION STUDIOS

EMPIRE WAY WEMBLEY

on TUESDAY, 28th APRIL from 9.00-10.30 p.m.

Doors open 8.30 p.m.   ADMIT ONE

FOR TEENAGERS BETWEEN 15 AND 18 YEARS
NO ADMISSION WITHOUT BIRTH CERTIFICATE
WE REGRET THERE WILL BE NO AUTOGRAPH SIGNING SO PLEASE DO NOT ASK

Nearest Underground Station
WEMBLEY PARK on Bakerloo & Metropolitan Lines

Bus Routes
46, 83, Alight at Wembley Park Underground

This ticket is issued subject to the following conditions :-
The ticket is complimentary and not for sale.
The taking of photographs during the performance is strictly forbidden.
The management of Associated-Rediffusion Ltd. reserve the right
to refuse admission.

My ticket to Around The Beatles

CHAPTER 26
FILMING A HARD DAY'S NIGHT

At the beginning of March 1964, The Beatles started working on their first full length movie. The title of the film had not yet been decided. I read in one of the teen magazines that it was possible to win a ticket to be part of the audience in the concert which was going to be the final scene in the movie. The article said that a request form to obtain one of these very special tickets will be published in a photography magazine. *(I can't remember the name of the magazine)* I immediately realized that this magazine was a special periodical for keen photographers, and that it was not going to be available at my local newsagents.

I remember my dad telling me that the area in London that sold rare books and all types of unusual magazine was Charing Cross. So, I knew that that was where I had to go. I immediately got out the map to figure out how to get there, and I left my house right after I had written down the directions. Once there, it didn't take me too long to find a shop that carried the unique magazine, and even though the price was outrageously expensive, I was more than happy to pay it. As soon as I left the shop, I ran over to a vacant bench. I immediately thumbed through the glossy magazine and right in the middle was the precious coupon that I needed. Now, I had everything that was required in order to own one of the most sought-after tickets in all of England.

The minute I got home I filled out the form, added my self-addressed stamped envelope, and put both things into another envelope. I carefully wrote out the address that was on the coupon and added a few stamps. I ran across the street, and dropped it into the postbox.

About a week later, my self-addressed envelope was delivered to our house. I thought it was very strange that the envelope had tape all across the top of the envelope. I carefully removed the tape, and a tiny piece of paper fell out. Printed on the paper was a typewritten note that said that they were very sorry, but all of the tickets have been distributed, and that I would not be receiving one. I have always wondered about that note. I truly believe that a ticket had been inside my self-addressed envelope, and that someone had opened the envelope, taken ticket and replaced it with the tiny note, and secured the envelope with tape.

My girlfriends and I were thrilled when we read that most of the filming for The Beatles' new movie would take place in and around London. Smiling broadly, Eileen gushed, "That means they'll be home in the evenings, so if we go around to their houses and we're bound to see them." Valerie added, "I've heard that working on a movie is very hard work, so let's hope they'll be totally *knackered and won't want to go out in the evenings." Christina cried, "We had better take full advantage before they go flying off on another tour." Rita sighed, "I'm getting fed up with having to share our Boys with the rest of the world." Valerie mumbled, "Yeah, the nerve of 'em! Why don't they get their own local group to love?"

While admiring the new centerfold in the latest Beatles Monthly magazine, Rita said, "I really don't mind when they go to France or Australia, but those Swedish girls are beautiful and I'm terrified that our Boys will go over there, fall madly in love, and never come back to England." Rita's statement made all of us a little bit weepy!

Once the filming began, we spent many a night standing outside The Beatles' homes.

Some nights I'd rush home, change out of my school uniform, and quickly put on my stretchy trousers and a long baggy *jumper. I would gobble up my dinner, and in record time I'd meet up with my girlfriends at Newington Green. On other days we'd go straight up the West End right after school. On most nights we'd go to William Mews, because we seemed to have better luck there, and saw George and Ringo quite a few times.

Paul was still living at The Asher's house on Wimpole Street, and occasionally we'd go there. There'd always be a horde of girls standing outside The Asher's five story home, and even though we never saw Paul, we'd always have a fun time chatting with the other girls who were also hoping to get a glimpse of him. Once in a while we'd go to John's flat on Emperors Gate. Just like the other homes, there were always lots of girls hanging around the doorway.

One night, John jumped out of a taxi and stood on the *pavement talking and laughing with all of us.

No matter which house we decided to visit we were never alone, and we got to know quite a few of the other fans. We'd always bump into someone we'd seen before, and one of us would say, "Fancy meeting you again!" One night, sitting on the curb outside George and Ringo's apartment building, we listened intently as two girls relived their incredible afternoon. They'd spent the entire day on the set of The Beatles' movie, and with a smug grin, one of them bragged, "We were standing with a group of people watching the filming when suddenly the director came over and asked us if we'd like to be in the movie. Can you imagine? Of course, we said yes! So, when the *picture is in the *cinema, don't forget to look for us, we're the ones chasing after The Beatles outside Marylebone train station."

Listening to them, it was plain to see that Valerie was seething, and whispering in my ear, she snarled, "Bloody showoffs!" Trying to pry more information from them, I asked in a nonchalantly way, "So how did you manage to find out about the top secret location?" With a rather smug grin, one of the girls answered, "My next door neighbor happens to be part of the camera crew, and he knows how much I simply adore The Beatles."

With a sulky pout, Eileen grumbled, "We've been stuck in school all day, and you're gonna be in The Beatles' first ever film. It's so unfair!" Valerie couldn't stand listening to their bragging any longer, and she pleaded, "Please, tell us where they'll be tomorrow. We haven't taken a day off from school in ages and just to watch The Beatles would be more than enough for us". The two self-centered girls glanced at each other, jumped up from the pavement and hurried off down William Mews. I yelled out to them, "How rude! Beatle fans are expected to share their information with other Beatle fans."

On many a night while standing outside George and Ringo's apartment, we began to notice a new girl who always seemed to be with George. This girl had long blond hair, wore fab clothes, and looked like a model. One night, while we were chatting with a group of girls, and leaning up against Whadden House, I watched with a pang of jealousy as George and his new girlfriend walked hand in hand into the garage. One of the other girls mumbled, "Cor blimey, I wish I looked like her. Isn't that the dress that Cathy McGowan was wearing on Ready, Steady, Go last Friday night?" George's girlfriend's mod dress was absolutely beautiful, and I sighed, "I'd give anything to be able to afford a gorgeous frock like that." Giggling, Rita replied, "You can have the dress, and I'll take George."

We smiled and waved to them as they drove away in George's silver E type jaguar, and they waved back. We soon found out that George's new girlfriend was named was Pattie Boyd, and that she had a small part in their new film.

*Charing Cross… The area of London that was famous for all the rare bookshops, and hard to come by magazines.
*Picture…Movie.
*Cinema…Movie House.

CHAPTER 27
AROUND THE BEATLES

April 28th, the long-awaited day for the taping of 'Around The Beatles' had finally arrived. It was an evening show, so my girlfriends and I made plans to meet at my house at precisely 6 o'clock. And at 6 o'clock on the dot, someone was pounding on our front door. I opened the door, and my giggling girlfriends came tumbling into the hallway. Her cheeks flushed with excitement, Rita squealed, "We're here, so can I please have my ticket."

One by one, I slowly removed the tickets from the envelope, and waving them above my head, I teased, "Before I give you these valuable tickets, I wanna know, what are you gonna do for me?" Each of my girlfriends promised me the world: From serving me breakfast in bed, to ironing my school uniform for a month. We all knew that once the show was over, the promises would be long forgotten.

Continuing to wave the tickets, I joked, "I could get a small fortune for these. A rich Beatle fan would give me at least twenty *quid for just one of these tickets." Laughing out loud, Rita said, "Sorry mate, you've left it too late. You'll never find a rich Beatle fan now, so you might as well just hand them over." Checking my watch I noticed that it was getting late, so I quickly handed each of my girlfriends one of the precious tickets, and together we ran down the stairs, and out into the street.

The directions to the television studio were printed on the back of the ticket. Rita was highly impressed when she saw that, "Can you believe it? They've thought of everything." Turning to face her, I joked, "A chauffeur driven car would have been even more impressive!" Following the simple directions, we took the 73 bus to King Cross Station, and from there we took the tube to Wembley Park Station. It was rush hour, and both the bus and the train were jammed packed with tired, and irritable commuters. So, we had no choice but to stand for the entire journey. On the crowded train, even though I was standing in a pile of dirty *dog ends, and jostling for a bit of elbow room, I didn't mind, because we were on our way to see The Beatles, and nothing was going to change my upbeat mood.

Thanks to the directions we made it all the way to The Rediffusion's Wembley Television Studios with plenty of time to spare. Hundreds of teenagers were circling the building, and we hurried over to take our place at the end of the long queue. The enthusiasm from the crowd was highly contagious and my girlfriends and I were having a difficult time trying to contain our excitement. Suddenly, the girl standing right in front of us, turned and said, "See the guard who's sitting by main entrance, he's warned everyone to have their tickets, and birth certificates out and ready to be inspected."

Hearing this, my happy-go-lucky demeanor came to an abrupt end. I gathered my girlfriends into a huddle, looked around to make sure nobody was listening, and in a rather shaky voice, whispered, "I'd completely forgotten about the bloody birth certificates. I was going to ask a few of the boys in my flats if they knew anyone who could make a couple of fake birth certificates for us, but I kept putting it off and now we're in a right old mess!"

From their panicked expressions it was plain to see that none of my girlfriends had even thought about the one essential document that was absolutely necessary to get us into this once in a lifetime show. Still huddled together Rita whispered, "Being as you and Teresa are supposed to be twins, shouldn't we have at least two birth certificates?" The guard was still a good distance away, but I knew that I only had a few minutes to come up with the most convincing explanation as to why both of us twins didn't have any form of identification with us.

I began to keep a close eye on the guard, and I noticed that he thoroughly examined each and every scrap of paper that was handed to him, and at the same time he managed to block the entrance to the studio with his enormous body. It was obvious that this *bloke was not about to take any nonsense from a bunch of teenage girls. I knew without a doubt that my girlish charm was not going to make a bit of difference with this mean old man.

The queue continued to shuffle forward, and the horrid guard kept screaming, "When you get to this table, you better be prepared! "My heart was pounding, my head was reeling, and I wanted to run away from the mess that my terrible lies had got us all into. In dreaded silence, my girlfriends and I inched forward getting closer and closer to the scary guard. My entire body was trembling from head to toe, my throat was parched, and I was sure that at any moment I could faint on the spot. Then, a true miracle happened and instantly everything changed.

The director's assistant came running out of the building and over to the guard. She looked quite flustered and whispered something into his ear. He immediately stood up and yelled to the remaining people who were still in the queue, "The show is about to start, we don't have time to check any more birth certificates, so just have your tickets ready." And with a nervous twitch, the director's assistant shouted, "And please, hurry up!"

At lightning speed, we hurried passed the unpleasant guard, ran through the doors and into the crowded studio. And after all the stress that we had just gone through, nobody even bothered to check our tickets. Unable to hide my excitement, I jumped up and down, and yelled out, "Yahoo we've made it, we're in!"

The tension was finally over and within seconds I began to feel like my old self. Waiting to be told which area to go to, my girlfriends and I stood with the other latecomers. Looking around the brightly lit studio, I noticed that three levels of balconies had been constructed specially for the show, and all the balconies encircled a small stage. At long last the highly strung assistant came over and told us all to go up to the second tier. As we clumsily climbed the narrow spiral staircase, the assistant screeched nervously, "You'd better get a move on, the show is about to start."

Finally, we made it to the second level, and one by one we cautiously stepped onto a long balcony. The balcony resembled a makeshift catwalk and surrounding it were two metal railings that kept us from falling down onto the audience below. Each of the three levels were filled with enthusiastic teenagers, and I noticed that the entire studio audience was standing.

Entering the crowded balcony an usher yelled to the people who were already in place, "In order to make room for the folks that are still coming in, please move all the way down."

While we waited for everyone to move, I carefully scanned the balcony and spotted a perfect space up against the railing. My girlfriends had noticed the same empty space, and looking at each other we ran over to it, and held onto the metal railing. The stage was directly below us, and for the second time that evening Divine Intervention had come into play. We'd miraculously managed to secure the most desirable spot in the entire studio. Holding onto the railing, I cried, "I'm not budging from here and if they want me to move, they'll need a crowbar to pull me away."

Minutes later, an American D.J. named Murray the K. came out onto the stage, said a few words, and the show began. That evening, along with The Beatles, many other popular acts performed. The list Included: Cilla Black, Millie Small, Long John Baldry, The Vernon Girls, P.J. Proby and several other performers. As the show proceeded we were in for yet another unbelievable treat: The Beatles came marching out onto the stage dressed in outrageous costumes, and George had an Afghan dog on a leash. As soon as the audience saw them, laughter and screams broke out from every corner of the television studio.

Mocking the original characters, The Beatles did a spoof of: Act V, scene 1 of 'A Midsummer Night's Dream.' George played Moonshine, Paul was Pyramus, Ringo was The lion, and John played Lady Thisbe. With deliberate exaggeration The Beatles performed their hilarious parts, when all of a sudden loud heckling came from the audience. In a panic, my girlfriends and I scanned the studio to see who was disrupting the show, but we soon realized that the heckling was clearly a rehearsed interruption. Causing all the commotion were a couple of actors, and Long John Baldry. The Beatles began to shout back at the hecklers, and this made the light-hearted parody even funnier. The entire spoof was hilarious and my girlfriends and I thoroughly enjoyed watching The Beatles act so silly. It was obvious that The Beatles too were enjoying themselves.

Once the skit ended, the other performers came onto the stage to entertain us, and to our complete surprise John, Paul, George and Ringo came into the audience to watch the other acts. They stood in their own little balcony, which lucky for us happened to be on the other side of the studio, right across from where we were standing. They were dressed in different colored jackets and shirts, and while Paul wore a tie, John and Ringo had open collars, and George wore a dark turtleneck sweater. Rita came up behind me, and whispered into my ear, "I say, who are those four lovelies *chaps standing over there?" Barely able to control my excitement, I replied, "Can you believe this? It's my dream come true."

While The Beatles were busy watching the other performers, I had an even better time watching them. Placing my hands under my chin, I leaned on the railing and stared straight ahead at the Fab Four. They were clapping their hands, swaying to the music, and singing along with the other acts. Without taking my eyes off The Beatles, I said to Maroula, "To be able to see them standing in the one place for such a long time is definitely a dream come true." Maroula was staring dreamily at The Beatles, and I soon discovered that she hadn't heard a single word that I had said. Rushing up behind me, Teresa squealed, "They're just yards away from us, how lucky are we?"

Still gazing at The Fab Four, I replied, "I really don't mind if they don't sing, I'm quite content to stand here and stare at them all night." Teresa sighed, "Yeah, me too!" At that very moment I felt as though John, Paul, George, and Ringo, and my girlfriends and I were the only people in that studio.

After watching the other performers, The Beatles walked out of their little balcony. My girlfriends and I gave a collective sigh, but then it dawned on me that this could only mean one thing; The Beatles were about to perform. Minutes later, The Fab Four came out onto the stage. The stage was tiny so the drums had to be set up at the far end of the stage, so from where we were standing all we could see of Ringo was his lovely back. However, we were fortunate to have John, Paul and George facing in our direction. The Beatles had changed into identical dark suits, with white shirts, colorful ties, and of course, their Beatle boots.

They started off by performing Twist and Shout, followed by Roll Over Beethoven, I Wanna Be Your Man, Long Tall Sally and Can't Buy Me Love. They also performed a special medley of their earlier hits: Love Me Do, Please Please Me, From Me To You, She Loves You and I Wanna Hold your Hand. Their performance ended with an amazing version of the Isley Brothers' song 'Shout' and the audience was encouraged to join in and sing along with The Beatles.

My girlfriends and I didn't need any encouragement and following The Beatles' cues, we happily sang along, getting louder at times and softer at other times. For the entire performance we hung over the railing, clapped our hands, swayed from side to side, and were very lucky that we didn't fall through the enormous gap that was in between the top and bottom railing.

When the show ended, my girlfriends and I stayed on the balcony, and waited until the studio had emptied out. Rita came over to me, and with a tear in her eye, cried, "Thank you Ursula for giving me one of the tickets." Hugging her, I sighed, "Wasn't it the best show ever? There aren't too many people that can say they've seen The Beatles perform both musically, and dramatically all in the one night's performance." Teresa added, "For me, the best part was staring at them on the balcony that was right across from us." Dabbing her eyes with a handkerchief, Rita continued, "As long as I live, I'll never forget this night." And in unison we all chirped, "Yeah, me too."

Walking to the underground station, I thought about how lucky we'd actually been. If we had arrived just minutes earlier everything would have turned out differently. The nasty guard would have insisted on seeing our birth certificates, and without those precious documents I'm sure he wouldn't have allowed us into the show. He was such a horrible man; it was obvious that he would have enjoyed humiliating us in front of all the other fans. Even though we had a few harrowing, nail-biting moments in the end everything worked out. We'd arrived at the perfect time and ended up in the most desirable spot in the entire studio.

'Around The Beatles' was televised on May 6th 1964. My family and I gathered around the television set, and because I hadn't stopped talking about that incredible evening, my mother turned it into a special occasion, and made one of her famous fruit cakes. So, while we waited for the show to begin, we nibbled on the cake and drank cups of tea.

While The Beatles were performing their hit song 'Can't Buy Me Love,' a close-up of Teresa, Maroula and me came onto the screen. Doing a double take, my mother jumped off of the couch and cried, "Ursula, am I seeing things or is that you up there on the *telly?" Laughing hysterically, I answered, "Yep it's me, I told you that one day you'd see me with The Beatles." Shaking her head in disbelief, my mother replied, "Well *fancy that!"

We're on the telly!

Closeup of Teresa, and me on YouTube

*_Twenty quid_... Twenty pounds.
*_Dog ends_... Cigarette butts.
*_Queue_... Line.
*_Bloke_... Man.
*_Get a move on_... Hurry up.
*_Chaps_... Men.
*_Telly_... Television.
*_Fancy that_... Used to express surprise.

CHAPTER 28
RINGO ADMITTED TO HOSPITAL

On the evening of June 3rd. while I was watching the six-o clock news a report came on about Ringo. As soon as I heard the word Ringo, I rushed over to the television set and turned the volume all the way up. In a serious tone, the newscaster informed the viewers that earlier in the day Ringo had been rushed to a hospital with tonsillitis, and a dangerously high fever.

The newscaster ended the news flash by announcing that John, Paul and George had flown off to Denmark for the start of their World Tour, and that Brian Epstein and George Martin had selected Jimmy Nicol to fill in for poor Ringo.

As soon as the report was over, I grabbed my bag and ran out the door. I hadn't read anything about Ringo's illness in the morning paper, so I needed to buy an evening newspaper. Ten minutes later I was back home with my copy of The Evening Standard. I spread the newspaper on the living floor, and frantically searched for an article on Ringo.

My mother came in, and with a puzzled look, said, "Why on earth did you buy another newspaper? Isn't one paper a day enough?" I was far too busy for a *chit chat, so I gave a weary sigh, and continued my search. Finally, I found what I was looking for. The Evening Standard had the exact same information that was on the news, but it also included one important detail that hadn't been mentioned on the telly. The newspaper informed it's readers that Ringo had been taken to The University Hospital on Grafton Way in London.

I jumped up, ran over to the sideboard and pulled out the giant map of London. I searched the index for Grafton Way, and soon discovered that the hospital was right off Gower Street. I was so happy because I knew Gower Street quite well. Not only did a boy in our class live on that street, but on my way to the shops on Oxford Street, the 73 bus drove right down Gower Street.

The following day at school my girlfriends and I chatted nonstop about poor Ringo's condition. So being as we knew which hospital Ringo was in, we decided to visit him as soon as we got out of school. Walking to the bus stop, Eileen turned and said, "We can't go empty handed, we'll have to get Ringo a present, but at the moment my funds are extremely low." Christina replied, "Flowers are the perfect present for someone in hospital, but right now I'm completely broke."

I peeked into my tiny purse, and all I could see were two thrupenny bits, so I moaned, "I barely have enough money for the bus fare to get to the hospital."

Being as we were all low on funds, we decided that Ringo had probably already received more than enough flowers. We all knew that he was a compassionate bloke, so if we showed up empty handed, he'd understand.

Realizing that no presents were necessary made all of us feel a whole lot better. In what seemed like a flash, we were standing in front of the main entrance to The University Hospital. We waltzed into the hospital lobby and tried to find a doctor or nurse who could direct us to Ringo's room. Suddenly, a loud arrogant voice came booming from the other side of the lobby, "*Oy, where'd you think you lot are going?"

I twirled around, and the scariest looking policeman I had ever seen was heading straight towards us. The five of us stood motionless. Rita decided to be the brave one and stepped forward. In a timid voice, she replied, "We're on our way to visit Ringo, he's been very sick, and we thought we'd try and cheer him up."

With an irritating smirk, he sneered, "I thought as much, well you lot are in the wrong place." In her usual cheeky manner, Valerie answered, "We've never been here before, so how are we supposed to know which way to go?" With a huge grin on his face, he pointed to the exit, and in a patronizing tone said, "You need to go around the corner to side entrance."

Rolling her eyes, Valerie said in a sarcastic voice, "Thank you so much constable, you've been ever so helpful." Walking away, Christina whispered, "Did you see that big smirk on his face? He had no right to treat us that way. I should have taken his badge number and report him to his superiors." Eileen who was busy combing her hair with her fingers, "Forget about him, we're practically in Ringo's room." She said.

With great excitement we swirled around the revolving door, and as soon as we were back outside, we began to run. The moment we turned the corner, the five of us skidded to a complete halt. I couldn't believe my eyes, the side entrance to the hospital was jammed packed with dozens of noisy girls. Maroula moaned, "Oh no, it's always the same! I was so sure that this time we'd be the only ones here," Reluctantly, we took our place among the rowdy crowd, and Rita whispered, "How did all these people find out about the hospital?"

Giving Rita a funny look, I huffed, "The same way we did, they read about it in the bleedin' newspaper." Valerie cried, I knew that bloody policeman was *having us on. We are so bleedin' gullible!

An hour later, a nurse came out onto the steps and spoke to the crowd. She informed us that she was the official spokesperson for the hospital, and reading from a card she announced, "Ringo is slowly improving, his temperature is back to normal, and he's resting comfortably."

Hearing the good news we and all the other fans began to cheer loudly, and with a sympathetic smile, she added, "So why don't you all go home.

There's nothing you can do for Ringo, and from the looks of it, it's going to start raining at any moment." Agreeing with the nurse, we decided to go home. On the way out, I giggled, "It's a shame we can't break into the nurses' room and borrow a few of their uniforms. Then we'd be able to see for ourselves how Ringo is doing." Laughing loudly, Valerie added, "And with our caring bedside manner Ringo would be as right as rain in no time at all."

A few days later, The Daily Mail published several photos of Ringo. He was sitting up in his hospital bed, smiling and looking like his usual gorgeous self! By June 14th he had made a complete recovery, and rejoined John, Paul and George on tour. This meant that Jimmy Nicol's life as one of The Beatles had come to an abrupt ending.

*Chit chat... Small talk.
*Oy...Hey.

CHAPTER 29

KEEPING BUSY

While The Beatles were busy touring the world, I tried my best to keep occupied. Each and every week, new articles about The Beatles appeared in almost every magazine, and along with the articles came never before seen absolutely gorgeous photos of John, Paul, George and Ringo. By this time, every square inch of my bedroom was covered in Beatle pictures, and the ceiling was reserved for my extra-large pictures. My favorite thing to do was to lay on my bed, listening to my Beatle records, and staring up at my fab collection of Beatle pictures. Beatles, Beatles, Beatles was all that I could think about!

Noticing my bedroom walls, my mother nagged, "I've allowed you to plaster The Beatles all over your bedroom, now that you've run out of space, I better not see them anywhere else in this house." Just by her tone I knew that she was serious, so I started buying scrapbooks.

As I glued the latest pictures into a scrapbook, I complained to Rita, "These books are costing me a bloody fortune, and between the collecting, the cutting and the gluing, it's like having a full-time job."

Admiring my work, Rita relied, "But you're doing a terrific job, they look absolutely fab." When I wasn't laying on my bed staring at The Boys, I was busy with my other passion which was writing letters. I spent hours writing to each of my pen-pals. I loved receiving letters, and I thoroughly enjoyed answering them. Thanks to our mutual love for The Beatles, a ten-page letter was my normal reply. My pen-pals loved reading about my latest Beatle sightings, and when John, Paul, George and Ringo were at home in London, I'd always have some new adventure to write about. My three pen pals all planned on visiting London in the near future, and of course, each of them wanted to see where The Beatles lived.

I'd write, "Come on over, I'd love to meet you and don't forget to pack your *brolly." Along with my letters, I'd always enclose some brochures, maps and whatever other fascinating facts articles I could find on London. My pen pals letters were very interesting too, and they'd always include clippings about The Beatles from their local newspapers. Beatlemania was sweeping across America, and my American pen pal sent me a bundle of magazines, with interesting articles, and never before seen photos of The Boys.

My Swedish pen pal also sent me lots of teenage magazines, including a giant one that was devoted entirely to The Beatles. Thumbing through the pages of the Swedish magazine, Valerie complained, "The pictures are fab, but I'd really like to know what they're writing about." I replied, "I only want the pictures, after all, what can they possibly write about that we don't already know?" Laughing out loud, Eileen squealed, "You're absolutely right, we're the Beatle experts, we could probably tell them a thing or two!"

I'd often read my pen pals' letters to my girlfriends, and I'd remind them, "We forget how lucky we are, living so close to The Beatles. My pen pals would give anything to see them just one time, and here we are seeing them on a regular basis." Laughing out loud, Valerie replied, "not quite regular enough for my liking!" Rita stood up, and with an impish grin, walked over to the front door, gave a little wave and chirped, *Ta ta for now, I'm off to visit George!"

*<u>Brolly</u>…Umbrella.
*<u>Ta ta</u>…Goodbye.

CHAPTER 30
THE PREMIERE OF A HARD DAY'S NIGHT

The World Premiere of 'A Hard Days Night' took place on July 6th. 1964 in London. For weeks, my girlfriends and I had been reading about the upcoming premiere, and from the moment we'd read the first press report, we'd made up our minds to be outside the theatre on the night of the big occasion.

Lounging on the couch, Valerie read yet another article about the fast-approaching premiere, and flushed with excitement, she cried, "This is going to be huge; they're expecting it to be the social event of the year." Hardly able to contain myself, I squealed, "Don't worry we're not gonna miss this. We may not have seen them making the film, but by hook or by crook we'll be there to see them walking into the premiere. Maroula added, "Who wants to watch it on the evening news, when we can be right there in the middle of all the glitz and glamour." We all nodded in total agreement!

Once again, the newspapers had provided us with all of the necessary information: The time, the place, and the long list of celebrities that had been invited to attend this very special first showing. Eileen gushed, "Oh it's going to be fab, I can't wait to The Beatles, and to see what all the other celebrities will be wearing."

On the afternoon of the premiere, we met at our usual bench in Newington Green Park, and together we took the bus, and then the tube to Piccadilly Circus Station. When we exited the train, but were still underground, we could hear all the commotion that was going on in the street above us. For this well publicized event, we never expected to have Piccadilly Circus all to ourselves, but when we reached the top of the stairs, we were flabbergasted to see such an enormous crowd. Thousands of people lined the streets, and Piccadilly Circus had actually been closed off to motor vehicles.

Most of the spectators stood across the street from the London Pavilion, but my girlfriends and I decided that we'd prefer to be on the same side as the theatre. So, we crossed over the street, and looked for a nice spot where we could witness all that was about to happen.

Hundreds of policemen stood outside the canopied entrance, and Rita gushed, "Never in my life have I seen so many policemen." As if on cue, Valerie raised her eyebrows up and down, and chuckled, "And may I add, most of them are good looking chaps, a real treat for the old eye! If you know what I mean?" Laughing our loud, Mary blurted, "And they're here for only one reason, and that's to protect The Beatles from people like us." Francis quickly reminded her, "I do believe they're here to protect Princess Margaret." Mary laughed, "Oh yeah, I forgot about her."

My girlfriends and I found a spot next to a group of rather handsome policemen, and while we waited for the celebrities to arrive, we chatted quietly amongst ourselves. Suddenly, out of nowhere, a giant police sergeant came bounding over to us and ordered us to stand on the other side of the street. With a quivering lip, Eileen cried, "But we won't be able to see anything over there, and we'll miss all the excitement." With his hands on his hips, he bellowed, "Now girls, don't make me say it twice!"

With his stern looking face, we knew that he meant business, and before he could say another word, we dashed across the street. As we pushed and shoved our way in amongst the noisy crowd, it was almost impossible to stay together. All the decent spots were already claimed, and it was plain to see that nobody was going to make room for us. By time we had found an opening where we could all stand together, there were at least ten extremely tall people in front of us.

Straining her neck, Christina suggested, "Let's wriggle to the front, then we'll have a great view." With my faced pushed into the back of a stranger's smelly *mackintosh, I moaned, "I can't even raise my arms. How do you expect me to wriggle anywhere?"

By now, the celebrities were starting to arrive, and every time a chauffeur driven car pulled up to the entrance of the theatre, the oohing and aahing from the people who were up front, made us green with envy. I heard a woman cry out, "Cor blimey, look at that gorgeous dress." Someone else blurted out, "In all my life I've never seen such sparkly jewelry." Gritting her teeth, Eileen moaned, "I wonder who that was that we didn't get to see?"

From all the noise, it was obvious that more luxurious cars containing glamour stars were pulling up in front of the theatre. But we couldn't see a thing, and the crowd of people that we were stuck in were getting rowdier by the minute. Finally, after being crushed, trampled, and almost flattened we decided that it was time to leave. It took another fifteen minutes to be free from the unruly mob.

Even though we were bruised, battered, and exhausted, if we had been able to see all the stars, and of course, The Beatles we would have happily stayed, and endured all the injuries. But our spirits had been broken, and the disappointment was just too much to bear. The premiere of 'A Hard Day's Night' had been a complete disaster for us. We didn't see The Beatles, we didn't see Princess Margaret or *Lord Snowdon. The only thing we saw were the backs of the giants that were blocking our view.

Fixing her disheveled hair, Valerie cried, "We're lucky we weren't suffocated in that mob!" Together, we hobbled to the underground station, and heartbroken, each of us went straight home. Later that night I watched the chaos on the evening news. The newscaster reported that over 12,000 fans had crammed into Piccadilly Circus, all hoping to catch a glimpse of The Beatles.

Standing outside The London Pavilion

Soon after the London premiere, 'A Hard Day's Night' opened in cinemas all across the country. My girlfriends and I were so excited to see The Beatles in their very first movie and going to the *pictures became a daily ritual. We'd pay for the early show, and as soon as the film was over, we'd casually walk into the ladies' *toilet, and hide in the cubicles. As soon as the lights dimmed, we'd walk out one by one, and take our seats for the second show.

Gazing up at the big screen, and seeing John, Paul, George, and Ringo was such an exciting thrill for all us. Listening to them speak in their lovely Liverpudlian accents, and of course, hearing them sing all those beautiful songs made us want to scream with joy, but we didn't want to get thrown out of the cinema, so we somehow managed to control ourselves.

By the end of the first week my girlfriends and I had seen 'A Hard Day's Night' at least a dozen times, and now we knew all of lyrics to all of the songs, and just about all of the script too. As we sat watching the film, we'd sing quietly and whisper the actor's lines before they had even spoken them.

On July 10th. 1964, the L.P. and the single, both titled 'A Hard Day's Night' were released. I'd read about the double release, so I had saved up my money, and on the very day that they came out, I rushed to the record shop, and bought both records. In less than two weeks, both of the records had reached the number one spot on the hit parade.

*<u>Mackintosh</u>…Raincoat.
*<u>Lord Snowdon</u>…Princess Margaret's husband.
*<u>Pictures</u>…Movies.
*<u>Toilet</u>…Bathroom.

CHAPTER 31
AN UNFORGETTABLE MOMENT WITH RINGO

On a balmy summer evening, Maroula, Rita and I decided to take a bus ride to George and Ringo's flat. There were no tours scheduled, so we knew that The Beatles were in London. As we strolled down William Mews, we were just in time to see George and Pattie Boyd drive away in his E type jaguar. Waving goodbye, Rita sighed, "There goes one lucky girl." Giving her a friendly shove, I joked, "Why couldn't it be one of us? We're just as gorgeous as she is."

Laughing out loud, the three of us continued walking down the mews. When we arrived at Whaddon House, there were two girls standing outside the building. We had never seen these girls before, so we walked over to them, and said hello, and began to chat with them. A few minutes later, an elegantly dressed older woman came out of the building. As she passed us, she smiled and said, "Hello girls" and continued walking towards the garage. I noticed that the door to Whaddon House hadn't quite closed, so I immediately stuck my foot between the jamb and the heavy glass door. The others realized what I had done, and from the look on their faces it was obvious they were about to dart inside. I wasn't sure how long more my foot could support the heavy door, and wincing in pain, I whispered,

"Don't move until that lady is completely out of sight."

As soon as the woman turned the corner, the five of us hurried inside the apartment building. Ready to spring into action, Rita ran to the staircase, and holding onto the railing, squealed, "I know the number of their flat, so come on, let's go!" Taking two steps at a time, the five of us bounded up the stairs, and by the time we had reached George and Ringo's flat we were panting heavily and trying to catch our breath. Without thinking, we pounded on the door and anxiously waited for someone to answer.

Seconds later the door swung opened, and to my surprise Ringo Starr was standing right in front of us. The five of us gave a collective gasp. I was expecting to see a *charwoman or maybe one of Ringo's friends, but the thought of Ringo actually opening the door had never entered my mind. I thought I might have been hallucinating, so I blinked repeatedly, rubbed my eyes, and dared to take another look. Yes, it was Ringo alright! He stood in the doorway, and with a blank face stared straight at us. He made no attempt to speak, and I'm sure he was quite annoyed by our rude intrusion.

My nerves got the better of me, and I knew that one of the other girls would have to break the ice. I was sure that once the conversation began, in no time at all I'd be joining in the friendly banter. But nobody said a single word, and the five of us stood there like a group of life-size statues, and even though the silence was making me feel very uncomfortable, I just couldn't take my eyes off of Ringo.

The awkward gawking went on for several minutes, we stared at Ringo, and Ringo stared back at us. Then all of a sudden, Ringo ever so slowly closed the door. I immediately breathed a deep sigh of relief and threw myself up against the door. The others were still rooted to the floor, and seeing their glazed expressions made me want to burst out laughing.

Leaning up against the door, I couldn't believe that the one and only Ringo Starr, drummer of the most popular group on earth was on the other side. Millions of girls all over the world would have given their right arms to be in my position. I was also fully aware that we had just ruined the perfect chance to have a nice chit chat with Ringo, and I was devastated.

From this unexpected, yet thrilling encounter that we had just experienced, it was plain to see that we were all in a state of shock. Without saying a word, we somehow managed to stumble down the stairs, and calmly walk out of the building.

Walking away from Whadden House, Maroula, Rita and I said goodbye to our two new friends and staggered down William Mews. On the bus ride home, we cried about the wonderful opportunity that we had totally messed-up. Annoyed at our wimpish behavior, I sniveled, "When did we become so bloody timid? Ringo was so polite, he could have slammed the door right in our faces, but he stood there waiting for us to say something. Rita replied, "You're right, if only one of us had been a little bit bolder, at this very moment we could be sitting in Ringo's living room enjoying a nice cup of tea with him"

Trying to make light of the situation, I added, "And maybe a nice piece of cake to go with it." And even though the look of disappointment was written all over Maroula's face, she sighed, "Don't worry, next time we'll be more prepared." Rita and I knew that a next time was highly unlikely, but stranger things have happened, so we nodded enthusiastically at Maroula's optimism.

Later that night, I spent hours writing to each of my pen pals. Letting them know all about our strange nonverbal meeting with the one and only Ringo. I knew that I was showing off, but I couldn't help it. After all, how many sixteen-year-old girls get to have a face to face with the gorgeous, and talented drummer of The Beatles.

*<u>Charwoman</u> ...A woman employed to clean houses.

CHAPTER 32
TWO FANCY AUTOMOBILES

In June of 1964, I started my first full time job. I was hired to work as a junior clerk at the corporate headquarters of Gestetner's (a company known for its duplicating machines.) I worked Monday to Friday from 9 a.m. to 5 p.m., and my pay was five pounds a week. The manager at Boots the Chemist offered me a full time position for the same amount of money, but I liked the idea of working in a beautiful art deco building that was right in the heart of London.

My time at Gestetner's was short lived, but in those few weeks I can recall two separate, and completely different events that reminded me of The Beatles' luxurious car. The first: Early one morning as I was walking down Matthias Road on my way to the bus stop, a chauffeur driven Rolls Royce pulled up alongside of me. Seeing the elegant car, I smiled and thought, "Ah, finally The Beatles have come to take me away." But as much as I would have loved my little fantasy to be real, I knew that it was highly unlikely.

I'd always been naturally nosy, and so I glanced over at the gleaming car. Sitting in the driver's seat was a uniformed chauffeur with the biggest grin on his face. He looked very familiar, but it took me a while to realize that it was Terry, the chauffeur for none other than Mr. Gestetner himself.

Walking over to the car, I cried, "You gave me such a fright, I couldn't imagine who was in this fancy car and I was sure you were going to kidnap me." Laughing out loud, he teased, "I can't believe you don't have a boyfriend who owns a car just like this one." I replied, "You must be joking, the boys around here don't even own a *Lambretta, never mind a fancy Rolls Royce." Grinning again, he said, "I didn't know that you lived around here. Hop in, and I'll give you a lift."

I couldn't believe what I was hearing, and I wasn't sure which made me happier, getting a ride in this beautiful car, or knowing that I'd be saving my bus fare. Either way I was delighted. I opened the front door and jumped in next to Terry. Panicking, Terry shouted, "Not in the front, if anyone sees you sitting next to me, I'll be sacked on the spot." I quickly leaped out of the front seat, climbed into the back and sank into the luxuriously soft leather seat.

From that day on, Terry picked me up on the corner of Matthias Road, and drove me to work. On the twenty-minute drive to Gestetner's, Terry chatted nonstop about all sorts of things. And while he chatted, I relaxed in the back seat, and hardly said a word. I'd often notice people in other cars looking at me, so I pretended to be *Helen Shapiro on my way to perform at the Royal Albert Hall.

With me in the car, Terry never acted like a proper chauffeur. He never opened the door for me, and instead of letting me out at the main entrance to Gestetner's, he'd drop me off around the corner, and I'd have to walk the rest of the way. Sitting in the back of the Rolls Royce, I'd often think about Mal Evans, and that very special ride that he had taken my girlfriends and me on in The Beatles' super luxurious car."

Then Mr. Gestetner's lovely car would come to a halt, and Terry would look back at me, and say "Alright me love we're here, so out ya get!" And I'd be forced back to reality. In the evenings after my long, hard day at work, I would have really appreciated my chauffeur driven ride, but Terry had to drive the boss home, so I had no choice but to take the stuffy, overcrowded bus.

The second car incident was completely different: One of my daily tasks at Gestetner's was to go to the post office to purchase various items for the mail room. One afternoon, as I was strolling down Euston Road on my way to the post office; a really elegant, chauffeur driven car pulled up alongside me. The car was stopped at a traffic light, and when I glanced over at it, I noticed that all of the windows except for the windshield were blacked out. The only logical reason for having blacked out windows was to hide whoever was inside. My immediate thought was: "It has to be The Beatles."

I knew that the light could change at any moment, so if I wanted to see who was inside, I'd have to hurry. I ran over to the car, and cupping both hands to shield my eyes against the glare of the glass, I peered inside. At first it was difficult to see, then all of a sudden everything came into view. And to my surprise, the person sitting in the back seat was none other than Queen Elizabeth the second.

The Queen looked over at me, and noticing the shocked expression on my face, she burst out laughing. I had always thought that the Queen was a rather serious person, but now I knew firsthand that she also had a great sense of humor. The traffic light changed, and as the car pulled away I waved to the Queen, and stood on the pavement until her car was completely out of sight.

That day, I may not have seen The Beatles, but I wasn't disappointed. After all, I had just had my very own private moment with the Queen of England, and for me it was indeed a very special moment.

*Lambretta…Motor scooter.
*Helen Shapiro… An English pop singer.

CHAPTER 33
A MOST UNREASONABLE BOSS

In August of 1964, my Swedish pen pal Lize Lottie, and I were about to meet. She and her two girlfriends who had been writing to Rita and Maroula were all coming to London for a *fortnight's vacation. Our parents had all agreed that the Swedish girls were more than welcome to come and stay with us, and my girlfriends and I couldn't wait to meet them.

Two weeks before the pen pals arrival date, Maroula, Rita and I sat down at my kitchen table to plan the upcoming trip. My mother had made a batch of her famous fairy cakes, so while we discussed the trip, we devoured the fairy cakes and drank cups of steaming hot tea. After finishing my third cake, I said to my girlfriends, "We have to make this trip really special, it's the pen pals first visit to England and in a couple of months I'll be leaving the country." Rita and Maroula shook their heads enthusiastically.

The week before the pen pals were due to arrive, I finally plucked up the courage to speak to my manager about taking some personal time off from work. I quietly opened her office door, and peeked in. She was sitting at her enormous oak desk, thumbing through a stack of papers, and drinking from a flowery porcelain teacup. In a timid tone, I asked, "May I have a word with you, please." She pushed the papers to one side, and with an ear- piercing shriek bellowed, "Please, come in Ursula!"

Her voice was so scary I jumped. I slowly tiptoed over to her desk and waited for her to look at me. She placed the delicate teacup onto its matching saucer and pointed to a chair for me to sit down. Finally, she looked up, and said, "Now tell me Ursula, what's on your mind?" Clearing my throat, I began my emotional plea, "My Swedish pen pal is coming to London next week for a fortnight. I know I haven't been here very long, but would it be possible for me to take a leave of absence?" I quickly added, "Of course, I don't expect to be paid for my time off." Smiling sweetly, she asked, "So how many days are we talking about?" I couldn't understand why she was asking such a ridiculous question, and I answered, "Well the whole fortnight, of course."

Taking her spectacles off, she looked straight into my eyes, and snapped, "But you've only just started the job! Young lady, I've been keeping an eye on you, and I do believe you have potential. It's quite possible that five years from now you could be managerial material." I had no idea what she was talking about, my only thought was, "What on earth does managerial mean?"

Cleaning her glasses with a special eyeglass cloth, she continued, "But tell me, how do you expect to be promoted if you're not willing to give one hundred percent?" The thought of getting a promotion hadn't entered my mind, and five years from now I'd be twenty-one years old, who could possibly think that far ahead? I was working purely for the money! Five pounds a week was a small fortune, and I was quite content with the way things were. So instead of answering her, I just shrugged my shoulders, and gave a little sigh.

She instantly noticed my calm, unconcerned reaction, and right before my eyes, my manager turned into a snarling witch. She picked up a letter opener with a gorgeous crystal handle, but the blade looked rather sharp, so I immediately moved my chair further back.

Pointing the sharp end of the letter opener at me, she sneered, "My dear, it's entirely up to you, but if you want to be irresponsible and take the whole fortnight off, then you needn't bother to come back."

I couldn't believe what I was hearing. After everything I'd done for the company, how could she treat me that way? Without saying another word, I stomped out of her fancy office, and found my way back to my overcrowded workspace. I spent the rest of the afternoon sitting at my desk, and pondering over my situation. I only had eight more weeks left in England, and so I weighed my options: Do I spend my time having fun with my girlfriends, or do I keep *slogging away day after day? The answer was crystal clear!

At four o'clock I left my desk and ran through the building searching for Terry. After all, Terry was the only person who really needed to know what my intentions were. After all, I didn't want him to be waiting for me at the corner of Matthias Road in his shiny Rolls Royce. Later that day, I walked out of Gestetner's vowing never to return.

*Fortnight...A period of two weeks.
*Fairy cakes... Similar but usually smaller than cupcakes.
*Slogging away...Working hard.

CHAPTER 34
THE ARRIVAL OF THE SWEDISH PEN PALS

Finally, the day had arrived, and our Swedish pen pals were on their way to London. Their journey took over thirty hours, included several buses, trains, and a long boat ride. Bright and early in the morning, Maroula, Rita and I headed off to the train station to meet them.

Remembering my yearly trip to Ireland, I said to the girls, "After such a long journey, they're bound to be completely knackered, so don't be surprised if all they want to do is to go straight to bed."

Rita started to laugh, and said, "I get worn out just walking around Chapel Market, so I can just imagine how they're gonna feel." As soon as we arrived at the enormous train station, we headed upstairs and stood on a balcony high above the main terminal. From there, we watched in awe at the never-ending stream of weary looking travelers.

Staring down at the crowd, Rita said, "It shouldn't be too hard to spot them, just keep your eye out for three girls weary looking dragging themselves and their luggage." Rita and I sat on the tiled floor while Maroula kept watch. Suddenly Maroula cried out, "Oh my God, that can't be them?" Rita and I immediately peeked through the balcony railing, and striding along the platform were three very tall, very blond, and very beautiful girls. I also noticed that every man in the train station had stopped to gawk at them.

Shaking her head, Rita said, "No, that's not them, they're too old. Those girls are definitely in their twenties." All of a sudden one of the blonde girls spotted us, and yelled up, "Hello, are you the pen pals?" Before answering her, I turned to Maroula and Rita, and mumbled, "Blimey, it is them!" I managed to put on a smile, and hanging over the railing, I yelled back, "Yes, we're the pen pals. Stay where you are, we'll be right down."

Plodding down the stairs, I moaned, "They don't look very tired to me. In fact, they look like they've just got off the runway." When we reached the platform, the pen pals dropped their rucksacks and came running over to us. They immediately threw their arms around us, and started kissing us on the cheeks. Being British, Maroula, Rita and I were not used to such public displays of affection and were quite relieved when the hugging finally came to an end.

The Swedish girls introduced themselves and trying to be polite we insisted on carrying their rucksacks. Stumbling with her heavy load, Rita whispered to me, "Did you see my one? She's at least six feet tall." I whispered back, "So is mine, and it's making me feel like a leprechaun."

By the time we got out of the crowded station it was lunch time, and we were all feeling a bit *peckish, so we ran across the busy street into a Wimpey Bar. Over hamburgers and chips, we and our pen pals chatted nonstop, and from all the letter writing we felt as though we'd known them our entire lives. The pen pals told us that they had decided that while they were in England they would like to try as many English meals as possible, especially things they couldn't even get in their own country. Laughing, I assured them that that would not be a problem, and that we would be more than happy to introduce them to our favorite choices.

They were so excited to finally be in London, and they told us that ever since they had first heard The Beatles on the radio, their dream had been to someday visit England.

After lunch we went straight to the post office, and each of the pen pals sent telegrams to their parents to let them know that they had arrived safely.

It was obvious that the pen pals were starting to feel tired, so we decided to all go home. Before splitting up we made plans to meet in Trafalgar Square at 10 o'clock the following morning. Then, Lize Lottie came home with me, Brigitta went with Rita, and Anita went to Maroula's house.

My mother was waiting at the front door when Lize Lottie and I arrived home. I introduced them to each other, and after shaking my mother's hand, Lize Lottie gave a little curtsy. I could tell my mother liked this greeting, and I joked, "Don't expect me to start doing that."

Three months earlier, my father and brother had left England, to go to America, so that they could have everything in order by the time my mother, sisters, and I arrived. Noticing how beautiful Lize Lottie was, the first thing my mother said was, "*It's a good job John isn't here. He' would be taking over the sightseeing, and he certainly wouldn't want you tagging along." Nodding in agreement, I laughed, "Don't I know it!"

Maroula, Rita and I decided to give the pen pals a really great sightseeing tour of London. We bought a guidebook, and for three days straight we dragged them from one tourist attraction to another: Trafalgar Square, Piccadilly Circus, The Tower of London, Westminster Abbey, Saint Paul's Cathedral, and, of course, Buckingham Palace. Everywhere we went, the Swedish girls snapped dozens of photos.

On the fourth day, the six of us met up at our usual stone bench in Trafalgar Square.

Maroula, Rita and I had a sneaky suspicion that our pen pals had seen enough sights, so I said to them, "Today we will be seeing something slightly different, today we'll be taking you to see The Beatles' homes." Squealing with delight, Lize Lottie cried, "This is what we've been waiting to see." I quickly reminded them, "Of course, we don't have the keys to go inside, so we'll only be seeing them from the outside." Giving me a huge hug, Brigitta gushed, "It's more than enough for me!"

Out of the blue, the pen pals held hands and began to dance around the fountain. Within seconds dozens of tourists had stopped to stare, and quite a few of them were actually taking photos of the girls. Rita yelled at the gawking crowd, "Ladies and gentlemen, the show's over so move along now!" After hearing Rita's bossy announcement, I just couldn't stop laughing. And finally, Maroula shouted to the dancing pen pals, "Come on you lot, let's go!" Ten minutes later, we were on a bus heading towards the top secret locations.

We decided that the first stop on the 'Beatles' Home Tour' would be to number 13 Emperor's Gate, and in less than a half an hour we were standing outside the four story, white building. We pointed to John's top floor flat, and the Swedish girls gazed up in awe. Standing in the entryway, the pen pals tried to peek through the tiny glass windows, but a curtain had been hung to hide the interior, so they began to snap dozens of photos standing next to the white pillars, and the black front door.

The Swedish girls were anxious to see where Paul lived, and so our next stop was to Jane Asher's parents' house at number 57, Wimpole Street. Once again, the cameras came out, but this time they handed them over to us. And while we pretended to be professional photographers, the pen pals pretended to be fashion models. We snapped photo after photo as the pen pals stood next to the front door, positioned themselves against the wrought iron railing, and posed next to a sparkling white Rolls Royce that just happened to be parked next door.

There were at least a dozen fans standing outside the Asher's home, and they watched with interest as the pen pals posed, and Maroula, Rita and I snapped one photo after another.

As we walked away, the six of us couldn't stop laughing. Our final stop was to William Mews, and before we had reached Whadden House, the pen pals' cameras came out, and the primping and posing began all over again. While the pen pals were changing their film, Rita reminded them, "You do realize that millions of girls would love to see these top-secret Beatle places." In her Swedish accent, Anita replied, "Oh yah, we are so grateful. It was nice to see Buckingham Palace and all of the other famous places, but this is what we were waiting to."

Lize Lottie sighed, "You're so lucky, I would give anything to live this close to The Beatles." My girlfriends and I were fully aware of how fortunate we were, so trying not to be showoffs, we just nodded our heads. On the way to the bus stop, Brigitta squealed, "Thank you so much, we will never forget this wonderful day." And immediately Lize Lottie and Anita chimed, "Oh yah, we'll never forget!" Laughing hysterically, Rita replied, "Once you get all those rolls of film developed, you're gonna have so many photos it will be impossible to forget."

It was obvious that the pen pals were enjoying their English *holiday. We'd taken them to all the tourist's spots in London, and now they had seen for themselves where each and every one of The Beatles lived. But on this trip, there was one rather important thing missing. On August 18th, John, Paul, George and Ringo had left for their second American tour, and this time they would be away until September 21st. So, by the time The Beatles would be back in England, the pen pals would be back home in Sweden.

On the bus ride home, while the pen pals were chatting to each other, Rita whispered to Maroula and me, "It's such a shame that The Beatles are three thousand miles away. I know the pen pals enjoyed seeing where The Boys live, but it's certainly not the same as actually seeing them in person. They're putting on brave faces, but it must be a huge disappointment. Can either one of you think of anything that could make this Beatleless trip a little more interesting?"

Laughing out loud, I said, "Beatleless, I do believe you've come up with a new word! And, as a matter of fact, there is something we could do that would definitely improve this situation." With a worried look, Rita cried, "Sorry mate, at the moment I'm a little bit *skint! I couldn't possibly afford a plane ticket to America, and besides I don't even have a passport." Maroula nodded, "Yeah, and that goes for me too!"

The thought of flying over to America hadn't entered my mind, and smiling, I replied, "No, what I'm thinking won't cost a fortune, and if we stick to my plan we could all definitely afford to do it." Giving me a sideways glance, Maroula sighed, "Okay, don't keep us in suspense, lets hear what your latest scheme is." Barely able to contain my excitement, I squealed, "We'll make a pilgrimage to Liverpool, we'll go and see for ourselves where it all began."

Rita's face lit up, and she screeched, "What a fabulous idea. I'd love to see Liverpool, and I've been dying to go to The Cavern. It'll be the adventure of a lifetime. Ursula, you're a true genius!" I was just about to say, "Why thank you darling." when she added, "But to travel that far sounds very expensive."

I quickly replied, "Ah, but not if we hitch hike, stay in youth hostels, and just eat the bare minimum." It was plain to see that Maroula liked what she was hearing, but with a sulky pout, she said, "There's one teeny weeny problem, do you think our parents will let us go all the way to Liverpool by ourselves." Giggling, I replied, "My Dad's in America, so I only have to convince my Mum." Looking at Rita I could see that she was deep in thought, then she leaned over, and whispered, "Have you noticed how our Mums and Dads are bending over backwards trying to please our pen pals?"

Nodding my head enthusiastically, I replied, "You're absolutely right, so if we get the pen pals to ask, I have a feeling our parents might actually say yes to our amazing idea." Grinning from ear to ear, Maroula squealed, "We've got nothing to lose, so let's give it a try." As soon as we got off of the bus, we went into a fish and chip shop, and while nibbling on our chips, we went over the plan with Lize Lottie, Briggita, and Anita. After hearing all the details, the pen pals could barely contain their excitement, and were more than willing to be the ones to step up and ask our parents. I suggested to make it impossible for our parents to say no, that each of them should give a little curtsey before they began their heart wrenching plea.

With a glint in her eye, Rita sighed, "Yes, that should definitely do the trick." In unison, the pen pals responded, "Oh yah!"

A Common Case of Beatlemania

Later that night, the pen pals got to work on their part of the scheme, and it didn't take too long for the parents to cave in, and each of them agreed to let us go to Liverpool. On Monday morning the six of us found our way to the headquarters of The Youth Hostel Organization on Charing Cross Road. Together, we filled out forms, stood in the queue, paid our dues and became official members of the YHA. We also bought maps, guidebooks, *rucksacks and lots of other travel necessities.

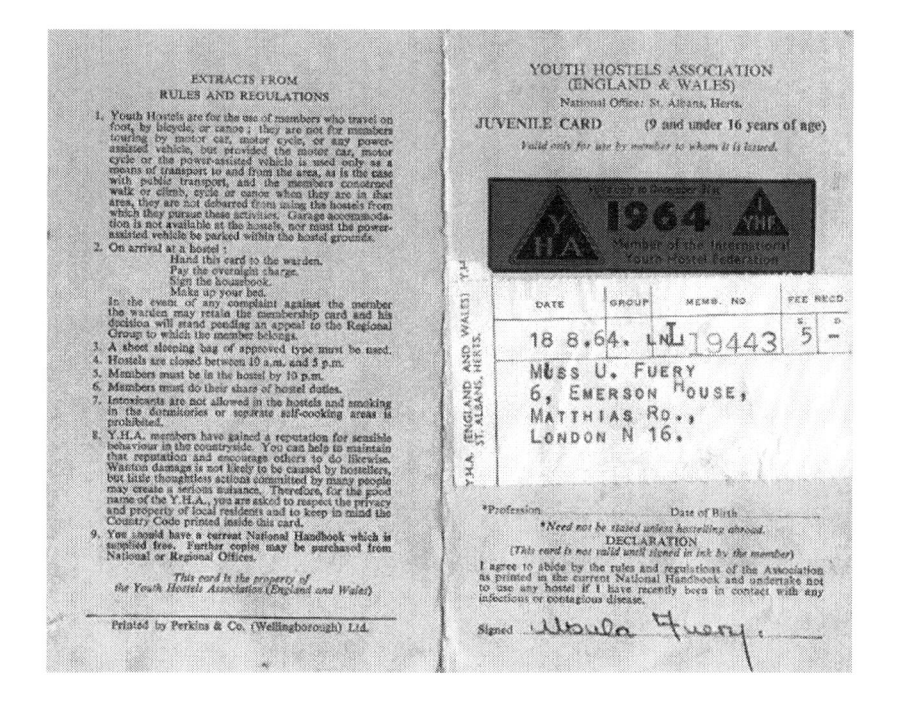

My youth hostel card

With our overflowing shopping bags, we sat in a Wimpy Bar, and while eating our hamburgers we went over our cross-country travel plans. Later that evening, Lize Lottie and I packed our rucksacks, laid out our clothes for the morning, and because we couldn't wait for our big adventure to begin, we decided to have an early night.

*<u>Knackered</u>...Exhausted.
*<u>Peckish</u>...Hungry.
*<u>Good job</u>...Good thing.
*<u>Cor</u>...An exclamation of amazement / amusement.
*<u>Holiday</u>...Vacation.
*<u>Rucksacks</u>...Backpacks.

CHAPTER 35
LIVERPOOL, HERE WE COME

The following morning, eager to start our exciting journey, Lize Lottie and I were up at the crack of dawn. My mother made us tea, and toast, and insisted that we each have a bowl of Weetabix too. Pouring the milk, she looked quite worried, and said, "You girls are going on a long journey, so you better make sure you eat something substantial before you leave." Looking up to heaven, I sighed, "Oh, Mum stop looking so upset, they're six of us, and we'll all be watching out for each other, so we'll be fine!"

Strapping the heavy rucksacks onto our backs, Lize Lottie and I said farewell to my mother, and my two half asleep sisters, and cautiously tiptoed down the two flights of stairs of our apartment building. By the time we were outside my mother had opened the bedroom window, and shouted down to us, "Be careful girls, stay together, and for sake don't get into any trouble, and if there's an emergency you can always call Eva downstairs. You have her phone number, but only call her if it's a true emergency." Laughing out loud, I yelled up, "Okay Mum, we've got it! Now stop worrying, and I promise I'll send you a postcard every single day. This way, you won't be tossing and turning all night."

As soon as we arrived at Euston train station, we spotted our girlfriends who were waiting by the main entrance. We staggered over to them, and I immediately dropped my heavy rucksack Rubbing my aching shoulders, I sighed, "Sorry we're late, but we had to wait over twenty minutes for the bleedin' bus." The previous day the six of us had a meeting to finalize all the plans. We all agreed that the sensible thing to do would be to start hitch hiking once we were out of London. After checking both the map, and the YHA book, we decided that our first stopover would be in the town of Shrewsbury. It was on the train line and had a rather nice-looking youth hostel.

Boarding the train, Rita sighed, "I'm ever so glad we're taking the train, my rucksack is so heavy, and my back is killing me already!" With a sympathetic sigh, I answered, "I know just how you feel." Sitting on the comfortable train, Maroula, Rita and I sat back and listened as the pen pals told us all about their families and life in Sweden. Up until now, we'd been so busy running all around London, that we really hadn't had much time to have a nice chit chat!

Rita was fascinated and had a million questions for the pen pals, and they were happy to answer each and every one of them. Rita said, "Sweden sounds like an interesting place, one day we'll have to go there, and visit you lot." In unison, the three Swedish girls replied, "Oh yah, we'd love that!"

As the train chugged along, the conductor came into our compartment to check our tickets. He reminded us that in order to get to Shrewsbury, we would have to change trains at Crewe. Just hearing the word Crewe made us English girls laugh, and as soon as the conductor left, Maroula, Rita and I began to sing: '*Old Mr. Porter.' The Swedish girls were grinning broadly but had no idea what prompted our spontaneous singing. When our singing ended, we told the pen pals about the popular song, and laughing hysterically, I blurted out, "I never thought I'd actually get to go to Crewe." Sitting on that comfortable train; the six of us became so relaxed, and before long I began to sing '*Summer Holiday' and once again, Rita and Maroula joined in.

Gazing out of the window, Lize Lottie sighed, "Oh my, I have never seen so many beautiful little fairy-tale villages." Brigitta chimed, "Oh yah, truly lovely." Rita said proudly, "There's nothing more beautiful than the English countryside." Maroula and I looked at each other and in unison answered, "Oh yah!"

After being on the train for just over two hours we arrived at Crewe. We sat in the 'ladies only' waiting room, and twenty minutes later we boarded the train to Shrewsbury. In less than an hour, the train pulled into our destination. Once outside, we opened our maps, but between the six of us we didn't have a clue as to which way we should go. We caught up with a man who was out walking his little dog and asked him for directions. Pointing to the left, he said, "It's quite a distance from here, so you've got a nice walk ahead of you." I thought to myself, "Now that doesn't sound too good!" We thanked the man for his help and after giving his little dog a quick pat on the head, I hoisted my rucksack onto my back.

On our rather long walk, I was quite surprised to see that Shrewsbury was quite a big town, with a fair amount of huge houses, plenty of shops, and lots of people walking around. After what seemed like an eternity, we finally arrived at the youth hostel. The hostel was a gigantic, red brick Edwardian manor house that looked a little bit scary.

We walked inside and dropped our heavy rucksacks onto the floor. The manager of the youth hostel was standing behind the reception desk, and in a cheery voice, said, "Hello girls, may I see your YHA cards, and how long will you be staying with us?" We handed him our crisp new cards, and in her lovely Swedish accent, Lize Lottie replied, "We are on our way to Liverpool, so we can only stay for one night." "*Right you are." answered the manager. He stamped our cards, and told us that the cafeteria will be opened at six o'clock for the evening meal, and breakfast starts at 7 a.m. He also told us that for a minimum charge, we could buy a packed lunch to take with us tomorrow. He also mentioned that the kitchen is also available if we prefer to cook our own meals.

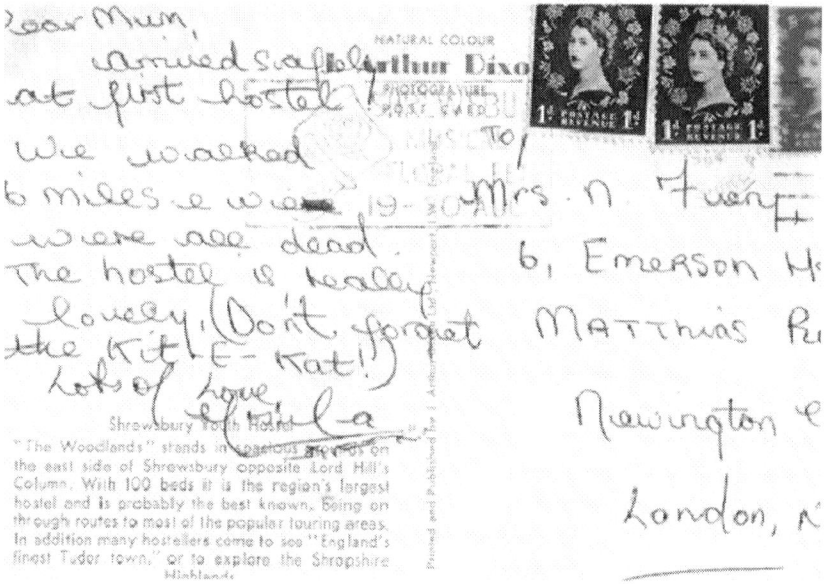

The first postcard that I sent to my mother

We hadn't brought any food with us, so we were more than happy to have someone else prepare our meals. I answered, "Yes please, we'll be here for dinner, and breakfast, and we'll have the packed lunches to go." He made a quick note in his book, and then he checked the register. He informed us that we would all be together in the same room. He told us the room number, we thanked him, and grabbing our rucksacks we ran up the stairs.

The room was quite small, with three sets of bunk beds, a little white table, and four wooden chairs. Within a minute, we had each decided on a bed. So, we threw our rucksacks onto the floor, and climbed into our chosen beds. My shoulders were so sore from carrying my heavy rucksack, and it felt so good to just lay there, and it was obvious that the others felt the same way.

A few minutes before six o'clock we found our way to the girls' bathroom and gave our hands and faces a quick wash. We hadn't eaten a thing in hours, and we were all quite peckish, so we ran down the stairs and straight into the cafeteria. There were quite a few people already standing in the queue, but we were happy to see that the line was moving at a fast pace. The main meal was *Shepard's pie, and for dessert we had a choice of either ice cream and *jelly or *jam roly poly*. The lady serving the dinner gave each of us a generous portion of both the dinner, and the *afters.

We sat at a long table and in the middle of the table was a caddy with cutlery and *serviettes. Also on the table were glasses and two large jugs of water. None of us spoke a said until we had eaten every last morsel on our plates! Once we had finished eating, we discussed our route for the following day. Brigitta volunteered to run upstairs and bring down her map. The YHA map showed all the hostels in Great Britain, and in no time at all we had decided on our next destination. None of us had ever hitch hiked before, so we chose a hostel that wasn't too far away.

Our next stop would be to a little town in Wales named Llangollen. It was only thirty miles from Shrewsbury, so just in case we were waiting for hours for somebody to stop and pick us up, we'd still have plenty of time to get there before dinner time. We realized that there weren't too many cars big enough to carry six hitchhikers, plus the driver, so we decided to split into two separate groups. The Swedish girls were one group, and us English girls made up the other.

One person from each group wrote down the address, and the directions to the Llangollen youth hostel. Once we had taken care of the following day's travel arrangements, we went to the front desk and each of us bought a couple of postcards. While we were busy writing out our postcards, the manager came over and reminded us that we still had our chores to do.

On the day that we'd gone to the headquarters to join the YHA, someone had taken the time to go over all of the rules and regulations. One of the rules was that each hosteler would be given some sort of chore to do after each meal, and again, before leaving the hostel in the morning. I whispered to the girls, "I'd forgotten all about the chores, and after all the walking we've done today, I'm really not in the mood to do anything too physical." Patting me on the back, Maroula giggled, "Don't worry, I'm sure it won't be anything too strenuous."

The manager came back and gave each of us a piece of paper listing our particular task. I was pleased to see that my job was to sweep the cafeteria floor, and in no time at all my chore was completed. After putting the broom, and dustpan away, I hurried upstairs to our room. Lize Lottie was already there, and the others came following close behind. An hour later, we were all fast asleep. The following morning at six o'clock sharp, we were woken up by the most unexpected alarm. Out of the speakers that were placed in each corner of the room, came The Dave Clark Five singing: 'Glad all over' and it was blasting at top volume. The six of us jumped out of bed, and covering her ears, Rita screeched, "I almost had a heart attack, they could have warned us about their super loud alarm system." Still half asleep, I groaned, "From now on, every time I hear that song I'm gonna get an instant headache!"

We somehow managed to drag ourselves to the bathroom. We each had a nice long shower, dressed, and hurried down for breakfast. We sat at the same table that we were at the night before, and we had a choice of either a *full English breakfast, or toast, with a banana and a bowl of cereal. We knew that we had a long day ahead of us, so we all choose the full English breakfast. We were eager to start our journey, so as soon as we were finished eating, we found the manager and asked which chores needed to be done. Once again, the chores were nice and easy, and after tidying up our room, we were ready to start the next part of our adventure.

Once we had found our way to the main road, we broke into our two separate groups.

We let the Swedish girls go ahead of us. In less than two minutes, a car skidded to a halt to pick them up. Shaking my head, I sneered, "I had a feeling that would happen." Maroula, Rita, and I stuck out our thumbs, and about five minutes later, a woman pulled up next to the curb, and asked us where we were heading. Then she said, "Hop in, I'm on my way to Oswestry, and Llangollen is only about fifteen miles from there. So, you'll be almost at your destination."

It felt so good to be sitting in a nice warm car, and as we drove along, the woman chatted nonstop about *this, that, and the other. We really didn't pay too much attention to what she was going on about, instead we simply smiled and nodded in agreement. Once we'd arrived at Oswestry, the woman pulled the car over and as we got out, she told us where the best place would be to get another ride. We thanked her for being so kind, and as she drove away, we waved until she was out of sight. As we looked around the area, Rita said, "I don't know about you two, but I fancy a nice cup of tea." I quickly added, "And a buttered scone would really *hit the spot." We found a workman's cafe, and ten minutes later we were enjoying our piping hot tea, and giant scones with *clotted cream and mounds of strawberry jam.

We had a nice chitchat with the waitress, and she assured us that we'd be in Llangollen in no time at all. "It's only about twelve miles from here," she said. Our next ride was with an older gentleman who was on his way to visit his daughter and her family. They lived in a town north of where we were going, so he'd be driving right through Llangollen. He wanted to take us all the way to the hostel, but it was only midday, and we knew that we wouldn't be allowed into the hostel until four o'clock. So, we thanked him, and he dropped us off on the main street.

Earlier that day, we'd each bought a packed lunch from the youth hostel, so we found a nice little spot right next to the river Dee and took our time eating our cheese and tomato sandwiches. Suddenly the three pen pals came into view. They were walking towards us, and as soon as they spotted us, they were overjoyed. They sat on the grass next to our bench, and while they nibbled away on their packed lunches, they told us all about the three rides they had taken. We checked our maps and knowing that the youth hostel was only a couple of miles away, the six of us decided to stay right where we were, and we had a nice long rest.

At three o'clock we began the two-mile hike to the youth hostel. The country road was quite narrow, with high bushes on either side. Lucky for us, only a couple of cars drove by. As soon as we came to an open field, we dropped our heavy rucksacks, and had another little rest. After what seemed like hours, a rather grand building came into view. I felt as though I was seeing a mirage, because it was the most beautiful half-timbered red brick mansion I had ever seen. I turned to the girls, and said, "This can't be right, it's way too posh to be a youth hostel! It looks more like a luxurious hotel." Just seeing this magnificent building gave each of us a second wind, and we started running towards the main entrance.

There were quite a few people waiting at the front door, and we still had fifteen minutes to go before it was 4 o'clock, so we chatted quietly with the other hostelers. I was surprised to learn that many of these young people were from all over the world. At 4 o'clock on the dot, the door swung open, and everyone picked up their belongings and rushed inside. When we got to the front desk, the manager went over the rules and regulations.

By now, we considered ourselves to be experienced hostelers, so we stood there nodding our heads but only half listening.

In this hostel we were given two separate bedrooms. Maroula, Rita and I took one, and the pen pals took the other one which was right next door to us. Our room was quite spacious and had two very large windows which made the room nice and bright. There were three single beds, each with the exact same green and pink *candlewick bedspread. We each picked a bed, and immediately plopped onto them. We were overjoyed that the beds were so comfortable and being as we had an hour to spare before dinnertime, we set the alarm on Rita's travel clock, and the three of us had a little snooze.

At six o'clock we were feeling quite refreshed after our nap, and more than ready to eat a delicious dinner. We followed the crowd into the dining room. This time we had a choice of either *bangers and mash, or fish and chips. The two desserts choices were *sticky toffee pudding, or *spotted dick. The tables were very long, and about a dozen people sat at each table. While we ate our dinner, we listened in awe to the other hostelers who were only a few years older than us, and they told us all about their unbelievable adventures. Once again, after dinner everyone was given a chore to do. Lize Lottie and I were asked to clean the tables, so in no time at all, we were finished.

We waited for our friends to complete their chores, and together we all went into the enormous living room. We found the perfect spot which had two enormous couches, and we plonked ourselves down. Minutes later, the people who were at our dinner table joined us, and we continued chatting with our new friends. By nine o'clock we were exhausted, so we said goodnight to everyone, found our rooms and crawled into our cozy beds. Just as I was about to drift off to sleep, Rita hissed, "I hope they have a different alarm system in this place!" Together, Maroula, and I said, "Let's hope so!"

At quarter to seven there was a light tapping on our door, and suddenly the door swung opened, and a lady popped her head in and said, "Time to get up girls." We sat up in our beds, and together said, "Thank you." As soon as she left, Rita said, 'Well, that was a pleasant wake up call." After taking a nice warm shower, I went downstairs to the dining room with Maroula and Rita. The pen pals were already sitting at a table, so we walked over and joined them. While we ate our breakfasts, the manager came over and handed each of us the daily task schedule. We also checked our maps, and just knowing that Liverpool was less than sixty miles away made me want to scream with excitement. After we had finished eating, we rushed through our super easy chores, and in no time at all our rucksacks were packed and we were ready to leave. Hoisting my rucksack onto my shoulders, I yelled, "Okay, everyone let's go!" And Maroula added, "Before you know it, we'll be in Liverpool."

We were so happy that our long journey was coming to an end, and that The Beatles' hometown was less than sixty miles away. Before splitting into the same two groups as the previous day, we had to decide on a place where we could all meet up. We chose the Liverpool docks, and being as it looked like a massive area we picked the exact spot where our gathering would take place, and marked it on our maps. Both groups wished each other good luck, and as we headed off I yelled out, "Get ready Liverpool, here we come!"

*<u>Emerson House</u>…The apartment building where my family and I lived.
*<u>Old Mr. Porter</u>…An old British music hall song.
*<u>Summer Holiday</u>…A popular song (and movie) by Cliff Richard and The Shadows.
*<u>Right you are</u>…An old fashioned British way of saying: "I understand."
*<u>Shepard's pie</u>…A meat pie with various vegetables, and a crust of mashed potatoes.
*<u>Jelly</u>…Jello
*<u>Jam Roly Poly</u>…A British dessert similar to a Swiss Roll.
*<u>Afters</u>…Another word for dessert.
*<u>Serviettes</u>…Table napkins.

*<u>Knackered</u>…Exhausted.

*<u>Full English breakfast</u>…A breakfast that typically includes bacon, sausages, eggs and beans, and a beverage such as coffee or tea.

*<u>This, that, and the other</u>…All sorts of different things.

*<u>Hit the spot</u>…Exactly what is needed.

*<u>Clotted Cream</u>… Is cream that has been cooked and is best described as something between whipped cream and butter.

*<u>Candlewick bedspread</u>…A bedspread that has been embroidered using a specific technique.

*<u>Bangers and mash</u>…Sausages and mash potatoes.

*<u>Sticky toffee pudding</u>…A British dessert consisting of a very moist sponge cake, made with finely chopped dates, covered in a toffee sauce

*<u>Spotted dick</u>… A British pudding, made with suet and dried fruit and often served with custard.

CHAPTER 36
WONDERFUL AND HEART- WRENCHING

Two car rides later, Maroula, Rita and I arrived at the prearranged spot. The pen pals had not yet arrived, so we found a bench and waited patiently for them to show up. An hour later the Swedish girls finally appeared. As they approached the bench, Rita cried, "Well it's about time, what took you so long? We were starting to get worried." Lize Lottie replied, "We've been in four different cars, and in the last car, the man got lost for over thirty minutes. We were beginning to think we'd never see you again"

I could see that Lize Lottie and the other girls were very upset, so I tried to change the subject, and said, "I don't know about you lot but I'm feeling rather peckish, so let's go and find somewhere to eat." And in unison everyone shouted, "Yeah." We found a workman's cafe and the six of us waltzed in. The place was packed with workers from the dockyards, so we hurried over to the only unoccupied table. Throwing our rucksacks under the table, we plonked ourselves down on the wooden benches, and each of us picked up a menu.

After studying the menu for quite a long time, I said, "I think I'll have the shepherd's pie with extra *Bisto gravy, and for afters I'll have the *treacle pudding with a nice cup of tea."

As I laid my menu down, the other five said in unison, "Yes, I'll have that too!" And of course, that collective response made each of us break into uncontrollable laughter. While eating my lunch, I realized that every man in the place was staring at us. I whispered to my friends, "I think we're the first females that have ever actually eaten in this place." Rita added, "I do believe you're right, there's nothing but old *geezers in here."

As soon as we had finished our lunch, we were all super eager to get out of the cafe and start discovering the great city that we had been reading about ever since that very first article on The Beatles. We were right next to the River Mersey, so it made perfect sense that our first adventure should be a ferry ride on the river that Gerry and The Pacemakers had made famous with their huge hit 'Ferry Across The Mersey.' Before that song, I had never even heard of The River Mersey.

While walking along the dockside, we stopped an old weather-beaten sailor, and asked him for directions to the ferry terminal. When he spoke, we stood back with our mouths wide opened, because he sounded exactly like George Harrison. He gave us the simple directions, and as he walked away, we squealed with delight. Twenty minutes later we had arrived at the terminal. Being as we had no idea where we were, we each bought a *return ticket.

Climbing up the gangplank we held onto the ropes for dear life! Even though it was the summertime it was quite chilly, and extremely windy. Carefully scanning the open deck, we spotted a long metal bench, and the six of us ran over to claim it. As soon as the boat set sail, my girlfriends and I broke into singing 'Ferry Across The Mersey.' Ever since the song came out, my dream had been to one day sing it while actually being on the ferry on the River Mersey.

Now, my dream had come true, and we were singing the popular song, swaying from side to side, and having the time of our lives. It was plain to see that the other passengers were enjoying our little sing song, and before long, most of them joined in the singing. The boat ride was really nice and very relaxing, but we were ready for something a lot more exciting.

So when the boat ride came to an end, we ran down the gangway, and Maroula yelled, "So what shall we do next?" Jumping up and down, Anita cried, "Lets go to The Cavern." The six of us had all agreed that The Cavern was the one place in all of Liverpool that we just had to see. After all, this was the place where Brian Epstein had discovered The Beatles, and within two months had become their manager.

Ever since I'd read about The Cavern Club and saw the numerous pictures of the dark vaulted cellar with the tiny stage, I'd been dying to go there. And here we were in Liverpool, and yet another one of my dreams was about to become a reality. The Cavern was located at number 10 Mathew Street and thanks to our trusty map, we were there in no time. The moment we turned onto Mathew Street we could barely contain our excitement, and the six of us began to run down the narrow street.

There were at least fifty people waiting to go into the most popular club in all of Great Britain, but before getting on the queue, we decided to have a look at the famous entrance. With mouths open, we peered down the familiar dark steps, and Anita screamed, "We've made it, we're at The Cavern." Rita's face was flushed with excitement, and jumping up and down, she gasped, "Can you believe this?" On my bedroom walls I had at least three pictures of The Beatles standing in the very spot that my girlfriends and I were now standing on.

The pen pals immediately pulled out their cameras and snapped photo after photo. Then we got on the end of the long queue, and slowly shuffled along getting closer and closer to the entrance. Holding our rucksacks in front of us, we carefully descended the poorly lit, extremely steep staircase. When we finally got to the end of the stairs, they were two men sitting at a table. One of the men was writing in a notebook, while the other was collecting the entrance fee. We had our money in our hands and were more than willing to give to him. Giving us a sideway glance, he scoffed, "You lot can't come in here! What are you, fourteen? You've got to be at least eighteen to get into The Cavern."

Rita looked like she was about to burst out crying, and she pleaded, "But you don't understand, we've come all the way from London and our pen pals are from Sweden." Briggita and Anita stood timidly behind Rita, and without saying a word, they frantically shook their heads up and down. Holding back the tears, Lize Lottie swallowed hard, and in her Swedish accent shouted at the man, "That's right, we've come all the way from Sweden to see The Cavern, so please let us in!" Folding his arms and glaring into Rita's face, the guard sneered, "I don't care if you've come from the moon. Unless you're the proper age and have you proof, you're not stepping one foot in here!"

Finally, I plucked up the courage, and stepping forward I barked, "I've read dozens of articles about The Cavern and I've never read anything about an age restriction." Taking a deep breath, I continued, "In London, once you've reached sixteen you can get into almost any club." Turning around to face me, he snapped, "Well, you're not in London now, you're in Liverpool and up here we've got our own rules."

While we continued our begging and pleading, the locals squeezed passed us, handed their entrance fee to the other man, and waltzed right in. Whispering to my girlfriends I said, "They look younger than us, and they were allowed to go right in without showing any kind of proof of age. For the next hour, one by one we each took a turn at trying to persuade the unrelenting man to please let us in, but sad to say, to no avail.

Standing next to the table we could feel the heat that was coming out from the overcrowded Cavern Club, and finally Rita cried, "We could be standing here all night, this mean old man is never gonna let us in." Rita was absolutely right, and the six of us knew that we were wasting our time. So, we slowly walked away from the table, and somehow managed to get through the horde of people that were descending the slippery steps while we were trying to go up. After what seemed like an eternity, we finally made it to the outside.

The six of us were completely devastated. The thought of not getting

A Common Case of Beatlemania

into The Cavern Club had never even crossed our minds, and we were crushed. To this day I still don't know how we managed to find our way to the youth hostel, but somehow, we did.

At the dinner table, instead of the noisy, giggling group that we normally were, we ate our dinners in complete silence. The day had gone from a perfectly wonderful morning to an absolutely miserable evening. Later that night, while lying in my bunk bed, I could hear one of the Swedish pen pals sobbing. The following morning, the six of us were up bright and early, and were determined to make the most of our time in the city where John, Paul, George, and Ringo *hailed from.

We had made arrangements to stay at the youth hostel for two nights, so we left our belongings piled neatly on top of our beds. We rushed through breakfast, and our mandatory chores and by nine o'clock we were all set to go. We all agreed that our first stop would be to Ringo's house. It was in an area of Liverpool known as Dingle, and after having a quick *gander at the map, it looked easy enough to find. Of course, we got lost, but thanks to the bus conductor, and the help of some very nice *Liverpudlians, in less than an hour we were standing outside: 10 Admiral Grove.

Looking at the little terraced house, it was hard to believe that we were right outside Ringo's boyhood home. I'd been dying to meet Ringo's mum and stepdad, so I knocked on the front door, and waited patiently for one of them to answer. When no one came to the door, I knocked again, this time much louder. Finally, a neighbor who had been watching us, came over and told us that Ringo's parents were away on *holiday. We couldn't believe it. How could they not be home? I had so many questions for Ringo's mum, and I had my heart set on meeting her.

Huffing and puffing, Rita sighed, "Yet another huge disappointment! So far not one bleedin' thing has gone according to plan!" Slumping to the pavement, Maroula and I watched in silence as the pen pals posed next to the little white house and snapped one photo after another. While the Swedish girls were busy taking photos, I decided to have a quick peek into the window. Holding my hands over my eyes, I placed my face up against the squeaky-clean window and peered into an extremely tidy little living room. My heart melted when I noticed a beautiful, framed photograph of Ringo right in the middle of the mantelpiece.

I sat on the pavement, and that's when I realized that all of the houses on the street were red brick, except for Ringo's parents' home, and the attached house next door. Both of the houses were painted bright white, and it was plain to see that they had both been recently done. I whispered to Maroula, "I bet Ringo paid to have his mum's house painted and the house next door too!" Maroula nodded in agreement.

Once the pen pals had finished taking photos we left 10 Admirable Grove, and spent the rest of the day wandering around the streets of Liverpool. After spending hours chatting with men, women, and teenagers, we all agreed that the people of Liverpool were the friendliest people in the world. Our main subject of conversation was, of course, The Beatles, and they were all so proud that John, Paul, George and Ringo all came from their hometown.

Sitting on a park bench, we met a local teenager who was amazed that we had traveled so far. In his lovely Liverpudlian accent, he said, "But there's nothing here!" Giving him a puzzled look, Rita replied, "You must be joking? This is where it all started for The Beatles, not to mention all the other groups. These days, Liverpool is the place where everyone wants to go." And he chuckled, "Well fancy that, I had no idea."

The following morning, knowing that we only had one more full day in Liverpool, we asked the manager of the youth hostel which was the best way to see a lot of the city without spending a small fortune. He suggested that we take a bus ride to the end of the line. The bus that he recommended went through many different areas of Liverpool. His suggestion sounded perfect, so he gave us the bus number and told us where the bus stop was.

Sitting in the front seats on the upper deck, we peered out of the window and had a fantastic view of the city. We were shocked to see that so many places still showed signs of the devastation from the Second World War.

A Common Case of Beatlemania

A Liverpudlian boy with me, Maroula, and Rita.

Staring at an enormous area of cleared land, I cried, "And I thought only London was bombed, I didn't realize that Liverpool got pounded too." After about an hour we had reached the end of the bus route. So, we jumped off the bus, and walked along the busy High Street, stopping every once in a while to peer into the shop windows. We were surprised to see that the same fashion styles that were popular in London, were all the rage in Liverpool too. Giggling, Lize Lottie reminded us, "You're not that far away, it's still the same country!" After hearing Lize Lottie's comment we all had a good old chuckle.

By one o clock, we were ready for lunch and in my best *scouse accent, I shouted, "I want a *jam buttie" Laughing her head off Rita turned to me, and said, "You've only been in Liverpool for two days, and already you've turned into a right Liverpudlian."

Ever since the pen pals had arrived in England, they had been saying how they wanted to experience real English food, so for this lunch we stopped at a fish and chip shop. We ordered cod and chips, and after unwrapping the *newspaper, we sprinkled both the fish and the chips with a generous amount of malt vinegar. The pen pals copied exactly what we did, and it was plain to see that they thoroughly enjoyed every morsel.

That afternoon, we spent hours strolling around the docklands and met many more fascinating characters. On the third morning, it was time to leave to Liverpool. Packing up her belongings, Rita chirped, "Every person we've met has been so helpful and lovely. No wonder The Beatles are so nice. It seems like everyone in Liverpool is the same way." Turning to her, I replied, "Yeah, you're right, everyone was nice, except for that one evil man who wouldn't allow us to go into The Cavern!"

*<u>Bisto</u>…*A well known brand of traditional British foods, most famous for it's gravy products.*
*<u>Treacle pudding</u>…*Treacle pudding is a traditional British dessert consisting of a steamed sponge cake with treacle cooked on top of it, usually served with piping hot custard.*
*<u>Old geezers</u>…*Old men.*
*<u>Return ticket</u>…*Round trip ticket.*
*<u>Hailed from</u>…*Came from.*
*<u>Gander at the map</u>…*Look at the map.*
*<u>Liverpudlians</u>…*Natives of Liverpool.*
*<u>Holiday</u>…*Vacation.*
*<u>Fancy that</u>…*Hard to imagine.*

*<u>Scouse accent</u>...Dialect associated with the city of Liverpool.
*<u>Jam buttie</u>...Jam sandwich.
*<u>Newspaper</u>...Newspaper was in 1964 the traditionally way to wrap the fish and chip.

CHAPTER 37
OUR MANCHESTER ADVENTURE

Our next stop was Manchester. Maroula wrote to her girlfriend Chris who lived in Manchester to let her know that we and our pen pals were going to Liverpool. Maroula's girlfriend wrote back immediately and invited us to come and stay with her and her family. In her letter she wrote, "Liverpool is so close to us, you must come and visit, and you can stay as long as you like." After reading the letter, I asked Maroula, "Are you sure Chris' parents know that there are six of us? Laughing, Maroula said, "In the letter Chris wrote that she had mentioned it to her dad, and he had answered, the more the merrier!'"

After a couple of days of not having to lug our heavy rucksacks around, we were totally spoiled. So, we had all agreed that instead of hitchhiking we would splurge and take a train to Manchester. We found our way to Lime Street Station, and each of us bought a one-way ticket to Manchester.

The journey by train was just over an hour, and in what seemed like a flash we had arrived at Manchester's Piccadilly train station. Maroula had visited Chris and her family many times, so she knew the way to their house. The bus stop was right outside the train station, and after a short bus ride we had arrived at our destination. Chris and her parents were waiting at the front door and as soon as we reached them, they welcomed us with open arms.

One by one, Maroula introduced us, and while Rita and I politely shook their hands, the Swedish girls curtsied. Chris' mother was not prepared for curtsies, and blushing she said, "Goodness gracious, I feel like the queen." We were led into the kitchen, where the table was set and the lunch was prepared. Chris' father turned to us, and said, "After the long journey, you girls must be famished." Each of us nodded enthusiastically.

We feasted on sausages, chips, beans, and buttered brown bread, and for afters, Chris' mother had made the most delicious jam roly-poly which was smothered in *Bird's Custard. We offered to help with the *washing up, but Chris' parents wouldn't hear of it, and insisted that we all go into the living room and relax. On the way to the living room, I whispered to Maroula and Rita, "This is like a dream, I may never leave!" And I knew that both of them felt the exact same way. While the seven of us relaxed on the comfortable couch, and matching seats we took turns telling Chris all about our amazing trip to Liverpool.

The pen pals were the ones who brought up the one and only disappointment of the entire trip. They told Chris all about the horrible man who wouldn't allow us to go inside The Cavern. Just thinking about it made us miserable all over again. Suddenly Chris blurted out, "That's great!" She immediately noticed our shocked expressions, and quickly added, "Oh, I didn't mean that! I feel awful that you couldn't get in, but we have our own Cavern in Manchester, and I think it's actually better than the one in Liverpool. I was wondering what we could do tonight, so now it's settled, we're all going to The Cavern!" Maroula cried, "That sounds wonderful." And in unison the rest of us shouted, "Yes it does!" We spent the remainder of the afternoon relaxing, taking nice hot baths, and getting ready for our evening out. At eight o'clock, we were ready to go.

On our way to the bus stop, we passed street after street of tiny, terraced houses with brightly colored front doors. I turned to the girls, and said, "I feel like I'm walking down *Coronation Street." Maroula laughed, "I was thinking the exact same thing!"

When we arrived at the main road, we caught a bus that was going towards Manchester City center. In no time at all we had arrived at Market Street, and The Cavern Club was right around the corner on Cromford Court. There was a long line of people waiting to go into the club and seeing the huge crowd it was obvious that this Cavern was just as popular as the one in Liverpool.

The queue moved along steadily, and twenty minutes later we had reached the ticket booth. Because of what happened in Liverpool, I was fully prepared for another pleading session, but to my surprise, the friendly girl behind the booth simply smiled, and said, "Hello, welcome to the Manchester Cavern, the admission charge is *half a crown." Breathing a deep sigh of relief, I smiled back, and handed over my money. Not only were we allowed to enter The Manchester Cavern without the slightest bit of commotion, but we were each given our very own Cavern membership card.

Admiring her card, Rita laughed, "Well that's more like it, pay your money, get your membership card, and *Bob's your uncle, you're in!" Descending the slippery stone steps was quite a challenge, and by the time we'd reached the bottom step, the entire place was pitch black. Holding onto Chris' jacket, I cried, "Cor blimey, I can't see a bleedin' thing!" She replied, "Don't worry, just hold onto me and you'll be fine." A minute later my eyes adjusted to the dark, and everything became clear. Looking around, I noticed that the curved walls, the barrel ceiling, and even the floor looked exactly like the pictures of The Liverpool Cavern.

Suddenly, the band started to play, and everyone in the club rushed up to the small stage.

During the evening, several bands performed, and my girlfriends and I danced the night away on the overcrowded dance floor. By the end of the evening we were totally exhausted. Holding onto the railing, we climbed up the slippery steps and staggered out into the cold night air. Holding up my membership card, I shouted at the top of my voice, "Who needs The Liverpool Cavern, when we've got The Manchester Cavern!" Hearing this, a crowd of people turned and cheered.

My Manchester Cavern membership card. Peter Noone (Herman) autographed it a few years later.

The following morning, the pen pals stayed with Chris' mother, while Maroula, Rita and I decided to go with Chris and her dad to their *allotment. We somehow managed to squeeze into his little truck, and off we went to the countryside. I had never been to an allotment; I was thrilled to have the chance to actually visit one. The huge field had dozens of tiny, divided plots, and each plot was unique. Some of the plots were growing the exact same things that my grandparent's in Ireland grew, potatoes, cabbages, carrots, and beans. While other plots were growing vegetables that I had never even seen before. Chris' dad noticed me staring at this huge shiny purple thing, and laughing out loud, he said, "Ursula, that's an *aubergine." Making a funny face, I relied, "I've never seen one of them before, and I don't think I'd want to eat it!"

Some of the other plots were overflowing with the most beautiful flowers I have ever seen.

We spent a couple of hours at the allotment, and it felt so good to be out in the fresh air. We helped Chris' dad carry some bags of soil off of his truck, and while he was busy gardening, we wandered around looking at the tiny gardens. Every once in a while, we'd stop to have a chat with some of the other friendly allotment owners.

When we got back to Chris' house, we spent the rest of the afternoon relaxing. We had already made up our minds to go back to The Cavern later that night. So, for several hours, we watched the telly, drank cup after cup of tea, and devoured Chris' mother's delicious scones.

At eight o'clock we were once again, back at The Manchester Cavern. The place was just as packed as the previous night, but we didn't mind. We were just happy to be able to spend another night at this amazing club.

Chris' brother had offered to drive us home, and as planned, at the stroke of midnight we left The Cavern, and he was waiting outside. I don't know how we did it, but the seven of us somehow managed to squeeze into his tiny car. Rubbing her aching feet, Rita sighed, "I've had a lovely time, and I'm ever so grateful that we don't have to walk all the way to the bus stop." In unison, the seven of us yelled, "Yeah, me too!"

The following morning, we said goodbye to Chris and her lovely family. We thanked them over and over for their warm hospitality, and for everything that they had done for us. They were one of the nicest families I had ever met. They told us, and our pen pals, that we were more than welcome to come back any time for another visit. Our enthusiasm for hitchhiking had completely vanished, and the six of us all agreed to spend the little bit of money that we had left on train tickets back to London. Chris' dad drove us to the train station.

On the train ride, we talked about the fascinating places that we had visited, the amazing people that we had met, and the dozens of fun things that we had experienced. We were all a little sad that our trip had come to an end, but Maroula quickly reminded us, "Cheer up you lot, we're only sixteen, we still have loads of places to explore, and we'll have lots more fabulous adventures." We all knew that Maroula was absolutely right, so we nodded enthusiastically.

When Lize Lottie and I arrived home, the first thing that I noticed were the postcards that I had sent, they were all neatly taped onto the front of the fridge. That night, my family and a few of my girlfriends gathered in the living room and listened, as Lize Lottie and I recounted the many tales of our unforgettable trip to Liverpool, and beyond.

While we were away, I had sent my other pen pals postcards from Liverpool, but I knew that they were waiting to receive a letter telling them all about our adventures in The Beatles' hometown. So, in the middle of the night, while everything was still fresh in my mind, I wrote a ten page letter to each of my pen pals.

Three days later our Swedish pen pals were ready to go home. Before leaving, Lize Lottie thanked my mother for allowing her to stay with us, and turning to me, she gave me a big hug and said, "It was the most wonderful trip I have ever been on, and I will never forget it." She also added, "And thank you for introducing me to so many delicious English foods, and my favorite dessert was definitely the *treacle tart." With a tear in my eye, I replied, "That's my favorite too." We were now so much more than just pen pals, we were truly the best of friends.

*<u>Jam roly-poly</u>...is a traditional British pudding (dessert) probably first created in the early 19th century.
*<u>Bird's custard</u>... Is the brand name for the original powdered, egg-free imitation custard powder. Made by combining the custard powder with milk, and cooking on the stove.
*<u>Washing up</u>...Cleaning the dishes.
*<u>Coronation Street</u>...Britain's longest-running soap opera, it started since its 1960.
*<u>Half a crown</u>...British money, equivalent to two shillings and sixpence.
*<u>Bob's your uncle</u>...An English expression meaning: And there you have it.
*<u>Allotment</u>...An area of land rented out for non-commercial gardening or farming.
*<u>Aubergine</u>...Eggplant.
*<u>Treacle tart</u>...A traditional super sweet British dessert, usually served with a dollop of cream.

CHAPTER 38
LITTLE MATCHBOX CARS

Once the pen pals had gone home, I didn't know what to do with myself, so I decided to get another job. I only had a few more weeks left in England, so I knew that it would only be a temporary position. My girlfriend Christina had been working at Lesney's toy factory for over a year, and we both agreed that it would be so much fun to work together. She knew the manager quite well, so she said with confidence, "Leave everything to me, and I'll arrange for you to come in for an interview, and don't worry I'll be sure to give you a glowing recommendation."

Later that night Christina came over, and told me that an interview was scheduled for ten o'clock the following morning. I made sure that I was at the manager's office on time, and after a brief five minute chat, I was hired on the spot. This job was completely different from my office job up the West End. At Lesney's I didn't have to get dressed up like I did at Gestetner's. I could wear anything that I wanted, as long as it was nice and comfortable. I worked on an assembly line with over a hundred other girls. Each day, we were given a different task. Some days I'd spend the entire day attaching wheels or other tiny parts onto colorful Matchbox cars.

And other days, my job was to drop a shiny new matchbox car into the opened end of a tiny box that came flying down the assembly line.

The work was quite tedious, and if it hadn't been for my happy go lucky co-workers, the job would have been mind numbing, and utterly boring. But, from the moment the conveyor belt started up, until the end of the day, my colleagues and I worked hard, and laughed even harder.

Every morning, Christina and I met on the corner of Matthias Road and Wordsworth Road, and together we walked to Dalston Junction, where the company bus (a green double decker) was waiting for us, and the dozens of other Lesney's employees. The bus driver drove us to Hackney and dropped us off at the main entrance to the enormous toy factory. The bus ride was free, and Christina and I both agreed that not having to lay out any of our hard-earned money to pay for bus fare was the greatest company benefit we could possibly want.

In the few weeks that I had worked at Lesney's, I made more money than I'd ever dreamed possibly. My days of living in England were quickly coming to an end, and so I spent my very generous wages on anything that was connected to The Beatles: records, magazines, books, posters etc.

CHAPTER 39
LEAVING MY BELOVED ENGLAND

During the first week of October 1964, I said goodbye to England. To leave from my girlfriends, my amazing carefree life in London, and of course, The Beatles; was the hardest thing that I had ever done. I knew that I had been living the ultimate dream, and that millions of Beatle fans all over the world would have given anything to have lived where I lived. To be able to jump on a bus, and in less than thirty minutes be standing outside the homes of John, Paul, George and Ringo was something that I never took for granted. My girlfriends and I were indeed very fortunate and saw The Beatles on numerous occasions. And no matter how often we saw them, each time was just as thrilling as the very first time.

And now, though no choice of mine, I was walking away from all the excitement that went along with Beatlemania. Before my father left for America, I begged my parents not to move.

They sat me down and tried to explain to me as to why they were making such a drastic move. They honestly believed that by going to America they'd be giving my siblings and me a chance for a better life. Trying to make them reconsider, I cried, "What's wrong with our life here?

Your children are happy, you have lots of nice friends, the shops are close by, and even *Oxford Street is just a short bus ride away." And turning to face my mother, I reminded her, " And don't forget, because we live in London, you can afford to visit your parents in Ireland every summer. If we move to America, you'll be far away from them, and it'll cost you a small fortune to go and see them."

Giving me a curious look, my mother asked, "Are you sure this has nothing to do with those Beatles? Your Aunt Bunny has written to me, and she tells me that Beatlemania is spreading all over America too. So just you wait and see, I'm sure The Beatles will be making a lot more trips to America." I quickly added, "Yeah, but that won't be living around the corner from us!"

I tried to make my mum and dad understand that they had a perfectly lovely life right where we were in jolly old England, but they just wouldn't listen. It was obvious that my parents had already made up their minds, and no matter what I said, it wasn't going to make a bit of difference. Once my father had left England, I knew that it was too late to try to change my mother's mind. She wanted to be with my dad, and of course, her brother and sisters who had been living in America for quite a few years already. So I knew that no matter what I said, it wouldn't make a bit of difference.

I spoke to my girlfriends about renting a *flat together, "Just think of all the fun we'd have" I pleaded. But even I knew that at sixteen none of us were mature enough to be living on our own. With a sympathetic smile, Eileen suggested, "Let's wait until we're eighteen, and then we'll get a nice big flat up the *West End, and go out every single night of the week." Rita chirped, "Oh, that sounds perfect. By that time, we'll have decent jobs, and money will be no object!" Trying to sound optimistic, she added, "Two years will fly by, and we promise to write to you every single week!"

As much as I didn't want to leave England, I knew that I was too young to be on my own and needed to be with my family for at least another couple of years. Just knowing that we'd be getting a flat together in the heart of London gave me something really special to look forward to.

A Common Case of Beatlemania

Before leaving for America, we had to apply for British passports. The first step was to go to a photographer to get our passport photos made. My first photo was a definite a thumbs down. The photographer told me that two things were wrong with it: First, because I wasn't facing forward, and second: because I looked profoundly unhappy. He approved the second photo, so that's the one we went with.

The rejected passport photograph

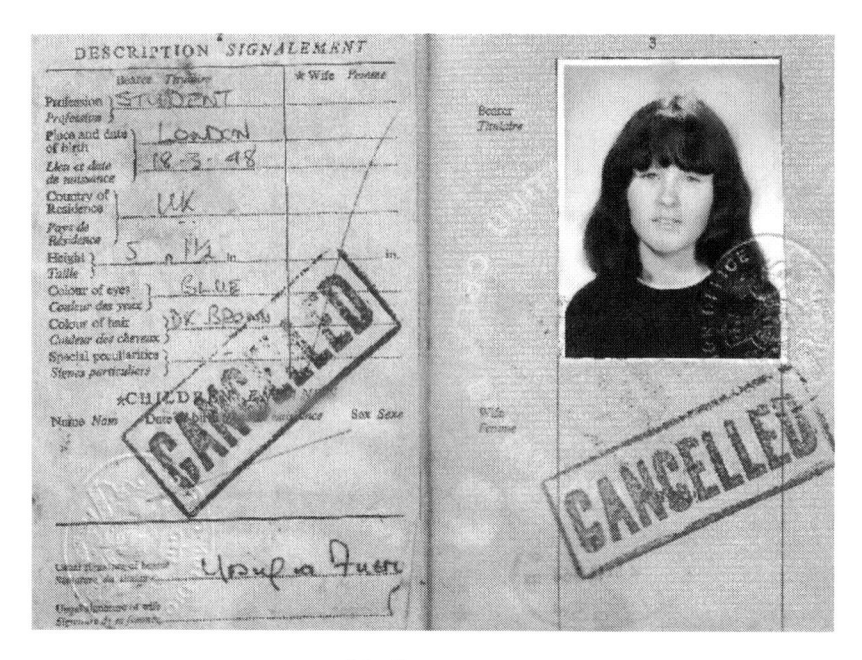

My first passport

A few weeks before our departure, I had given my mother an ultimatum. If she wanted me to go to America, two things would have to come with me: My cat Fluffy, and my extremely large collection of Beatle memorabilia. My mother instantly agreed to both of my demands.

The week before we were due to leave, I took Fluffy on a bus ride to the *R.S.P.C.A. at the Angel in Islington. He was thoroughly examined and was given a couple of injections. The veterinarian assured me that Fluffy was in perfect health and handed me a certificate which allowed our beloved cat to travel with us to America.

My second task was to pack up all of my Beatle memorabilia. With my girlfriends' help, we carefully removed each and every one of Beatle pictures from my bedroom walls, the ceiling, and the bedroom door. We lovingly wrapped the pictures in tissue paper and placed them into a neat pile. This task should have taken a couple of hours, but because of all the reminiscing, the job went on for days.

My mother surprised me with the most perfect present. She went to the *Kingsland Waste in Dalston and found an old steamer trunk. I don't know how, but she somehow managed to haul the gigantic trunk onto a bus, and once off of the bus, dragged it all the way home. She gave the trunk to me for my Beatle stuff, and I was absolutely thrilled. Later that night, using an entire bottle of *Dettol, I washed both the inside, and the outside of the ancient trunk. I thoroughly dried it with loads of rags, but just to make sure, I stuck it in the *airing cupboard overnight.

The following day I spent hours gluing images of The Fab Four all over the ancient trunk, and using a black marker, I wrote on the lid: 'My Beatle Trunk'. The night before we left England, my girlfriends came over for a final visit. In between the tears, we drank pots of tea, and ate mounds of chocolate digestive biscuits. I gave each of them my new address in America, and we all promised to always keep in touch.

My mother wanted to spend some time with her parents before heading to the new world, so we left England and travelled to Ireland. At Paddington Station, I dragged my heavy Beatle Trunk with one hand, and I held the wicker basket that contained my beautiful cat Fluffy with my other hand. Boarding the boat to cross the Irish Sea was a nightmare, and climbing up the metal gangplank was next to impossible. The wind was howling, and a stiff breeze almost knocked me down. I was about to leave the one place that I truly loved, and I was miserable!

A sailor offered to help me and tried to take my Beatle trunk off of me. But I refused to let go of it, and snapped at him, "Thank you very much, but I'm quite capable of carrying it myself!"

Through sheer determination I managed to hold onto The Beatle Trunk, and poor old Fluffy. Once we arrived in Ireland, my sulky attitude improved. My grandparents lived in Kanturk, Co Cork which is a beautiful little town surrounded by the most incredible countryside. We were very fortunate, and spent every summer there, so I immediately felt at home.

We were there for two glorious weeks, and I was so happy to be back again with my amazing grandparents. Looking at my mother it was obvious that she too was thrilled to be spending time with her beloved parents. While we were there, my mother took my sisters and me to the woolen shop; where we each picked out our favorite-colored wool, and my grandmother got to work making each of us an Irish sweater to take with us to America.

My grandfather also kept us entertained. Each day he took us on a thrilling excursion through their town, and into the countryside on his donkey and cart. My sisters sat up the front with him, while I laid on a bed of hay in the back of the cart. Just listening to the donkey's hooves going clippety clop was the most magical sound I had ever heard. We also enjoyed spending time with our Irish girlfriends who we had known since we were five years old, and were always so much fun to be with.

On October 22nd, my mother, my sisters and I said farewell to my grandparents, and travelled to Cobh, Co Cork, where the' S.S. America' was waiting to take us to our new home. The S.S. America was the biggest ship that I had ever seen, and I couldn't wait to get onboard to explore it. A nice-looking steward immediately took Fluffy away from me. I was sure that Fluffy would be allowed to stay with us in our cabin, but the steward assured us that Fluffy would be treated like a king in the spacious top deck kennel. Just knowing that we could visit him at any time, day or night, made me feel a lot better.

We found our cabin, which to me, was quite a disappointment. I was expecting something a lot more luxurious, but the cabin was quite a plain, and it didn't even have a window. There were two gray metal bunk beds, and in the middle of the beds was a night table with a lamp.

Immediately, Angela and I claimed the two top bunks, so my mother and Veronica had the lower beds. The cabin also had the tiniest bathroom that I had ever seen. But whoever built the ship had somehow managed to put a toilet, a sink and a shower stall into the tiny space. We also had a closet with some hangers and a few shelves, so while we waited for the ship to set sail we unpacked our suitcases, and to our surprise we got everything into the teeny closet. Finally, the ship sailed away, and our next stop would be New York City Harbor.

We were now ready to explore the gigantic ship, and for next two hours we went from one deck to another discovering all sorts of fascinating things. With all the oohing and aahing coming from my mother, it was plain to see that she was highly impressed with all the onboard amenities: An indoor swimming pool, a brand-new gym, several enormous dining rooms, a well-stocked library, a *cinema, and so much more. Looking from one corner to the next, she cried, "I've never seen anything like it. It's like a floating hotel, isn't it just grand?" My sisters and I nodded our heads in agreement.

At dinner time, we searched the enormous dining room looking for our assigned table. We thought we'd have a table for the four of us, and when we finally found our table, we were quite surprised to see that six other people were already sitting at it. It was a huge round table, and all of the people sitting were giving us smiles. So, my mother quickly introduced herself, and us to the other passengers.

We were the last people to arrive and as soon as we were seated, the waiter suddenly appeared from nowhere. Wearing white gloves, the perfectly groomed waiter handed each of us a large red leather folder with a gold tassel dangling from it. Inside the folder was a menu that had been written in the most beautiful italic handwriting. While everyone else at the table were busy staring at their menus, I was busy staring at the waiter. His movements were so graceful and deliberate, and I felt as though we were dining at the Ritz.

I finally opened my menu, and looking at the extensive wine list I leaned over, and whispered into Angela's ear, "La de da!" Reading the menu, I noticed that the roast beef dinner had a choice of either mashed potatoes or french fries, and turning to Angela I said, "Mmm, french fries, now they sound rather continental, and I do believe I'm in the mood for something a little exotic."

Angela replied, "I've heard that French cooking is done in a rich creamy sauce, and yes, french fries definitely sound scrumptious, so I'll have 'em too." In my poshest accent, I gave the elegant waiter my order, and taking the menu from me, he bowed and said, "Thank you Miss." Giggling, I whispered to Angela, "I do believe I could easily become accustomed to this lifestyle." Angela looked at me, and just rolled her eyes.

The dinner finally arrived, and when the waiter lifted the silver dome that covered my plate, that was the moment that I learned that french fries were nothing more than plain old chips. What a huge disappointment! After dinner, my mother decided that seeing a movie would be a rather nice thing to do, so while she went to check the showtimes, my sisters and I peeked into the fitness center. Inside the gym a group of middle-aged women were dancing and twirling to Chubby Checker's hit single: 'Let's Twist Again' and seeing this unexpected scene, made the three of us burst out laughing.

Suddenly, my mother came running towards us, and grabbing my arm, she gasped, "You're not going to believe what's playing tonight." And before I had a chance to even think about it, she squealed, "A Hard Day's Night." Later that night I found out that 'A Hard Day's Night' would be shown twice a day for the entire transatlantic crossing, and so for the rest of our journey my mother knew exactly where to find me. Each afternoon, my sisters and I would go to the little theater to watch The Beatles, while my mother enjoyed a little nap.

After dinner I'd go back for the second showing of 'A Hard Day's Night' while my mother and sisters went to the main lounge and played bingo for two hours. While watching the movie, one minute I'd be laughing at The Beatles' silly behavior, or tapping my feet to the music. And the next minute I'd be in tears, wondering if I'd be able to cope with living so far away from all the excitement that went along with Beatlemania. And with each passing day I was sailing further away from England, and I just couldn't bear to think of my life without John, Paul, George and Ringo.

For the entire crossing, my onboard activities consisted of: eating way too many delicious meals, sitting alone in our cabin, spending time in the kennel with Fluffy, and of course, watching 'A Hard Days Night'.

The' S.S. America'

<u>Oxford Street</u>…Europe's busiest shopping street with approximately 300 hundred shops, both small ones, and enormous department stores.
<u>A flat</u>…An apartment.
<u>West End</u>…An area of Central London, whack has many restaurants, pubs, and nightlife. R.S.P.C.A.…The Royal Society for the Prevention of Cruelty to Animals. Which is an animal hospital.

*<u>Dettol</u>…A very strong household disinfectant.

*<u>Airing cupboard</u>…An airing cupboard is a warm closet where you can put clothes and other things that have been washed and partly dried, to make sure they are completely dry.

*<u>Kingsland Waste</u>…A marketplace that sold mainly old household items

CHAPTER 40
SETTLING IN, AND MEETING ANOTHER PEN PAL

On October 28th, 1964, my mother, my sisters, Fluffy, and I arrived in New York City.

My father was waiting at the dock along with my Aunt Brenda, my Uncle Jack, and my adorable little cousin Jane. I hadn't seen my father in almost six months, and he looked completely different. This was the first time I'd ever seen my dad with a tan, and his hair was extremely short, almost a crew cut. His clothes were different too. He was wearing a blue and white checkered shirt, with beige trousers. In England he had always worn plain white shirts, and black trousers, so seeing him dressed in such colorful clothes was quite a shock.

After giving him a great big hug, I stepped back, and said, "Well, look at you, you look like a proper *yank!" Putting on his best American accent, he joked, "Gee whiz, I can't help it if I'm good looking." Taking me to one side, he whispered, "You'll be happy to know that The Beatles are quite popular over here too." Giving him a sideways glance, I replied, "Yes Daddy, quite a few people have already made me aware of that!"

After stuffing all of our luggage into the trunk, we piled into my Uncle Jack's station wagon, and drove away from the port. As we drove along the

Expressway, I couldn't decide which way to look. Not only was the road the widest road I had ever seen, but the speeding cars were almost as long as a double decker bus.

When we arrived at our new home on Irving Street in Westbury, the entire family, including my brother John were waiting outside to greet us. We hadn't seen most of the relatives in years, and a few of the younger cousins who were born in America, we had never met. My Aunt Bunny gave me a big kiss and handed me three letters. I immediately found a quiet spot in the corner of the garden and read the letters. I felt a little guilty, while I was enjoying my time in Ireland, and my transatlantic cruise, my girlfriends in England had taken the time to write to me. I realized how lucky I was to have such good friends, but after reading the letters I felt even more homesick than before.

The aunts and uncles gave us the grand tour of our new home. Every room was filled with furniture, including rugs and a television set that was twice as big as the one we had in England. All of these items had been donated to us by our relatives, and some of their friends. My mother didn't know what to say, and she became quite emotional. My cousin Ursula took Angela and me upstairs to show us our new bedroom. There were three single beds in the large room, all with the same blue flowery *eiderdowns. I immediately started to examine the walls, and the slanted ceiling. Finally, I stood back and announced, "Yes, this will do quite nicely."

It was obvious that my cousin didn't have a clue as to what I was talking about, but it was plain to see that Angela did, and she just shook her head knowingly. The following day my cousin Jimmy came over to take us for a drive around our new neighborhood. My mother and sisters were excited to go, but I refused. I had work to do, and until my Beatle pictures were hanging up on my new bedroom walls, I couldn't think about anything else.

My brother and one of my cousins had brought the Beatle trunk up the steep flight of stairs and placed it in the corner of the bedroom. As I opened the truck I pulled out the tin box which contained everything that

I would need; rolls of tape, a bottle of glue, and a container of thumb tacks! I took each picture out of the trunk, and laid them carefully on the floor. After much consideration, I decided where each and every picture should be placed. I had spotted a step ladder in the kitchen, so I dragged it up the stairs, and began to decorate our new bedroom.

At four o'clock, my mother and sisters came home from their sightseeing tour, and Angela came running up to our bedroom to see the progress. Looking from one wall to the next, and smiling from ear to ear, it was plain to see she approved. Finally, she spoke, "You must be feeling right at home. It looks exactly like your old bedroom in Emerson House."

Two weeks after arriving in America, I was on my way to New Jersey to meet my American pen pal Melanie. She was one of the many girls who had written to me after reading my letter in The Beatles' Monthly magazine. We had been writing to each other for almost a year, and with our mutual love for The Beatles, we had so much in common, I couldn't wait to meet her.

In our new American home, not only did we have a lot more channels on the telly, but for the first time ever, we actually had a telephone. Melanie called on Thursday evening, and I was pleasantly surprised that she had taken care of all the travel arrangements. With my girlfriends in England, taking care of all the details had usually been my job, but now that I was living in a place called Long Island, I didn't have a clue as to where I was.

While Melanie spoke, I sat on the floor, untangled the long telephone wire, and listened carefully to every word she spoke, because at times, her American accent was quite difficult to understand. Finally, she said, "Okay, so my parents will pick you up at two o'clock tomorrow afternoon. By the time you get to my house, I'll be home from school. Gee, I'm so excited, I can't wait to meet you."

My father had bought a giant atlas of America, and each state had its own detailed map. I studied the map of New Jersey, and soon realized that Perth Amboy was quite a distance from Long Island. So, while Melanie was still on the other end of the phone, I asked, "Are you sure your parents don't mind driving all the way to Long Island?" She replied, "Don't worry about it, it's no problem."

The following afternoon at two o'clock sharp, Melanie's parents drove into the driveway.

I ran outside to meet them and brought them into our house. My mother and two of my aunts were sitting on the couch in the living room. Angela took me to one side, and whispered, "I hope your pen pal's parents are ready to get the third degree."

My mother went into the kitchen to make a pot of tea, and my aunts had a chit chat with Melanie's parents, while I sat there anxiously waiting to leave. An hour later, we were finally our way. I was so excited to be going on my first adventure in America, and all the way to New Jersey. Driving along the highway, I peered out of the back seat window, while Melanie's parents told me fascinating facts about the different landmarks that we were passing.

Going across an enormous bridge was absolutely thrilling, and everything seemed so much bigger in America.

An hour and a half later we pulled into their driveway. Melanie was waiting at the front door, and before the car had even stopped, she opened my door. Dragging me out of the back seat, she gave me a huge hug, grabbed my suitcase, and ushered me into the house, and straight into her bedroom. Melanie's bedroom was exactly how I'd imagined it: pictures and gigantic posters of The Beatles everywhere and taped onto her dressing table mirror was the postcard that I had sent to her from Liverpool.

While I unpacked my suitcase, Melanie and I chatted nonstop. She wanted to hear about every single Beatle adventure that I had experienced, and even though I had given her all of the details in my super long letters, she insisted on hearing them again. To relive my Beatle escapades was just as exciting for me as it was for Melanie. So, after removing my shoes, I jumped on her bed, crossed my legs, and began from the very beginning.

Melanie listened intently, and as I came to the end of my long list of exciting adventures, she sighed, "Gee Whiz, what a thrilling life you've led." Looking out of her window, my only thought was: "Yes, but those days are clearly over now."

Melanie's father and brother had gone to the store to pick up dinner. When they arrived home, they were each carrying a gigantic white box, and I couldn't imagine what was inside these unusually large boxes. Melanie's father noticed my puzzled look, and said, "It's Friday, and on Fridays we always have pizza."

In our house on Fridays, we always had fish and chips, and I had never even heard of pizza! Melanie's mother placed the box in front of me, and ever so slowly opened it. I stared down at the round, flat, colorful looking food. I had never seen anything like it before, and Melanie's mother explained that the bottom of the pizza was like bread, and that the red runny stuff was tomato sauce, and the topping was mozzarella cheese. (Mozzarella cheese? something else that I had never heard of.)

She placed a triangular slice on my plate, and everyone eagerly waited for me to try it. I finally plucked up the courage and took a teeny bite. I couldn't believe it, I actually liked it, and minutes later I was enjoying a second slice. I couldn't wait to get home to tell my family all about this new savory delight that everyone in America called pizza!

Later that evening, Melanie took me downstairs to show me her basement. Melanie's mother was a hairdresser, and to my surprise the basement was a complete hairdresser's salon, which included three sinks, special hairdresser's chairs, mirrors everywhere, and quite a few hooded hair dryers. While the two of us chatted continuously about John, Paul, George, and Ringo Melanie washed my hair, and followed with a deep conditioning treatment. As we discussed the many scenes in 'A Hard Day's Night' she rolled my hair in extra-large rollers, and sat me under the dryer. To keep me occupied, Melanie handed me the latest edition of The Beatles' Monthly magazine, and even though I had already read it, I didn't have the heart to tell her.

By the time she had finished with my hair, it was perfectly straight, and ever so shiny. Melanie said I looked like a dark-haired version of Marianne Faithful, which to me, was quite the compliment. Melanie and I spent the weekend going from house to house visiting all of her girlfriends. They were the nicest girls, and of course, they were all true Beatle fans. Once again, thanks to The Beatles, we were never at a loss for words. Her girlfriends told me that every time Melanie received a letter from me, she would read them out loud to all of them. So now, they too wanted to hear firsthand all about my many Beatle sightings. While I, once again, recounted my numerous exciting escapades, Melanie's girlfriends sat there oohing and aahing!

The week before, Melanie had asked her principal for permission to bring me to school for just one day, and the principal had said yes. So, on Monday morning I went off to school with Melanie. Melanie's classmates and the teachers made me feel so welcome, and I thoroughly enjoyed answering all of their questions about being brought up in England. At the end of the school day Melanie, two of her girlfriends, and I were taken into an office. A rather serious looking boy was sitting at a desk, and he asked me if he could interview me for the school's newspaper. I looked over at Melanie, and together we replied, "Okay."

In between our laughter, the poor boy managed to write a few things down, and then he asked permission to take a couple of photographs. Melanie quickly fixed her hair, then mine, and her two of her girlfriends came rushing in to be included in the photos.

The following day I said goodbye to Melanie, and as she left to go to school, her wonderful parents drove me all the way back to Long Island. Less than a week later, I received a ten page letter from Melanie, letting me know how much fun my visit had been. In the same envelope were two copies of the article that had been published in her school's newspaper all about my special day that I had spent with Melanie, and her lovely friends at Saint Mary's Catholic High School.

BLIMEY! IT'S A LIMEY
by Melanie Slater

"I feel like a right and proper lady," replied our English visitor in her singsong Cockney accent. I took her aside when it was all over and asked her how she felt about her first visit to a Catholic high school in America.

"It's lovely, really; a bit like my old school in England. I notice the kids have the same niceness about them. The uniforms were quite different though. We had summer and winter ones. That's because in England school runs right trough to the end of July. Fancy starting vacation in June!"

Perhaps you missed out in meeting her personally. Well, our little visitor's name was Ursula Fuery, a 16 year old Londoner who has immigrated to New York. I've known her for 9 months, via paper and pen. Neither of us ever thought we'd go to classes together, yet it all happenend. She loved St. Mary's, especially the Tribute photographer that popped in to say "cheese." I told her her picture would be in our school paper. She replied, "Fancy that! And I'm not even from Liverpool!"

Melanie Slater reads Amboyan English to pretty Ursula Fuery while Franc Nemeth and Patricia Clougher look on.

Making the school newspaper

I immediately ran to show Angela the article. And hardly able to contain herself, she laughed, "Cor blimey, who do they think you are, *Pattie Boyd?"

*Yank...An America.
*Eiderdown...Quilt.
*Pleased as punch...British saying that means: Happy and content.
*Pattie Boyd...George Harrison's girlfriend (soon to become his first wife)

CHAPTER 41
UNHAPPY SCHOOL DAYS

Less than a month after arriving in America, Angela and I were enrolled in high school.

Angela was now fifteen years old, and neither one of us had any intention of going back to school. I begged, pleaded, and cried to my parents, "But I've already finished school. Why on earth would I want to go back?" My cousin Jane sat both of us down, and tried to explain, "You're in America now. Nobody finishes school at fifteen over here. Most kids don't graduate high school until they're at least eighteen."

Bright and early the following morning, one of my aunts drove my mother, Angela and me to Westbury High School to have a conference with the principal. The principal decided that Angela would be a junior, and I was placed in the senior class. And the very next day, before I had a chance to even think about any other options, I was standing at the school bus stop with Angela. It was freezing outside, and it was only 7:30 in the morning. There were at least eight other students waiting for the bus, and shivering with the cold, Angela whispered to me, "Can you believe how early it is?" I was so cold, and so annoyed, I replied, "This whole thing is ridiculous!" Finally, a big yellow bus came along, and that's when I realized that in America the schools provided the buses, and that we didn't have to take public transportation. Piling onto the bus, I said to Angela, "Something else that's completely different."

The previous day, the principal had told Angela and I that before going to our homerooms, we would meet our guidance counselor. We had no idea what a guidance counselor was, but after a quick talk with her, we both agreed that she was rather nice. Then we went our separate ways and found our homerooms.

Standing next to the teacher's desk, the teacher introduced me to the class. Staring at my new classmates I was dumbfounded, because some of these people look old enough to be the actual teacher. Taking me to one side, the teacher asked, "Now that I've told your classmates that you've just arrived from England, they may want to ask you some questions. Would you be willing to say a few words?" Hearing this, I wanted to run away as fast as I could, but I didn't even know the way home, so what choice did I have?

Standing in front of the class, the mature looking students began to fire question after question at me, and to my surprise just about every question had something to do with either The Beatles or the English music scene. Listening to the questions, the teacher's face became quite flushed, and frantically waving a blackboard pointer, she screamed, "The questions should pertain to geography or history, not The Beatles! So, I suggest you start asking sensible questions, or say nothing at all!" Smiling broadly, I turned to the teacher and said, "Oh, it's no bother, no bother at all. In fact, I know a lot more about The Beatles than I do about the history of England." Giving me a disapproving look, the teacher told me to sit down.

Later that evening, Angela and I discussed our first day at our new American high school.

Angela sighed, "I've got so much to learn. They were talking about things I've never even heard of." My only comment was, "I know one thing for certain, there are plenty of Beatle fans in our new school."

A week after we enrolled at Westbury High school, 'Around The Beatles' was aired for the first time on American television. The following morning, when I entered my homeroom, my new classmates came rushing up to me. They had all watched 'Around The Beatles' and after seeing me in the audience, everyone wanted to hear all about the show.

Most people couldn't believe that someone in their school had actually seen The Beatles in person. I told them about 'Around The Beatles' and how I had managed to get six free tickets. Now, most of my them wanted to hear all about my other Beatle adventures as well. Now that I was in America, I realized that to see The Beatles as often as I had was indeed a rare, and wonderful thing. But now, after seeing the stunned reactions from my American classmates, it made me even more grateful for having lived in London, and for being so close to John, Paul, George and Ringo's homes.

My time at Westbury High School was very brief. The entire time that I was there, I was so homesick and quite sad. This school was so unlike my old school Cardinal Pole, and I just couldn't get used to all the differences! Westbury High School was enormous, and had over two thousand pupils, and my school in London only had about 500 pupils. In my old school, the boys and girls were always separated from each other. We each had our own playground, our own set of stairs, plus, we never had lunch or gym together. We were in the same classroom, but the boys were on one side of the classroom, and the girls were on the other side of the room. So there was very little interaction between the two genders.

Westbury High School was practically the opposite. The hallways were packed with boys and girls running in every direction, yelling at the top of their voices, and no one there to control them. The most shocking thing that I witnessed was in the girls' bathroom. On that first day, as I entered the bathroom, I walked into a huge cloud of cigarette smoke. Dozens of girls were standing around, smoking cigarettes, fixing their hair, applying makeup, and talking to each other. Once again, the noise was deafening! At Cardinal Pole, we were never allowed to wear makeup or jewelry, and if a teacher had caught us smoking, it was grounds for instant expulsion. (It's not that we were goody goodies, and most of us did enjoy a sneaky cigarette, but never anywhere near our school.)

There were two other incredible differences between my school in England, and this new school in America. First was: The parking lot at Westbury High school was huge, and almost completely full. And to my surprise, most of the cars were actually owned by the students. My school in England didn't even have a parking lot, and even the teachers got on a bus to go home. I don't remember any of the teachers at Cardinal Pole owning their own car, and at this new school the pupils who were still in their teens, had their very own personal cars. I was flabbergasted!

The second most amazing difference was that Westbury High school had the most magnificent indoor swimming pool right in the school building. At Cardinal Pole my classmate and I would have to take a bus to the local swimming pool for our swimming lessons. The swimming pool was the one thing that made me just a little bit happy, but most of the time I was miserable, and so homesick.

Looking bewildered in a strange, new country

Not all things were bad at Westbury High school. After being there for only a few days I met a girl who soon became my best friend. We had so much in common, and of course, she too adored The Beatles. Her name was Josefa but everyone called her Joey, and we remained best friends until the day she died in 2002. And little did I know, that while I was attending Westbury High school my future husband was also there. I've often wondered how many times we passed each other in the hallways.

My time at Westbury High School was short-lived. On Thursday, February 11th, 1965 I had gone to school, and just like every other day I was my usual miserable self. Later that night, as I watched the evening news, the reporter said that Ringo Starr had married his Liverpudlian girlfriend, Maureen Cox. Ringo had always been my favorite Beatles, I was heartbroken. After being depressed for what seemed like an eternity; this horrible announcement was just too much to bear!

I stayed in bed all day on Friday, and for the entire weekend. Finally, on Sunday night I stumbled out of bed, and informed my parents that I had made up my mind, and that I would not be going back to school! Even though John, Paul, George and Ringo were now three thousand miles away, I knew without a doubt, that one day I would see them again!

CHAPTER 42
RUNNING AWAY FROM HOME

I knew that The Beatles were coming to America in the summer of 1965, and I had read that they were scheduled to perform at a place called Shea Stadium. I had no idea where Shea Stadium was, or how to go about getting a ticket for the show. I was also fully aware at how popular The Beatles had become in America, so I was sure that a ticket would cost a small fortune; way too expensive for a poor girl like me. So, I had made up my mind to not even think about the upcoming show, and to cherish all of the wonderful memories of The Beatles that I was fortunate to have. Having this attitude was the only way that I could cope with this terrible situation.

I read in one of the teen magazines that Herman's Hermits were also coming to America, and lately Joey, Angela, and I had been quite captivated by this new group who hailed from Manchester. The article stated that they were going to be performing at The Steel Pier in Atlantic City, New Jersey. I had no idea where Atlantic City was, but I had already been to Perth Amboy, so I was somewhat familiar with the New Jersey area.

I suggested to Angela and Joey that we should go there to see Herman's Hermits. Their faces instantly lit up and were totally on board with my brilliant idea. For me, seeing Herman's Hermits would definitely take my mind off of The Beatles' super expensive upcoming concert. We got the atlas out and tried to figure out the best way to get to Atlantic City. After much research, the cheapest way would be to take a bus from the Port Authority bus station in New York City.

That night, Angela and I spoke to our mother about our well thought out plan, while Joey did the same with her mother. Both mothers said. "Absolutely not!" The three of us were shocked by their unreasonable reactions, and we decided to go anyway. So bright and early on Monday, August the 9th. I left a note on the kitchen table, letting my mother know that the three of us had already left to go to Atlantic City, and could she please call Joey's mother, because Joey was too afraid to tell her. I ended the note with "P.S. Don't worry, we'll stay together, and we'll be fine. After all I'm seventeen years old, and Joey will be next month"

Joey was waiting for us at the Westbury Long Island train station, and three of us jumped on the train and headed towards Manhattan. Once off the train, we asked a friendly policeman for directions to the Port Authority and were relieved to hear that it was just a short walk away. We bought round trip tickets to Atlantic City, and when boarding the rickety old bus, we ran to claim the back seat. It was a scorching hot day, but unfortunately for us and the other passengers, the bus was not air conditioned. And because of how hot and uncomfortable the bus was the long distant bus ride soon became an agonizing nightmare.

Herman's Hermits were going to be performing at Atlantic City for three days, and our plan was to stay for just two days. This way, we could see them on Monday, and again on Tuesday, and then we'd head back home. There were thousands of girls all waiting to see Herman's Hermits' performance, and the entire show was absolutely amazing. Joey, Angela and I had each had our own favorite guy in the group. Joey loved Keith, Angela adored Karl, and I was quite partial to Herman.

Peter Noone (Herman) in Atlantic City

    While they performed, we danced in place, and stared up at them on the stage. We soon became friendly with the two sisters who were standing next to us. Their names were Brenda and Susan, and it was plain to see that they were enjoying themselves almost as much as we were. Once the show had ended, we asked the sisters if they would like to join us for something to eat. They said they would love to, so we found a little restaurant that was close by the Steel Pier. While eating our hamburgers, we tried to figure out where we could stay that night. The sisters also wanted to stay overnight, so we decided to look for a cheap motel, and to keep the price super low, we all agreed to stay in one room.

We found a rundown motel that looked quite scary, but the price was very reasonable, so we agreed to take our chances and stay there for the night. Angela wanted to call home, just to let our parents know that we were still alive. But I was having such a good time, and the last thing I wanted was to get a lecture from my mother, so I persuaded Angela not to make the call.

From the long, overheated bus ride, and the exciting show we were exhausted. The room had two double beds with scruffy looking bedspreads that looked like they hadn't had a good wash in months. The two sisters slept in one bed, and in the other bed Joey slept down the bottom, and Angela and I squeezed into the top. Within minutes, the five of us were sound asleep.

The following morning, we were up with the birds, and ready for another fun filled day. Once again, Herman's Hermits put on a fabulous show, and the five of us had a most enjoyable time. Later that evening, Joey, Angela, and I took the greyhound bus back to New York City, and the sisters went home to Pittsburg. Before leaving, we exchanged phone numbers, and after our exciting couple of days together, we made plans to meet up in Central Park in a few weeks.

We actually kept in touch with Brenda and Susan for a couple of years. It was quite late when we arrived home, and we were exhausted and extremely sunburnt. My mother suggested that Joey should sleep over, so Joey called her mother and was quite relieved that she didn't have to face her. My mother called me into the kitchen, and I whispered to Angela, "Oh, boy, here we go!"

But instead of nagging, she handed me a ticket. When I read what was on the ticket, I almost fell to the ground. It was a ticket to see The Beatles at Shea Stadium. I couldn't believe it, and I could barely contain my excitement. Staring at the ticket, I realized that it was only five dollars, and all along I thought the cheapest ticket would be at least one hundred dollars. I looked over at my mother and asked, "But where did you get it?" She told me that she had given the money to my cousins Ursula and Jane. They had been planning for months to go with their girlfriends and would love for me to come along with them.

That night, I was expecting to be in a lot of trouble for running away, but instead, my lovely Mum had bought me a ticket to see my beloved Beatles again, I only had to wait for a few more days. Angela was very disappointed that my mother hadn't bought a ticket of her too. But weeks later Angela told me that my mother had bought the ticket for me to try to cheer me up.

She could tell that I was deeply unhappy, and extremely homesick. She was terrified that one day I would pack my bags and move back to London. This was the second time that my lovely mother had bought me a ticket to see The Beatles, and once again, I was ever so grateful.

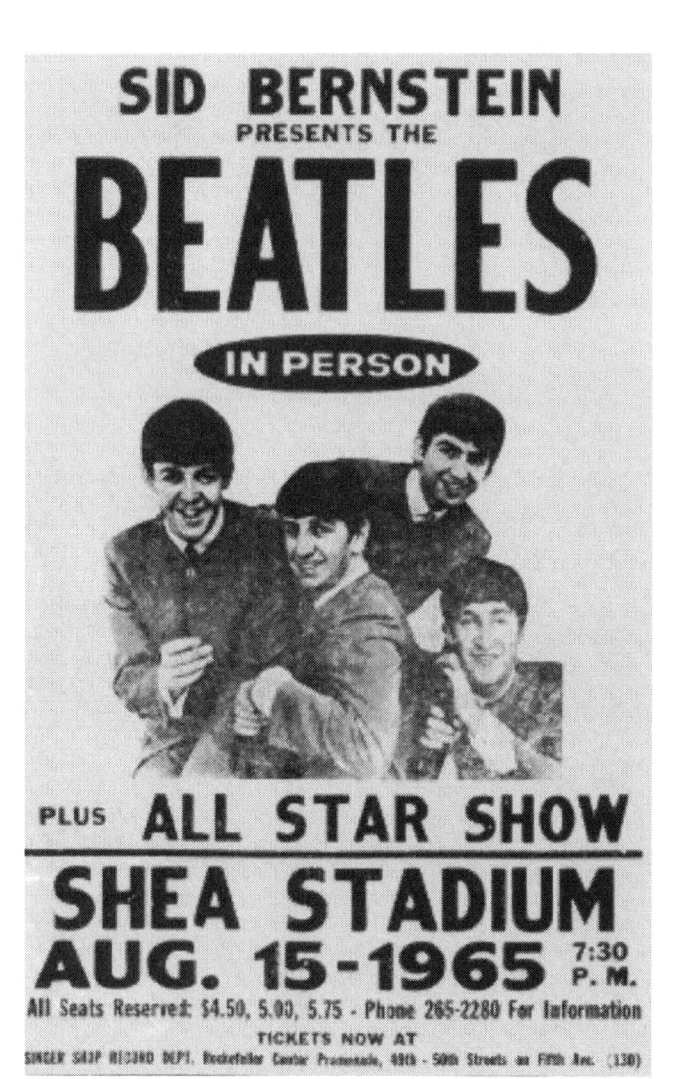

The flyer advertising The Shea Stadium concert

CHAPTER 43
SHEA STADIUM 1965

Ten months after immigrating to America, I was once again enjoying a live performance of my all-time favorite group: The Beatles. On August 15th 1965, along with my cousins, their two girlfriends Kathy and Elaine, and 55,000 other lucky Beatle fans I attended The Shea Stadium concert.

A few months earlier, Ursula and Jane had each bought a Ford Mustang. Jane's was a pale blue convertible, and Ursula's was a bright red hardtop. On the day of the concert, they drove to Westbury, and picked me up in Jane's convertible. It was a roasting hot day, and I was relieved to see that the top was down. I jumped in the backseat and sat in between Kathy and Elaine. My parents were standing on the front porch, and as we drove away, I gave them the royal wave, and they stood there laughing.

We wanted to be at the stadium in plenty of time, so we left hours before the show was scheduled to start. Everything was going according to plan until Shea Stadium came into view, and that's when everything came to a screeching halt, and we were stuck in a massive traffic jam. Sitting in the car, just like all of the other cars that were at a standstill, Jane had the radio blasting. On all of the radio station, the D.J.'s were playing one Beatle song after another and talking about the fast approaching concert. Just listening to the over excited D J's made me even more excited than I already was!

After one and a half hours of driving at a snail's pace, we were finally in the parking lot. We quickly closed the car's roof and ran to the stadium entrance. The line moved quite fast, and within ten minutes we were showing our tickets to the ticket taker. This was the first time that I'd been inside a stadium, and I was totally flabbergasted by the sheer size of the place. I couldn't believe that we had to take an escalator to get to our designated level.

Standing on the moving staircase, I turned to my cousins and gushed, "I've never in my life seen anything like this. I thought The Royal Albert Hall was enormous, but it's teeny compared to this place!"

As the escalator continued upwards, I watched as people on each level rushed around in the sweltering heat. Some were looking a little frazzled as they searched for their specific sections, while others were on the long line waiting to buy hot dogs, and ice-cold drinks.

Others were just standing around trying to comprehend what was happening all around them. After pushing our way through the rowdy crowd, we eventually managed to reach our assigned seats. The fold down seats looked rather hard, but we didn't mind. We were delighted to finally be sitting. I sat in between my cousins and stared in awe as the crowds kept pouring into the massive stadium. The minute Jane sat down, she kicked off her sandals and rubbing her ankles, cried, "Oh my, would you look at my swollen feet. This always happens to me when the temperature goes above eighty-five degrees."

With a sympathetic glance, my cousin Ursula sighed, "Oh you poor dear, I bet the high humidity has a lot to do with it too." While the cousins continued to discuss the weather, I looked around our section, and I began to notice familiar faces. Then I remembered that these people had probably all bought their tickets at the same shop in Westbury that our tickets had come from. Twenty minutes later, I was still staring at the crowds, and I said to the cousins, "I just can't get over it, I can honestly say I've never seen so many people in one place!"

Looking surprised, Ursula said, "But surely you've been to an *Arsenal or Spurs game, and they get quite a crowd too." Shaking my head, I replied, "Nope, can't say I have! Football really isn't my cup of tea!"

We still had another half an hour before showtime, so while I sat fanning myself in the unbearable heat, I began to think about all of my previous Beatle sightings. Meeting, and occasionally chatting with them outside their homes. Watching them run into a waiting taxi, or inside of a theatre. Brazenly going around three times to shake their hands at the Fan Club Get Together. Banging on Ringo's front door and staring at him while he stared back at us. Standing across from John, Paul, George and Ringo at the taping of 'Around The Beatles'. And seeing them perform at seven separate shows.

I knew without a doubt that I was one of the lucky ones. I was also aware that ninety nine percent of all the people who were sitting in this gigantic stadium had never actually seen The Beatles before, and that this special day was something that they will remember for the rest of their lives.

After pondering for a long time, I turned and said to my cousins, "I'm so happy to be here, but I know that this concert will be completely different from all of the other shows I've attended. Everything about this place is huge: the stadium, the field, the audience, and even the noise. Compared to this, the shows in England were like private parties."

This was my first summer in America, and I truly believe that on the day of the Shea Stadium concert, it was the hottest day I had ever experienced. I was having a difficult time adjusting to the blistering heat, not to mention the humidity. Wiping my brow, I moaned, "I can honestly say in all the years that I lived in England I don't ever remember sweating, and I have a feeling I'll never get used to this bloody heat?"

While my cousins laughed, I continued my ranting, "And today of all days it feels like the hottest bleedin' day of the whole flipping summer!" Laughing out loud, and in her poshest accent she sighed, "Oh Ursula, your language is simply appalling!" I quickly retorted, "Bleedin isn't swearing!"

Then the three of us had a good old laugh! And after what seemed like an eternity, the concert was about to start.

The stage had been erected in the middle of the field and was quite a distance from the stands. In between the stands and the stage were long wooden barricades. And now that the show was about to begin, hundreds of New York City police officers came marching out onto the field and stood beside the barriers. Giving me a nudge, Jane whispered, "And just in case you get the urge to join The Beatles on stage, may I remind you that with all these cops, you won't stand a chance!" Giggling, I cooed, "Just to be able to see them again is more than enough for me, and besides I'm way too hot to even think about running."

Suddenly, a hush came over the crowd, and the concert began. The opening acts were King Curtis, Cannibal and The Headhunters, Brenda Holloway, Sounds Incorporated, and The Young Rascals. All of these performers were truly amazing, and at any other concert I would have been delighted to see them. But I was at Shea Stadium for only one reason, and that was to see John, Paul, George and Ringo.

While the other performers were trying their best to entertain us, I sat in my wooden seat, and wished that I had brought a cushion. Knowing that The Beatles would be coming on stage at any moment, I just couldn't concentrate on the other acts. So, I spent most of the time wiping the sweat off of my forehead and gawking at the people who were sitting all around us.

At long last, it became clear to everyone what was about to happen: Ed Sullivan appeared on stage, and the entire audience gave a collective gasp, followed by loud cheering. Ed Sullivan spoke into the microphone, but nobody paid any attention, until he announced, "And here are The Beatles," At that very moment, John, Paul, George and Ringo came running out of the dugout. Everyone in the stadium rose to their feet, and flashbulbs began to pop from all directions. The roar from the crowd was deafening, and screaming at the top of our lungs, my cousins, their friends, and I did our best to add to the pandemonium!

To see The Fab Four again was a tremendous thrill and to witness my Beatles being adored by all of these American fans was also very emotional. Surrounded by dozens of policemen, The Beatles continued to run down the field towards the stage, and I noticed that John, Paul and George already had their guitars strapped on. When they reached the stage, one by one they climbed up the steps, and shook hands with Ed Sullivan. Also on the stage was a very tall man wearing a white shirt, who was busy untangling wires, and checking the sound equipment, and even though he was far away, I knew without a doubt that it was Mal Evans.

The Beatles were dressed in identical beige Nehru collared jackets, dark tee shirts and dark trousers, and each of them had a shiny star on their stylish jackets. Yelling into Ursula's ear, I screeched, "They look gorgeous, but those jackets look like they're wool, and in this heat, they must be roasting up there." With a sympathetic look, Ursula shook her head and mouthed, "Poor dears."

As soon as Ringo took his place behind the drums, The Beatles were ready to perform. They began with 'Twist and Shout' And from the moment John sang the opening line, the continuous screaming from the enormous crowd continued for the entire thirty-minute set.

I read in the newspaper the following day that The Beatles had performed twelve songs: starting with 'Twist and Shout' and followed by 'She's A Woman,' 'I feel Fine,' 'Dizzy Miss Lizzy,' 'Ticket To Ride,' 'Everybody's Trying To Be My Baby,' 'Can't Buy Me Love,' 'Baby's In Black,' 'Act Naturally,' 'A Hard Day's Night,' 'Help,' and finishing the set with 'I'm Down.

Not to be able to hear them didn't matter one bit. Just to be able to see them again was more than enough for me, and having a good old scream felt so exhilarating. All of the other shows that I had been lucky enough to attend were all quite noisy, but this one was like nothing I had ever experienced! While The Beatles performed one song after another, dozens of fans tried to reach the stage. I watched in awe, as the daring fans sprinted down the field, jumped over the barricades, and seconds later, were dragged away by dozens of policemen.

I also saw several other fans who had been either injured or had fainted and were being carried off by paramedics who were carefully taking them to the first aid area. After thirty minutes of non stop playing, The Beatles performance came to an end.

Stepping off the stage, John, Paul, George and Ringo waved enthusiastically to the cheering fans, climbed into a big American station wagon, and were whisked away. And in what seemed like a flash, The Beatles were gone!

From all of the screaming that we'd done, my cousins and I were totally knackered, so we decided to sit back and wait for the crowd to thin out. Sounding hoarse, I turned to my cousins and croaked, "Wasn't it absolutely *smashing?" Both of my cousins nodded enthusiastically, and the girl who was sitting in front of Jane turned around, and looking just a little bit puzzled, said, "Gee, I'm so confused, what does smashing mean?" Giggling, I answered, "Why, absolutely fab, of course!"

Two hours later, we were finally in the car and on our way home. To see The Beatles again was definitely another dream come true, even though I always knew that one day I would. But this concert was like no other Beatle concert. The audience was huge, the screaming was deafening, and I'm sure it was the hottest day of the entire summer. I have no idea how The Beatles, who were certainly not used to that kind of oppressing heat and humility, even managed to get through it!

It was like nothing I had ever experienced, and I and the other 55,000 fans thoroughly enjoyed every single minute.

*<u>Arsenal or Spurs</u>... Two English football (soccer) teams.
*<u>Smashing</u>... Wonderful, marvelous, and of course, Fabulous.

CHAPTER 44
SHEA STADIUM 1966

The following year on August 23rd, 1966, I was once again back at Shea Stadium for yet another spectacular Beatle concert. This time, my sister Angela and my best friend Joey came with me. They had read dozens of articles about the record-breaking Shea Stadium concert of 1965, and of course, they had to listen to me going on and on about it for almost the entire year! So this time they were determined not to miss out on any of the excitement.

My father drove us to Shea Stadium and dropped us off by the main entrance. The concert was expected to end at 10 p.m., so we picked a spot where we would meet up.

Last year's mass exit was still fresh in my mind, so I told my dad not to be in any rush. Jumping out of the car, Angela laughed, "Don't worry Dad, we won't leave without you." Laughing out loud, I quickly added, "Unless of course, The Beatles insist on taking us with them." And Joey chimed in, "And their next stop will be to sunny California, which sounds good to me." And Angela added, "And if that should happen, we'll be sure to give you and Mum a quick phone call the minute we get there." As he drove away, my father was laughing his head off, and he yelled out, "Ta ta for now, enjoy the show, and you girls better be outside when I get back here."

The three of us ran towards the line, and took our place among the hundreds of other over excited Beatle fans that were waiting to get into the stadium. It was another hot, humid day, and when I turned to look at Angela and Joey, I burst out laughing. Before we had left the house, the three of us had spent over an hour carefully ironing each other's hair. And in the car, we had kept the air conditioner on so that our hair would stay nice and straight. But after standing in the line for less than five minutes, we had all gone back to our natural state of uncontrollable frizz. Angela knew what I was laughing about, and touching her hair she said, "I'm so excited, I really don't mind how it looks."

The big difference at this year's concert was that Joey was with us, and Joey always came prepared. She had brought a huge picnic basket which was full to the brim with all sorts of goodies, and she had three plastic containers full of ice-cold water."

Feeling guilty, I offered to help carry the heavy picnic basket, and confessed, "The only things that I've brought are some Life Savers, and my brother's binoculars." Joey answered, "Don't worry, I've been planning this ever since the day we bought the tickets, and I have more than enough for all three of us."

An hour later, we were finally inside the stadium. Angela and Joey had the same reaction that I'd had the year before, they just couldn't believe the enormous size of Shea Stadium.

Angela was baffled, "I had no idea. It just doesn't look that big from the outside." she said.

As soon as we found our seats I plonked myself down in between Joey and Angela, and yelled out in pain. Shaking my head in disbelief, I cried, "I knew there was something I'd forgotten, cushions for these bleedin' hard as a rock seats."

Joey started to laugh, and Angela sighed, "Oh well, never mind, it's too late now." As soon as I was settled, I looked at Joey and said, "I do believe I'm a little bit peckish! Can I please have something to nibble on? Angela added, "Oh, me too please, I'm starving." Joey opened the picnic basket, and we each took a peanut butter, and jelly sandwich. While we feasted on the endless treats, the three of us watched with fascination as the never ending crowds kept streaming into the stadium.

And as I sat there, I had the exact same butterfly feeling in my tummy that I had felt the previous year and knowing that I was about to see The Beatles once again, this strange, but rather pleasant feeling kept increasing. Looking out over the crowd, I noticed that once again, the barricades were all over the field, and when it was almost time for the concert to begin, hordes of policemen came marching out onto the field.

After sitting in our seats for what seemed like an eternity, the concert finally began. The Disc Jockeys known as 'The Good Guys' from the W.M.C.A. radio station introduced each act. The support acts were: The Remains, Bobby Hebb, The Cyrkle and The Ronettes. Angela, Joey and I sat in our seats, and while we listened to all of the performers we ate dozens of cookies, devoured several candy bars, and sipped on our iced water.

At 9 p.m. at long last, it was time for The Beatles to come out. The popular Disc Jockey Bruce Morrow, (who was known to everyone as Cousin Brucie) had the honor of introducing The Beatles, and as soon as The Beatles came into view, the entire audience erupted into loud cheers, and the usual high-pitched screaming. Peering through the binoculars was a real treat, and John Paul, George and Ringo looked as if they were standing right in front of me.

For this concert, I was happy to see that The Beatles were more prepared for the stifling heat. They were wearing identical lightweight pin striped suits, and fab flowery shirts. As always, they looked absolutely gorgeous, and as I peered through the binoculars, I was pleased to see that they seemed to be a lot more comfortable in their carefully thought-out outfits. After a few minutes I handed the binoculars over to Joey, and after she adjusted the focus, she began to jump up and down and screeched, "Gee whiz, they're adorable! "Seeing Joey's excitement, Angela begged, "Oh please Joey can I have a quick gander?" Joey reluctantly shoved the binoculars into Angela's hands, and just as I had expected, Angela began to scream uncontrollably.

After five minutes, it became clear to me that Angela was not about to give the binoculars back, so she left me no choice but to grab them right out of her hands. Just like the previous year the audience screamed from the moment The Beatles came on stage and continued screaming until the very end of the concert. The three of us screamed along with everyone else, and the only time that I was quiet was when it was my turn to stare at them through the binoculars.

From all of the screaming nobody heard anything, but just like every other time, it didn't matter. John, Paul, George and Ringo were standing right in front of us, and we were on cloud nine.

For me, seeing The Beatles again was definitely the highlight of the summer of 1966, and from the reaction of all the people that were around us; I knew without a doubt that it was for them too!

That evening, The Beatles performed eleven of their hit songs: 'Rock and Roll Music,' 'She's A Woman,' 'If I needed Someone,' 'Day Tripper,' 'Baby's In Black,' 'I Feel Fine,' 'Yesterday,' 'I Wanna Be Your Man,' 'Nowhere Man,' 'Paperback Writer' and ending the set with 'Long Tall Sally.'

When the concert ended, and The Beatles had left the area, I turned to Joey and Angela and said, "There's no point in rushing out. Dad won't be here for another hour, so we might as well sit back and relax." Laughing out loud, Joey cried, "I was hoping we'd be going home with The Beatles. Then your poor father wouldn't have to drive all this way to pick us up."

Giving her a funny look, I sighed," No such luck, but who knows, maybe next year we'll have better luck!" Waiting for the stadium to empty out, we chatted about The Beatles' unbelievable performance, and somehow managed to finish off the last remaining goodies that were still in the picnic basket.

As we were going down on the escalator, Angela moaned, "All of a sudden I'm feeling quite nauseous." Joey replied, "Yeah, me too!" And I asked. "I wonder if it has anything to do with all the goodies we've just finished off?" And the three of us laughed hysterically!

My father was waiting patiently at the spot where we had agreed to meet. Angela jumped into the front seat, and Joey and I climbed into the back. And before he drove off, my father chuckled, "I was just about to leave. I was sure The Beatles had taken you away with them!" Sighing loudly, I answered, "No such bleedin' luck!" My father adjusted his rear-view mirror and asked, "So girls, how was the show?" In her fake English accent, Joey cried, "Oh, Mr. Fuery, they were absolutely fab, and I was chuffed to bits!" Staring at Joey, I said, "In all my life, I have never said the word chuffed, I don't even know where you got that one from!" And Angela and I just looked at each other and started laughing.

CHAPTER 45
KEEPING UP WITH THE BEATLES

On August 29th, 1966, just six days after the Shea Stadium concert, The Beatles final live concert took place at Candlestick Park in San Francisco, California. (Although they did make an unannounced live appearance on January 30th, 1969 on the rooftop of the Apple building on Savile Row in London)

For the next three years, The Beatles remained together, and most of their time was spent in the studio recording numerous singles, and albums. They also worked on two films: 'Magical Mystery Tour' and the animated 'Yellow Submarine.'

At the end of January 1967, The Beatles made a promotional film to publicize their latest single: Strawberry Fields Forever, and on the B side: Penny Lane. This film was an early example of what later became known as a music video. It was released in America on March 11th, 1967. (14 years before MTV was launched.) And on June 25th, 1967, The Beatles, along with many of their friends did the first live international satellite television production on the show 'Our World.' They sang 'All You Need Is Love' and it was seen by over 400 million people across 5 continents. So between the records, the movies, and the numerous articles that were written about them, The Beatles were never far from the spotlight or from me.

On March 12th, 1969 my sister Angela and I were in California when I heard the news that Paul McCartney had married his American girlfriend Linda Eastman in London. At first, I was a little bit upset about it, but what could I do? After getting over the initial shock, I was actually quite happy for him, and of course, for his extremely fortunate wife!

I can't remember the date; but when my husband and I were newly-weds, we read that one of the movie houses in Manhattan were going to be showing all four of The Beatles' movies.

So, one afternoon we took the train to Penn Station, and spent the entire day, and into the night watching: A Hard Day's Night, followed by Help, then Magical Mystery Tour, and ending with Yellow Submarine.

We had filled my gigantic hippy sling bag with some sandwiches, a few packets of potato chips, and even a paper bag filled with cookies. A cooler would have been way too conspicuous, so we purchased some large cokes from the concession stand. We thoroughly enjoyed watching all four movies, but by the time we got out, we were both quite blurry eyed.

In 1974, my husband Ronnie and I attended the first Beatlesfest which was held at The Commodore Hotel in Manhattan. We had made plans to meet up with my girlfriend June, and her boyfriend King at Penn Station. They too, were huge Beatle fans, and we decided that it would be fun to all go together. Ronnie and I were so surprised when June and King showed up wearing the most amazing Sgt. Pepper outfits that June had whipped up on her sewing machine. They looked like they had just stepped out of the album cover and walking to the hotel everyone turned to look at them.

The Beatlefest was so different to anything we had ever experienced. They had dozens of stalls selling everything connected to The Beatles; books, records, pictures, and so much more. Hundreds of fans attended, and we had a fabulous time. It wasn't until twenty six years after The Shea Stadium concert of 1966 that I finally attended another concert that included one of the members of The Beatles.

On June 23rd, 1992, my girlfriend June and I went to see Ringo and his

All Starr Band perform at The Jones Beach Theater on Long Island. The All Starr Band included Ringo's son Zak Starkey, Timothy B. Schmitt, Niles Lofgren, Dave Edmunds, Todd Rundgren, Joe Walsh, Burton Commings, and Timmy Capell. They were an amazing group of super talented musicians, and along with Ringo they performed one great song after another. For several of the songs both Ringo and his son played their drums simultaneously, and for other songs Ringo jumped down from behind his drums, and holding a microphone, sang one song after another, and of course, being as the audience knew all of the songs, we sang along with him. I was amazed at what a fabulous dancer Ringo was. He pranced from one end of the stage to the other, and had more energy than most teenagers.

He also told quite a few jokes, and the audience laughed hysterically at Ringo's very unique sense of humor and witty personality. Sitting in the audience, I realized that something was very different about this performance, but I just couldn't put my finger on it. I knew that John, Paul and George were missing, but something else just wasn't quite right. And suddenly it dawned on me. Nobody was screaming! For the first time ever I could actually hear Ringo singing live, and what an amazing voice he had.

Ringo was outgoing, full of energy and quite the comedian. He definitely knew how to engage the audience, and he certainly wasn't the shy, reserved Beatle that I remember from the early sixties. And June and I thoroughly enjoyed every minute of the amazing show.

After all those years to see Ringo again was such a special treat, and as I sat watching him I couldn't help but think about the time he opened his apartment door and probably got the fright of his life, when all he could see was a bunch of young teenage girls with their mouths wide opened, gawking at him!

27 years later, I was fortunate to see Ringo, and his All Starr Band again. At the beginning of August 2019 my son Nick called me. At that time, he and his wife Lindsey had two little girls. After a quick hello, and how are you and dad doing? He asked, "What are you doing on August

18th?" I chuckled, "Don't know, I'm a very busy woman, I'll have to check my appointment book." I was sure he wanted me to babysit my adorable granddaughters, which would have been my pleasure, but he quickly replied, "Oh, it just that I have these two tickets to see Ringo on August 18th., and I thought you might like to have them."

I immediately began to scream, and without giving it another thought, I yelled, "Yes, I'm definitely free that day. I just hope you're not joking." He answered, "Nope, I wouldn't do that to you! I have the tickets, and two special wristbands that will allow you into the after party."

I could barely contain my excitement and told him that I will get the train into Manhattan the very next day to pick up my wonderful surprise. He replied, "That's okay Ma, I'll put them in the mailbox right now, and you'll have them in two days!" I thanked him over and over until he hung up the phone.

I invited my girlfriend Georgette to come with me, and she was almost as excited as I was.

Two weeks later Georgette and I met in the Seaport district of Manhattan. We had a lovely early dinner and headed towards the venue. The concert was being held at Pier 17. We were there nice and early, and the line moved right along. The concert was being held on the rooftop, and when we saw the amazing view, we couldn't believe it how beautiful it was.

Our seats were in the fifth row, and we were so excited to be that close to the stage. In no time at all, the entire rooftop was packed with people. Finally, the show began, and Ringo and his All Starr band came on stage, and performed one great song after another. Ringo was amazing, and even though he had less than a year to go before his 80th. birthday, he still sang, and danced better than most teenagers.

Unlike the last time that I saw Ringo in 1992, this time I had an iPhone, and was able to take loads of photos, and videos. Even though everyone had their own seat, most of the audience stood for the entire show, and just about everyone sang along with Ringo. I was amazed at how many young people knew all the lyrics to his songs.

All too soon the fabulous show came to an end, and as he performed the last song which was: "With A Little Help From My Friends" not only did Ringo sing, but at the end of the song he did quite a few jumping jacks.

August 18th. 2019. Ringo and his All Starr Band.

After the show, Georgette and I showed the guard our special wristbands and were allowed to enter the private bar area. We each ordered a soda and sat patiently waiting for Ringo to appear. But alas, he never showed up!

Before leaving this unique venue, we took one more breathtaking look at the New York City skyscrapers, and with its glittering lights The Brooklyn bridge. Georgette dropped me off at Penn Station, and she drove home to New Jersey, I took the train back to Bethpage.

CHAPTER 46
SAD TIMES, AND GOOD NEWS

A date that will always stay with me is December 8th. On the evening of December 8th, 1980 John Lennon was shot outside of his apartment building in New York City by a crazy man. He was pronounced dead on arrival at Roosevelt Hospital.

It wasn't until the following day when I turned on the morning news that I heard about this unbelievable tragedy. I just stood next to the television set unable to comprehend what I was hearing. I was completely numb, and I kept the television on all day, just trying to make sense of this heinous crime.

As the hours went by, the crowd that had gathered outside The Dakota, (John's New York City apartment building) kept growing, and by the evening, thousands of people had come together to mourn his untimely death. I wanted to join them, but my son who was only fifteen months old and needed me to be with him.

The following Sunday, just six days after John Lennon's murder, a memorial was held in Central Park. It was reported that nearly two hundred thousand fans had attended, and after singing many of John's songs, there was a ten minute silent vigil where everyone was asked to pray for John's soul. At the exact same time, many other vigils took place all over the world.

The next few months were very hard for me. I felt as though I had lost someone that I had known all of my life. At that time, my girlfriends in England and I wrote to each other more often than usual, and I felt as though they were the only people who truly understood how I felt, and I knew without a doubt that they too were going through the same grieving process.

These days, whenever anyone comes for a visit from either England or Ireland, one of the first places they ask to see is Strawberry Fields. This is the memorial that is dedicated to John Lennon in Central Park, which has the Imagine mosaic where many people come to pay tribute to his memory. It is also right across from the apartment building where John's wife Yoko Ono still lives.

Visiting Strawberry Fields with Eileen, and my sister Angela.

In 1997 George Harrison was diagnosed with throat cancer, which was treated with radiology. In May of 2001 he had undergone an operation to remove a cancerous growth from one of his lungs, and later that same year he was treated for a brain tumor. Sadly, on November 29th. 2001 George Harrison died. His ashes were scattered in the Ganges, and Yamuna rivers in India by his wife Olivia and his son Dhani.

On a much happier note, Paul McCartney and Ringo Starr have both been knighted for their services to music, and for their numerous charitable deeds. They are now rightly known as: Sir Paul McCartney and Sir Richard Starkey.

Over the years, I've stayed in touch with most of my English girlfriends. I've been back to England at least ten times, and some of my girlfriends have crossed the pond to visit me.

I was thrilled when in 1972, Rita came to New York for our wedding, and was one of my bridesmaids. Eileen and Mary were also present at the wedding. In 1964, my girlfriends and I promised to stay in touch, and I'm happy to say that most of us have kept that promise.

These days, our lengthy letters have been replaced by emails, messages on Facebook, and the occasional greeting card.

Outside Abbey Road Studios with Maroula and Christina. 2012

Crossing Abbey Road. Angela, Maroula, me, and Christina. 2012

Back for the Queen's Platinum Jubilee. Walking across Tower bridge with my sister Veronica, and Christina

A Common Case of Beatlemania

With Christina, Rita, and Rita's sister Liz. June 2022

Still friends after all these years

After all these years The Beatles are still a huge part of my life. Whether it's watching them on YouTube, listening to them on the radio, playing their CD's, or reading one of the many Beatles' articles that can be found on Facebook. There really aren't too many days that go by without hearing or reading something about them.

This memoir has taken me many years to write and rewrite, and I can honestly say I have thoroughly enjoyed writing it. Each chapter has brought me right back to the exact moment that I was writing about, and I can remember precisely how I felt.

All those years ago, to have John, Paul, George and Ringo living practically around the corner from me was nothing short of a miracle. And all I can say is: What more could a teenage girl possibly want?

THE END

We didn't realize we were making memories,
we just knew we were having fun.....A.A. Milne

ACKNOWLEDGMENT

Thank you to all of my girlfriends who are a huge part of this book. Especially Maroula and Rita who were always right there with me chasing after The Beatles all over London. Also thank you to Eileen and Christina who were also part of so many of our adventures. I'm so fortunate to still have them all in my life; even if they are 3,000 miles away.

Thank you to my dear friend Adam Timmerman for designing the fabulous Book Cover.

Also, thank you to my lovely niece Rebecca Levin who changed my PDF into a word document, and added all of my photos into a zip! Without Becky's help, and encouragement both the book, and the photos would be stuck on my computer forever after.

I would also like to thank John Grappone for suggesting that at the end of each chapter I should include a glossary.

Printed by Amazon Italia Logistica S.r.l.
Torrazza Piemonte (TO), Italy